TEST PILOTS

Test Pilots

BY WOLFGANG SPÄTE

Independent Books

Test Pilots
by Wolfgang Späte

1st edition (Germany)
AVIATIC VERLAG

Translation from the German original by:

Harald Böhnke, Translation Services,
Cohrsweg 6,
27339 Riede
Germany

Tel: +49 4294 919103
Fax: +49 4294 919105

English Language edition by:

Independent Books
3 Leaves Green Crescent
Keston
Bromley
BR2 6DN
United Kingdom

Tel: +959 573360
Fax: +959 541129
e-mail indbooks@globalnet.co.uk

Edited by David Tindall

Jacket design and page layout:

Rob Taylor – GDi studio
Brunswick Mill
Pickford Street
Macclesfield
SK11 6JN

Tel: +1625 618655
Fax: +1625 618622

Photographs:

Baist (1)
Beauvais (1)
Eisermann (8)
Airport Frankfurt (1);
Kloeckner (26)
MBB (6)
Roloff (1)
Jean Marie Saget (6)
Schäfer (10);
Schieferstein (11)
Schmid (3)
Späte (8)
Thomas (2)
Treiber (2);
Zübert (7)
all others, private archives.

ISBN: 1 872836 20 8

In co-operation with

Walter Baist

Heinrich Beauvais

Wilhelm Buss

Hans Dieterle

Jochen Eisermann

Erich Klöckner

Hanna Reitsch

Helmut Roloff

Jean Marie Saget

Fritz Schäfer

Karl Schieferstein

Lukas Schmid

Dieter Thomas

Helmut Treiber

Georg Wollé

Hans Zübert

Kurt Zwickau

CONTENTS   PAGE

THE AUTHOR:

Wolfgang Späte

Wolfgang Späte was born in Dresden 1911 and attended High School and College in Saaz, Sommerfeld and Dessau. From 1930 to 1936, he was a trainee with the newspaper *Tageszeitung*, in Chemnitz. A glider pilot since 1927, he started in 1934 to participate in national and international Gliding Competitions with gliders he had himself built. In 1938, he advanced to the lite of German glider pilots as overall winner of the Rhöne Glider Competition and holder of the seventh Golden Achievement Award.

Having trained as a pilot of piston engined aircraft, at the beginning of World War II he became a reserve officer in the rank of *Leutnant*, serving as an Army Reconnaissance pilot, chiefly employed in the Polish and French campaigns. Thereafter, he served as a fighter pilot, operating mainly in the East. In 1942, he became Head the *Erprobungs-Kommando 16*, tasked with the development of the *Me 163* Rocket Fighter. Returning to operations as a Wing Commander in 1944, he continued flying until the end of the war, by which time he had been promoted *Major:* he was credited with ninety-nine aerial victories and was awarded the Knight's Cross with bar.

After the war he became Managing Director of a photographic company in Frankfurt, but from 1956 to 1967 served again in the German Air Force. From then until 1971 he worked with Dr. Lippisch (designer and constructor of the Me 163) on the trials and testing of the Ground Effect Flying Boat X 113 Am.

Wolfgang Späte died in April 1997, leaving a widow and two sons.

INTRODUCTION:

The words 'Test Pilot' describe to the layman, as well as to the expert, a man who lives his life at full risk and therefore has an experience to share. It is his task to test aircraft. In order for him to be able to carry out this task, he has to take the flying machines as well as himself to the limits, asking the most of both. Above all, he has to determine whether the aircraft is good or bad. In doing this, he often experiences very exciting moments.

When man began to lift off the ground with machines built heavier than air, each and every attempt carried the risk of losing one's life. The individual who, 80 years ago, climbed into an aircraft to risk a flight, was accompanied by the dangers of a crash at all times. Therefore, it was very important to know which flight regime ensured safe flight, and which limits not to exceed in order to minimise the risk. To try, test and make these facts known, played a very important part. The one who was committed to this task, the *Versuchsflieger* (literally: *trial pilot* – Test Pilot) enjoyed the highest respect and recognition.

During the few decades in which man conquered the air by means of gliders and engine driven aircraft, the quality of aeroplanes improved at an enormous rate. Designers and constructors were able continually to improve the flying abilities of aircraft. When a new 'flying machine' showed a fault, it was to be diagnosed, researched and corrected. This was the duty of the test pilot. The abilities and collective experience of designers grew over the years, resulting in fewer faults being found during the maiden flight of a prototype. But it still took a test pilot to perform the first flights, his duty being to discover whether the aeroplane fulfilled the requirements of modern technology and to explore 'the envelope'.

The performance which the test pilots asked of their aircraft at that time represented the prevailing knowledge and 'state of the art' of the aircraft in their epoch. If it were possible to put together original reports from test pilots, reflecting the past eight decades, it would be a superb and interesting work of art with regard to the History of Flight. In this book one would be able to read about the development of flying as seen through the eyes of the pilots.

With this thought in mind, I began my search for such

reports. The search was encouraged by the fact that I have had my flying licence for over 50 years and have experience in gliding as well as piston engine, turbine powered, rocket and jet flying. These experiences were published in their time. This inspired confidence among different pilots who opened their diaries and minds in order for me to put all this on paper and so help to prevent this accumulated knowledge and experience from falling into obscurity.

The fact that I was able to find reports from Erich Klöckner and Karl Schieferstein as part of the history of the DFS (German Institute for Research of Gliding) and keep them from being forgotten, gives me the greatest of pleasure.

It took years of travel, meetings, interviews, long distance telephone calls and an enormous amount of correspondence in order to obtain the necessary documents for this book. I owe thanks to all co-authors, who allowed me to re-arrange, trim, expand and or shorten their contributions to match the title of this book. The chronological connection of the individual reports lays out an important aspect of German Aviation History. In order to maintain coherence and to introduce the individual test pilot to the public, I have prefaced each contribution in italic print. Some of the reports have been previously published in different German Aviation Magazines and or newspapers, but never as such an anthology.

My thanks to all the companies, institutions and private owners of photographs and sketches who enabled me to illustrate the book. Some reports describe a time in aviation history which goes back as far as half a century. In a few cases, these circumstances forced me to use a picture of poor quality, rather than no picture at all.

Last but not least, I thank the instructors at the EPNER (Training Centre for Trials, Inspection and Acceptance) at Brétigny, who gave me the skills and knowledge which enabled me to become a test pilot myself and to evaluate the deeds and feats in this sector of aviation.

Wolfgang Späte   Edewecht, Autumn 1995

CHAPTER ONE

Kurt Zwickau

Jumping in the Air

This report was published 50 years ago by a man who was already known as an 'old eagle' at that time. Kurt Zwickau, born 5th November 1886, would be over 100 years old today. In an old aviation circular, dated 1940, he describes what young pilots had to put up with at the beginning of aviation: – No publications, or pilot's notes: in those days each pilot was his own Test Pilot. However, Zwickau gives an account of how resourceful the young pilots were required to be in the pioneer days of flying, and of the things they had to do in order to get safely airborne and just as safely back to the ground.

The Grade-Monoplane in flight.

The year 1910 was the first 'German' flying year! The only flying available up to that time was in foreign countries. Only two names, the only Germans, who, despite all prejudice, took up the 'battle' in the air, August Euler and Hans Grade, pioneers and doyens, come to mind.

I still remember precisely that, in 1910, an altitude of 400 metres (1, 300ft) meant an altitude record. A long distance flight was more than 120km (74.57 miles) and it took 2 hours and 41minutes. These records had been set by foreign pilots, flying foreign aircraft at Johannisthal and at Bornstedt airfield, near Potsdam.

Hans Grade was the first pilot to win the 'Lanz Award'.

Winning this award required a German pilot, piloting an aircraft which had been entirely manufactured in Germany, to fly the so called 'triangle' over the airfield of Johannisthal. Our decision to learn to fly with Grade was final. The way the decision was made illustrates the first essential characteristics required by a pilot, both then and today: Toughness, tenacity, daring – and stoicism!

Celebrating Grade's success with a hefty evening drink, we developed our battle plan. It is a pity that I no longer have the letter we wrote with the courage of drink that evening. Filled with burning desire and excitement, I sent it off to Hans Grade, in Bork. The content of the letter was briefly this: 'We are thirsting to fly, full of energy, but we have no money!' The answer arrived promptly: 'Yes...but any damage will have to be paid for by you: everything else is free of charge!'

We were off to a good start, although we really did not know where the 'flight' would take us! We did not think any further. We had been given the opportunity to learn to fly! This was the only thought in our minds! All else was pushed aside and left to take care of itself.

In November 1910, the Beelitz Railroad took us to Bork. A clear, cold wintry day which led us to believe flying was possible. This was not to be taken for granted, bearing in mind that the aeroplane had to be serviceable and the wind on the airfield just right.

On our walk from the station to the airfield, we listened out for the sound of a propeller. This listening out accompanied us through many years of flying, and it inspired our steps or calmed our conscience when we were late. This feeling was with us when we searched for a downed comrade, and it released the tension when the missing aircraft finally made itself heard on the horizon.

On the day we arrived at Bork, there was no flying. This was not because of the weather, but due to the fact that we had dressed up in coats, overcoats and long trousers. Hans Grade was barely able to hide his amusement during the formal introduction. We had a look around the 'factory' instead. Even though I put this in quotation marks today, in those days it *was* a factory. These 'aircraft works' were mostly just single sheds containing everything, including the accommodation for the 'factory owner'! This was the beauty of flying – everything was sacrificed in order to fly!

The visit to the 'factory' made it obvious that the four of us had to share one aircraft, which was also to be used by Grade until his new 'plane had been built and was ready to fly. With 'expert' eyes we looked at the aeroplane which had just won the 'Lanz Award', including the 40,000 Marks that came with it. With admiration we also looked at the man who had achieved this.

Without having actually flown, our first 'flying day' was filled with new impressions. As we left for home, full of confidence, we knew that we were going to have a part in the realisation of Leonardo da Vinci's fantasies and Lilienthal's achievements as a pioneer of flight.

We used the journey home to discuss our future dress code. We did not view the problem from the aspect of 'looking good' as we were later to experience with some of the first pilots, especially ladies. We looked at it with regard to expense and practicality. Climbing into the seat of the 'Grade' for the first time left an 'oily impression' on our coats, as did Grade's hint that the 'engine feels best' when it spills gas oil all over the 'aviator' sitting below. 'Look at my leather jacket! It could easily be used as a spare tank for gas oil!'

The question of proper attire was finally solved by the one whom we called 'Pioneer Klinke'. His father owned a boiler factory and he remembered the men working there, dressed in boiler suits. A less expensive and more practical piece of flying clothing called a 'flight suit' was not available at that time; at least not at the time when we required it. Later, when the use of this suit became commonplace, the prices in the shops increased by a considerable amount. These were all minor things considering today's standards. Today's flight suit is nothing but a modern boiler suit with all the practical improvements such as pockets, zippers, back and parachute straps. Things we had to do without!

Then we were ready to start! – Aircraft and instructor were standing before us. We were ready for take off! – At least this was what we thought! – 'Now,' said Hans Grade, his hand making a friendly inviting gesture towards the aircraft, 'first of all we want to look at the pump handle!' (joy stick).

The pump handle was the fully automatic steering. All steering movements were combined within this handle and you operated it with only one hand, namely the left. Yes, there we stood, looking at the pump handle. It indeed looked as if it had just been taken off a pump in the yard. But this 'aircraft pump handle' was something special! It could be moved in all

Hans Grade, standing to the right of the propeller, introducing the aircraft to his students.

different directions, left, right and, to describe a circle, it could even be turned. A real miracle in itself, as we were to find out later. The simplest and best known movement, by definition, was up and down: 'pulling up' and 'pushing down'. The elevator was connected to this handle movement. Pulling the pump handle up and moving it towards your body meant steering up. Pushing the handle down and moving it forward meant steering down. And then unusual moves for a pump handle, namely left and right, the sideways movements resulting in left or right aileron deflection. But the most difficult movement a pump handle could ever dream of was turning left and right around itself. 'Twisting' was what Grade called this and we acknowledged it by nodding understandingly, even though we had no idea what he was talking about. When Hans started to show us the inherent moves of the pump handle on the ground, we were astonished by what an experienced left 'pump handle handling hand' was able to do, and what could be done with a simple pump handle.

And this was our first lesson: Each of us had to 'pump'. It worked like this: Hans stood in front of the aircraft and moved his arms, simulating the 'air'. Arm up, meant elevator up. Arm down, elevator down. Arm right or left, aileron input right or left. When he dropped his torso sideways, this meant setting the aircraft upright, 'Twisting'! Now we knew. Fully satisfied with his own

18

physical exercise, he left the continuation of practice up to us.

The sight of our automatic reactions was rather funny. A bystander could have had the impression that we were all a bit 'loony': One standing in front of the aircraft contorting his arms and body, and one in the aircraft swinging the pump handle like a madman! However, we knew what we were doing and we also knew that our automatic reactions were of the utmost importance.

The next exercise concerned the engine. Grade flew a two-stroke engine, which he had designed and constructed himself. This engine had one great advantage: Compared to its weight, it produced a high HP and was air cooled. The disadvantage was that it did not hold out very long. The regulation of fuel flow lay firstly in the hand and, secondly, in the 'ears' of the aviator. This meant that the right hand, with the arm extended towards the engine, installed forward and above the pilot, had constantly to hold on to the fuel spindle. If he took his hand away for only a second, you could be certain that the engine did not like it and after a few coughs 'lost its breath'. Instead of the engine running, the fuel was running! The engine was flooded. Many a Grade pilot lost control at the last moment due to a flooded engine. And this engine was to blame for the pilot 'flooding' himself in the end.

We then practised handling the engine. This was very strenuous. One of us had to swing the propeller. The worst of it was that this always had to be performed by the one not practising 'running the engine'. The one practising sat calmly in the aircraft, adjusting the fuel spindle for too much – or not enough – fuel, causing the engine to stop and the propeller-swinger to swing. We soon worked out a way to spread the workload. Each of us was allowed three practice runs to 'stop the engine', then the prop swinger scornfully walked away and sat down to watch. The sights which were then to be seen are difficult to put into words. Our ground aviator turned the fuel spindle so that there was just a little fuel flow, then he climbed out of the seat, crawled through the wires and rushed around the aeroplane to swing the propeller! Wroooomm, engine start. Back into the aeroplane the same way, back into the seat and – just as his hand reached the fuel spindle to increase fuel flow, the engine went ...blubb...blubb...blubb, end of dream! This was also allowed to happen three times before it was time to let the next ground aviator try!

Eventually, we all mastered the technique. During all this time we also studied the aircraft itself. The wings with their moveable ends, and the tail assembly, were made of bamboo canes. A host of simple, thin wires led from the wing to the tail, bracing a strong single bamboo cane leading to the tail. An equally large number of wires braced the wings and the undercarriage, making it difficult to climb into the seat. The seat, in the shape of a deck chair, practically hung under the wings like a hammock. The engine was installed in front of the wings, connecting the undercarriage to the wings. The aviator sat in the centre of the aircraft, just like a spider in its web, surrounded by a forest of wires in which, when climbing in or out of the aircraft, he either lost his cap or entangled his arms and legs. What seems primitive today was highly admired at the time. What is seen as impossible today evaded judgement then. This judgement and experience had to develop over the years, with courage and loss of life.

The propeller was a work of art. A gas pipe with a stretched metal shovel connected to each end. A propeller is a dangerous thing in itself, but this one, with its sharp metal edges, seemed like a rotating guillotine. This thing put the fear of God into us, especially when the ground was frozen and slippery. Soon our ground training had been completed. We now knew how to handle the controls and the engine. We were ready to go! Grade demonstrated flying to us by saying: 'To accelerate, push the pump handle forward, thus raising the tail, and roll straight ahead.' This was fabulously simple. Well then,... let's go!

Then the funniest 'rolling around' on the airfield began. Just imagine: Right hand raised up high, adjusting the fuel spindle, left hand firmly on the freely moving pump handle. One was hanging under the 'bird' more than sitting, while a valuable part of the body was hanging close to the ground. We still, rather uncomfortably, remember the large mole hills and the small tree stumps. Mind you, this airfield had been constructed on a clearing in the woods.

What an airfield! Those like Grade, who were able to fly, were happy to have a field like this all to themselves. For those of us who were just beginning, however, the woods around the field were very much like 'the single tree' for the cyclist. For us, the field was far too small, and for our early rolling exercises (taxiing), we had selected a special path which led diagonally across the field to a corner of the woods. This was the longest straight line available, but not very wide, and it fell to us to widen it as time went on. The 'rolling exercises' began, and the craft would just start to move when one or another of the following would occur, depending on the temperament of the aircraft's occupant. When he was a 'daredevil', he opened the throttle, pushed the pump handle forward, resulting in the tail lifting and exposing the propeller to the danger of 'pecking' (digging into the ground). In order to avoid this, he then pulled back on the handle and the craft would lift off. The engine would not like this at all, due to fuel starvation and would simply stop. Then the 'aviator' would stir the handle as if he really expected it to help.

All this happened within split seconds, and during these involuntary jumps, we never reached dangerous altitudes; we just jumped around the field with our somewhat vulnerable rear end making the odd solid contact! The cool, calm and collected aviator moved the throttle carefully, and when the aircraft started to move, he pushed the handle forward. The tail, however, could not be persuaded to lift off the ground, due to the lack of speed, thus slowing the craft. The small tail wheel, sooner or later, became the fixed centre of a circle, around which the stunned pilot and his craft spun with increasing speed. Trying to regain control with the pump handle resulted in the wheel deciding to search for another holding point as centre, and producing a sudden change of direction. During this merry-go-round, throttle control and all the other points of the practice were forgotten, usually resulting in the craft coming safely to rest. In both the case of the 'daredevil' and his more timid colleague, the craft ended up in the middle of the field.

During the first days of training, we all behaved as comrades and marched over to help start the propeller and give the pilot a push. This comradeliness did not, however, last very long, and at the same rate as our taxiing experience increased, our readiness to run and help decreased. The very careful ones among us took a solid rock or two, or maybe a stick, to use as primitive chocks to stop the bird from moving off while starting. When they finally sat in their hanging seat again, their attempts to kick the obstacles away from the wheels sometimes looked very dramatic.

Yes, the legs! Sitting in the hammock, you braced your feet against the axle, on which the wheels were mounted, and when not in this relaxed position the feet were used as brakes, in just the same way you steered a toboggan. One simply dug one's heels into the ground to slow down the speed of the rolling aircraft, resulting in a few sprained ankles; not to mention the damage to the heels on our shoes. This did not mean that our aircraft had no real brake; on the contrary, it was just that we were all scared stiff of it! The brake operated on the axle between the wheels, right where the feet usually found a hold. The brake itself was an iron claw which was prone to dig deeply into the ground, and especially favoured the small tree stumps which I have mentioned. We usually got off lightly when the propeller and the brakes wanted to demonstrate which of the two was the better.

If the effect of braking was more than the pilot had anticipated, one could not predict what the aircraft was going to do. Sometimes it flipped onto its back, other times it spun around the wing tip and stopped, tilted on its side. Either of these situations was rather uncomfortable, but it was less expensive when you executed a clean somersault, landing upside down. This would mean that only the metal propeller was bent, and this was easily put right using a solid hammer. Dropping a wing tip normally snapped the bamboo member on top of the wing, which supported the flexible upper surfaces (wing warping preceded ailerons). This produced an instant 'crash fee' and free drinks for those who were not able to practice because of the aircraft being out of action.

We were soon able to get down to business, after each of us had had the opportunity to assess his temperament and to be classed as either a 'jumping' or 'gyro' type. Soon we were buzzing around the field like wild bumble bees and poor Hans Grade was really worried! We took care of the required extension of the airfield, but it was remarkable how quickly one arrived at the edge of , or even made one's way into, the woods. It was not easy to cut off the engine and stop the aeroplane before reaching the end of the 'runway'. When you tried using the rudder, you could rest assured that you arrived at another corner of the woods, and that was the only certainty: you always ended up in the woods. Success came down to not being too ambitious in enlarging the practice ground. The propeller and wings did not appreciate this very much either. Normally our 'scooper' was satisfied with cutting down brush, bushes and thin trees and then coming to a halt after the job was done. So, within four months, we had helped considerably with the extension of the boundaries of the field.

The 'rolling' handling of the aircraft made us feel like half pilots, at least on the inside. We all admired Grade when he flew, and criticised the civilian students who had already made it to their first solo flight. When Grade flew we all had to look up, because he always flew at a height of 8 to 10 metres! When the two or three private students flew, we had to look down – or hit the ground. One was never sure if the wheels were airborne or if they were still rolling along the ground. We thought of them as boys in a 'non-swimmers' pool who were pretending to swim, while their feet touched the bottom. Occasionally a humorous (and sometimes serious) dispute developed over the question as to whether they had flown or not! We laugh about all this today. There is a considerable difference between having made your first flight all alone in 1910 or, later, having been accompanied by an instructor.

Grade did not have a two seat aeroplane at the time, as it was still being built. Everything one had to know and do in the aircraft could only be explained on the ground, and not demonstrated in the air. Before your first flight you felt like a child standing before the fireplace, waiting for Santa to come down the chimney. The question of having been airborne or just rolling on the ground became a matter of great moral importance. The breaking away from the ground, which nowadays loses its psychological pressure for those attempting their first flight, then required the highest concentration and willpower, as well as great strength. This strength was provided for us by the pure excitement of flying itself. Many others, however, were driven by the urge of earning more money and the sensation of adventure. These types of pilots mostly paid with their lives, and did nothing to enhance the reputation of flying in general.

At last came the day when we had practised enough 'tail in the air' and wanted to get on with it! We had often heard – far too often – how it was done in the air. We finally wanted to try, experience, feel and live it ourselves! The 'opener' was drawn by casting lots, and the order was set. Grade said over and over again: 'When it flies, throttle back immediately.' This was the safest recipe – if indeed there was one at all – to avoid stalling immediately after take off. The most important aim for us was to fly the short distance we had previously only 'rolled' across the field.

As soon as the first candidate was rolling we all lay down on the ground – as if at a single command. When all wheels had lifted above the height of the grass, an excited 'BRAVO!' was to be heard. Followed by the confirmation 'Flown!' One after the other... Thereafter we all went proudly to the Station Restaurant in Bork, a public house opposite the station. We carried pictures of ourselves, framed and glazed but still covered. The first 'flight' entitled each one of us, after a free beer, to hang it above the sofa reserved for us 'regulars'. The still covered 'memorial' bore the name and the date of the first flight, followed by: Pilots Examination...? Whilst hanging the pictures, we already looked forward to the unveiling ceremony. Many pictures were added later though, sadly, a cross was marked behind some of them.

From flying straight ahead we gained the confidence to use our wings. The first steep turn either took you up to tree top level or pulled you back to the ground. It took me to the tree tops and I will never forget the sight I was able to enjoy – the whole of the Bork forest -for the first time. Grade's altitude gave me a feeling of security which continued to drive me into the air during my long flying career. The confidence I felt then took me a step further and I flew a complete pattern around the field. Down below I could see all my comrades waving their hands and scarves. Hans Grade was waving his handkerchief to indicate the direction in which to land.

The engine understood the up and down of the handkerchief much more quickly than I did. It stopped completely and all by itself, while Grade only wanted me to throttle back. What came next was only the first of the surprises I was to experience in my future flying career. I pushed the handle down, and most probably all the other controls as well, because I was able to move the damned handle in all directions. Between the downs it went up , every so often – also to the left and right. Finally the aeroplane took me towards the ground for landing. The wing tip touched the ground first, then the propeller, then a wheel, and around all this, the aeroplane spun with me inside it.

'That went well,' was my first thought. The second was put to me by the engine: 'Cut the fuel.' It was pouring all over my head. Then, quickly out of the aircraft to inspect the damage.The propeller was a question mark and looked as if it was asking: 'Why did you shake me back and forth, when all was going so well?' Nothing else had been damaged. The propeller was quickly straightened out again. The aircraft had tagged a wheel. That was the best thing to happen. That way the wing was spared.

All was okay! That afternoon we were not able to fly any more, but this 'round trip' was worth the free beer! Everyone was expressing congratulations and, at the same time, telling me how I should have done it! When, later, everyone had had their first 'experience', the advice ceased. We all knew why. We were so happy that all had gone well and that nothing disastrous had happened.

CHAPTER TWO
Wolfgang Späte
Dr. Justus Schneider – the Doctor of the Wasserkuppe.

Dr. Med. Justus Schneider –
The Doctor of the Wasserkuppe, taken in 1932.

A man whose ambition is to drive a lorry powered by a roaring engine and having several axles, and who drives it recklessly on the road and motorway, does not require a medical examination in order to receive his licence. But every young glider flyer who wishes to perform his sport without an instructor (to fly solo) has to undergo a thorough medical examination, performed by a flight surgeon, before the officials will allow him to fly.

Well, doctors are human, just like you and I. They have been driven by their compassion and care for others (if we disregard the urge to earn vast amounts of money) to take up their profession. Sad to say that, sometimes, an unwavering obedience to the rules affects some flight surgeons, especially those who are not naturally equipped with a strong and indefatigable character. They have occasionally been known to pass harsh judgement where a tactful hint would have been much better. The relationship of a flyer to the flight surgeon has – in respect of medical examinations – always been under a certain tension. Pilots have closed ranks and taken up a fighting stance when they have had to deal with a psychologist. From an aviator, you will rarely hear an appreciative word about these 'worried' government officials, especially when they have had decisive powers over a pilot's future. These are the kind of 'soul doctors' who believe they are serving aviation best by preventing unsuitable individuals from entering the profession. Many false decisions in this field are proof of that.

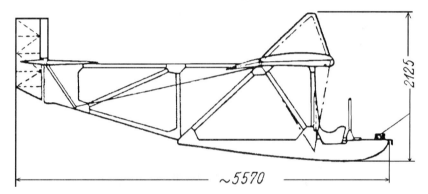

1932 Zögling (Pupil) Glider.

Having said this, it must also be said that there was one flight surgeon who was admired and highly respected by us 'gliders'. Symbolically 'carried shoulder high', for he fully represented the ideal of a 'Flying Doctor', he was Dr. Justus Schneider, well known for many years as the senior consultant at the Marien Hospital in Fulda. He, as a surgeon, had continuously to operate on the accident victims of the Wasserkuppe. Many a competing pilot owed the restoration of his health, even his life, to Dr. Schneider. A larger number of casualties, however, came from the students who were learning to fly gliders at the Wasserkuppe: more often than not the ambulance had to take one of the injured students to the hospital.

Dr. Schneider was not content merely to treat the human 'cases of repair' to the best of his ability following their crash landings. It did not take long for him to contact the training centre, the designers and constructors of these gliders at the Wasserkuppe. His experience led him to realise that fractures and damaged organs were operated on in higher numbers than in a so called 'normal' hospital. Dozens of 'Talus fractures' (fractures of the ankle bone) were brought to him in the early 1930's; nearly as often he had to deal with broken spinal columns or broken backbones; bruised and crushed livers were daily business for quite some time; serious head injuries (all experienced in the same type of glider) did not seem to end.

Dr. Schneider not only did his best conscientiously to cure the injuries his patients had sustained, but also searched for the cause of these injuries, especially for the 'how and where' they had occurred. He found that the Talus fractures were all caused

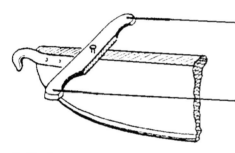

Rudder bar.

by the feet dropping down on landing and the heels hitting hard on the unsuspended rudder steering bar. The workshops then designed and built rudder pedals which supported the whole of the foot. From that time on there were no more broken ankles. The seats of the training gliders had an elegantly proportioned and anatomically shaped mould. During an 'elevator landing' and hard touch-down, this mould prevented the pilot's body from sliding forward in the seat, and compensated for the abrupt deceleration. As

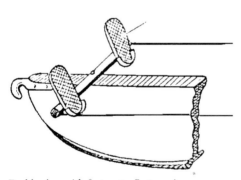

Rudder bar with foot rests, first version.

the horizontal seat was installed and fitted with suspension, spinal injuries were reduced considerably. Crushed livers were caused by narrow, inflexible and uncushioned lap straps. The straps were widened and a useful support and suspension added. The crushing injuries to the liver were reduced to practically nil. Dr. Schneider also succeeded in the pilots

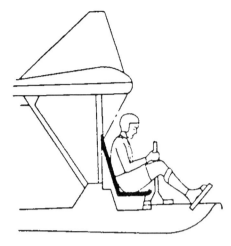

Upright, straight-backed seat.

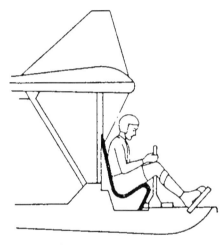

Anatomical aircraft seat.

wearing protective helmets, even during the most basic of flights for beginners. This measure resulted in the virtual absence of head injuries.

These examples could be continued and expanded. We will leave it at that, for this book shall not become a guideline for medicine. In all fairness, it has to be said that many other doctors have done their share for the protection of health and life in aviation. In this connection, the names of Dr. Ruff and Dr. Strughold must also be mentioned. However, Dr. Schneider stands out, not only because he helped to heal injuries with his great knowledge and experience, but also because he did everything in his power to prevent the accidents which brought the victims to his operating table.

In a post doctoral thesis, which was required to qualify as a university lecturer in1942, he wrote: 'A doctor who is sitting in front of the X-ray, and putting right the mutilations of the moment with his eyes and hands, has to repeat the event of injury in reverse... His view, and he himself, will be expertly trained if and when he perseveres in his work. His awareness of the external mechanisms of an injury will increase. This remains true for as long as there is medical education and training in this world in order to understand the mechanics and mechanisms within'.

Dr. Justus Schneider not only had excellent medical knowledge, but was also very skilful in handling the scalpel,

29

bone saw and all the other numerous utensils at his operating table. Mother Nature had provided him with the gift of a clear mind, which enabled him to understand the physical and mathematical backgrounds of his work. It let him comprehend their logical sequence. While searching for the cause of the injuries suffered in a plane crash, he found not only the kinematic explanation but, more importantly, he discovered the formula for their future prevention.

His lectures about flight medicine, held at the *Technische Universität* Darmstadt in 1938 and 1939, are unforgotten by those who attended. These lectures ended with a flight to high altitude in the pressure chamber, installed at the Kerkhoff Institute in Bad Neuheim. These 'flights' were followed by a visit to a local Inn, including free beer. In this way the students were, among other things, able to experience personally how co-ordination and mental dexterity diminish under the influence of altitude sickness in a way similar to that in which alcohol affects the same functions.

Dr. Schneider was the very first flight surgeon who had patients carried from their gliders and delivered straight to his hospital beds, immediately after these pilots had been taken to their physical limit by low temperatures and high altitude. During the Rhöne gliding competition they had been taken to altitudes of up to twenty-five thousand feet by upcurrents in thunderstorms, subsequently landing by parachute, with frostbite and exhaustion previously unheard of, unknown and not to be found at that time in any textbook.

What he thought of flight medicals is expressed in a few sentences published in 'Aviation Medicine' of 1952: '...the reflex apparatus of the human being is relatively complex and complicated. Naturally it is not possible, by medical examination only, to find out if the person examined will later become a good and safe flyer. Not everyone who has healthy fingers can become a good violinist, and not every healthy man can become a good pilot. Many a problem awaits psychological research.'

If anyone ever came near to the Hippocratic ideal of a doctor, then it was Dr. Justus Schneider. His scientific mind, combined with his sound medical experience, observation, critical views, great medical art and highest degree of medical and human ethics, made him 'The Doctor of the Flyers and the Wasserkuppe'.

CHAPTER THREE
Georg Wollé
Parachute Trials and Testing

While the first account in this book takes you back in the history of flight, practically to 'ground zero', Georg Wollé reports from the middle of the twenties, and writes about the trials of the parachute as rescue equipment for pilots.

Georg Wollé.

Rechlin was a very large flight test centre to the north of Berlin, located on the banks of Lake Müritz. In the thirties, thousands of technicians and engineers, as well as hundreds of pilots, worked at this centre. All were busy testing flying equipment which had, for the most part, been designed, developed and built in Germany. During my time at Rechlin, the remit for 'Rescue and Safety Equipment' fell to me. My colleague and very old friend, Siegfried Oswald Schade, was responsible for parachutes, and the two of us were supported by Karl Haubold, who was initially a member of the DVL – *(Deutsche Versuchsanstalt für Luftfahrt –* German Institute of Aviation Research and Development).

The testing of parachutes, and this fact must be mentioned here, was not an easy task to perform properly, especially in the face of the limited funds allocated. A proper test programme was not going to be cheap, mainly due to the fact that a systematic test series meant numerous flights, during which the dropping speed of the parachutes was to be increased to destruction point. This, of course, meant the eventual loss of the test 'chutes, which were of different design and make. All this had to be taken into account and accepted as losses in a very tight budget. Although the DVL checked and authorised the different parachutes, it would have been very difficult for both the Institute and the manufacturer to complete an extensive test series as it was performed at Rechlin.

A largely unknown fact should also be mentioned here: Hermann Göring, the *Reichsmarschall*-to-be, was virtually unknown at the time, but had already started a career in the NSDAP. He had previously been married to a Swedish girl, and through this marriage came into contact with a parachute company by the name of Thörnblad. He worked as a representative for their parachutes, one of which had been taken to Rechlin for testing. The 'chute was not introduced to us by Göring himself, but by his good friend 'Pilli' Körner, the future Prussian Secretary of State. During the time we tested the parachute he stayed at Rechlin and quietly beat the drum for the NSDAP. We were not interested in politics and, therefore, his words had no effect whatsoever on us. It is worth noting that, for all their efforts, the Thörnblad parachute proved unsuitable for our use and was not brought into service.

At the risk of bringing condescending smiles to the faces of most readers, I have to go into a few basic details for those who may have no knowledge of parachutes. (For the more knowledgeable I ask your indulgence.) There are basically two types of parachute, one operated automatically by a static line, and that which is operated at will by the wearer. Tests showed that the increasing speed of aircraft (and many other factors) made it necessary – in order to be able to use the 'chute as a life saving device – for the person leaving the aeroplane to be able to pull the ripcord and open the 'chute at an altitude of his choice. By pulling a handle which opened the pack around the parachute, a device drew out a small drogue 'chute which, in turn, pulled out and opened the main canopy. This type of parachute is called a manual parachute because it is opened at a selected altitude. Its disadvantage is that it can only be operated by a paratrooper or pilot who is still mentally and physically capable: on the credit side, the clearing of the aircraft is ensured.

For our tests we used man size dummies with a weight of 170 – 220 pounds (78 – 100 kilos), solely constructed for this use. They were made of hemp ropes and had ballast weights inside in order to achieve the required dropping weight. For manual 'chutes we had similar dummies, but they had the addition of a powerful clockwork mechanism installed on or inside their 'torsos' which was started at the commencement of the drop. After a pre-set time lapse, a powerful lever opened the 'chute, thus simulating the manual opening. These dummies were robust enough for them not to be 'fatally' harmed by repeated free falls from great heights.

For special trials we had a special dummy weighing 170 pounds (78 kilos). This also had a clockwork mechanism inside, and was dressed in a light flying suit and a leather cap in order to make it lifelike. We called it 'Löwenstein', after a banker who had disappeared after jumping from a small aeroplane while crossing the English Channel. (It was thought, although never proved, that he had committed suicide). During the tests with our Albatross L 76 the question arose: 'Is the crew, when in a steep spin, able to clear the aircraft whilst baling out?' It was I who had to answer this question through a practical test. Our fitters removed the observer's seat from the aircraft and replaced it with a wide strap. The view was now towards the tail, rather than the normal forward lookout. The whole thing was designed for me to have sufficient space available to wear a parachute pack on my back. The pilot and I had to be prepared for the worst, i.e. immediate bale-out should the dummy strike the tail or one of the wings of our biplane when released from the aircraft during the spin. This was the sole purpose of the test. If this trial went wrong, our chances of survival during the subsequent bale-out would be minimal.

All was made ready and I was sitting on the strap, facing the tail. The 'Löwenstein' dummy was put onto my lap, ready to be thrown overboard at a given time. Hoppe, a very reliable pilot, was flying, and the take-off was normal, as was the climb to a relatively high altitude. The heavy dummy was sitting on my lap, awaiting its fate and slowly numbing my legs. 'Löwenstein' was wearing a seat-pack parachute (as opposed to a back-pack), which proved quite a hindrance. However, I was not able to do anything about it and, as Hoppe flew towards the airfield, the tension was understandably high – would this test be successful? Soon we arrived overhead and Hoppe, in his usual easy manner,

Georg Wollé (right) with his pilot.

rolled the aircraft into a steep spin. I was half lying and half sitting with my view being only of the sky rotating above me. The rotational acceleration, as well as the increasing weight of the dummy, due to centrifugal force, pressed me into the seat strap and the side wall. By gathering all my strength and energy I managed to lift 'Löwenstein' and push him over the side. The tension had reached its climax! Would I have to jump after the dummy? My eyes looking towards the tail, I gave the dummy a last push! Then I observed 'Löwenstein' describing an elegant arc – relative to the spinning aeroplane – around the elevator

34

without touching it! Hurray! After a few more turns in the spin, Hoppe applied opposite rudder, levelled the aircraft out and we landed safely. We both felt highly satisfied, with an intensified sense of life and achievement.

A different and most uncommon parachute adventure is also worth recounting but, before doing so, I must mention that we initially strapped the dummy, fitted with the parachute, somewhere to the outside of the aeroplane: sometimes it was on a wing, but always in a position to enable the trial engineer to release it easily. For implementation of the test series with increasing dropping speeds, we were also required to release the dummies in a steep dive. In order to do this, we had to think of a re-usable tie-down or attachment point for the dummies.

Our *Meister* (master mechanic) Schubert, found a functional solution: he attached a very solid staple in the neck area, and another near the 'coccyx' on one of our continuous-use dummies. The dummy which had been fitted with a parachute was attached under the fuselage, held by two claw-shaped double hooks. These claws had to be opened by pulling a handle inside the cockpit, connected via a wire which, in turn, simultaneously opened the two claws and released the dummy. It then dropped away from the aeroplane, either pulling the static line attached to the 'plane, thus opening the pack and releasing the drogue, or, alternatively, triggering the clockwork within the dummy, to open the 'chute automatically after a set time and drop. The jettisoning device, which had been attached to the lower fuselage of an Albatross L 76, had proven itself during many of our trials, and we were fully confident of its performance. However, our faith was to prove slightly misplaced...

One day, during a trial, I was to release an automatic 'chute which had been made of Egyptian cotton instead of natural silk. The flight was routinely performed, the dummy with its static line parachute hanging under our aircraft as usual. The pilot was Hans-Jochen Keibel and the 'plane took off and climbed to working altitude with ease: it was a routine test. At the required airspeed we turned towards the airfield and I calculated the direction and speed of the wind and made the appropriate changes in track so that, when released, the dummy would descend onto the airfield. I pulled the handle to open the claws which would release the dummy to free fall. In a host of trials these claws had worked perfectly: why should they not work now? Instead of looking overboard as usual, to observe the release and clearing of the falling dummy, my main concern that day was to bring in the static line which actuated the parachute pack before it could cause any damage by whipping around in our slipstream. I was calmly hauling on the line when Keibel turned around and looked at me with a look of abject horror on his face, pointing toward the tail plane. When I turned my head in that direction, I observed the parachute rotating in our slipstream behind the tail. It was fully deployed and partially torn! Luckily it continued to rip and tear without damaging a single thing. An ugly situation, which Keibel mastered by immediately initiating a landing: in the circumstances, this went well despite the parachute lines and straps fluttering in the wind and dragging behind us.

How could this have happened? The claws had partially failed. The claw in the area of the coccyx had released the staple properly, but the corresponding claw in the neck of the dummy had not opened. Therefore the dummy was held 'by the scruff of the neck', being buffeted in the slipstream. It was my fault for not having looked overboard. Had I done so, I would have seen that the dummy had not released and fallen free of the aircraft. Instead of observing, as was my duty, I had drawn in the line which, in turn, had pulled the safety pins of the 'chute pack, causing the sudden deployment of the 'chute. Keibel felt this effect on his stick, and was understandably angry with me. No one has ever held this against me, and my actions were accepted, although they could have been the cause of a catastrophe... Luck had been with us!

CHAPTER FOUR
Helmut Roloff
Life at Rechlin

Helmut Roloff paints an atmospheric picture of the work at the Luftwaffe's Trials and Test Centre at Rechlin. The problems described in this report were all new at the time, but are common knowledge to every pilot today.

Helmut Roloff.

What drove us as young high-school and college graduates to go into aviation engineering, technology and flying as an occupation? What exactly was it that caused us, following our studies and some work experience in mainly non-flying-related jobs, to come back to aviation? Germany had gone through bad economic times between 1930 and 1935, but yet we returned to flying. What kept us in aviation and particularly in test flying, even when we had seen so many of our comrades pay with their lives while fulfilling their duties, even before the war?

I am only able to speak for myself; however, many of my comrades thought and felt as I did. Many more engineers in other lines of business, who had come into aviation after 1935, shared the same feeling. We were young, fit and enterprising. After our studies we did not want to work as mechanical or construction engineers in the well worn field of civil engineering. We were mostly interested in the new ideas and lines of work which aviation promised: areas such as airframes, engines, the actual science of flight and instrumentation – now called avionics. We saw possibilities for development after the aviation industry had taken its first new faltering steps after World War I.

We were lucky to be able to complete specialised studies in 'Flugzeugbau' (Aircraft Construction) at the 'Technische Universität' (Technical University) of Berlin. Also, in 1927, during our time with the 'Akademische Fliegergruppe' (Academical Flying Group) and in the years to follow, we not only acquired practical experience in all aspects of aviation engineering but, as working students with the DVL (Deutsche Versuchsanstalt für Luftfahrt – German Institute of Aviation Research and Development), we were able further to improve our knowledge. The goal of flying was achieved by each and every one of us, although financial grants from the Government were low and insufficient for most to complete their training. Many were forced to complete their pilots' licences and training in some other way elsewhere.

My appointment to the trial site at Rechlin came after spending eighteen months at the Luftfahrtministerium (Ministry of Aviation). This appointment offered the possibility of working not only as a trial engineer, but also as a professional pilot – to an extent we were unable to imagine during our studies. Now I think back to the trials we completed: the altitude chamber flights, the ejector seat tests, the acceleration flights measuring g-force and, especially, the efforts of Department E 2 during research into the speed of sound and the possibility of breaking the sound barrier in a dive. For some of our comrades these trials ended in disaster and, without exaggeration, I may say that these activities, in our world as it was at that time, corresponded to the achievements of astronauts in space two decades later. We were every bit as much at the cutting edge of technology

It was especially attractive for an engineer to combine the laboratory tests, which were partly performed on test equipment which they themselves had developed, with the practical flight tests. All this was followed by analysis at the desk, sometimes with results of major importance.

We were free and far less restricted in our flying than pilots nowadays. The aircraft were relatively inexpensive compared with those of today, and there was a commonality in their controls. We often flew different types of aircraft, fast, slow, large, small, on the same day, depending on the requirements of the tests and trials to be performed on that particular day. The test pilots at the Centre were very calm, exceptional men, inspiring confidence in all around them; they were all experts and we had complete confidence in them. While flying with any of them, as a trial engineer during tests, observing the course of events, one had the same confidence in them as if one were flying oneself – perhaps even more so. I would compare this to the confidence one had as a child during PE classes. While performing exercises at the horizontal bar, one knew very well that there were two students lending a helping hand to catch one if anything were to go wrong. In this situation one had faith and confidence, one risked everything and, usually, all went well.

This mutual trust was evident during cross-training, or when flying a new aircraft for the first time. For instance, when the first Bf 109 G6 (Gustav) arrived for trials at Rechlin, fitted with a significantly more powerful engine, fielding a much higher gross weight and with a rudimentary pressurised cockpit, comrade Beauvais, as the official in charge of fighter planes, merely said, after a brief introduction: 'Try her out'. And I went out and flew her. Although I had flown all of the Bf 109 series up to the Gustav, as well as the Fw190, I thought this simple invitation was invaluable proof of confidence. To gain such confidence, and to be trusted by everyone involved, was the goal of every pilot at Rechlin. It was needed to gain strength, calmness and self confidence in order to be able to handle calculated risks and survive.

Nevertheless, we were not infallible. The following incident happened to me on take off with a Do 335 – an aircraft with two engines arranged on the centre line, one behind the other, one propeller pulling and the other pushing. As usual, I had taxied across the field to the take-off position, using the forward engine. A good looking young lady in uniform waved the appropriate signal, clearing me for take-off. After briefly checking over the instruments, flap position etc., I opened the throttle for take-off and realised at that moment that I had not even started the rear engine. With only one engine and this heavy, fast aeroplane, I would not have been able to lift off. I throttled back, taxied back to take-off position, started the rear engine, nodded towards the astonished young lady and, again with her permission, I took-off safely. Of course, even today, I do not know if she was ever aware of my near-fatal mistake.

For flying at high altitudes – initially performed without a pressurised cabin – we had to undergo many a test conducted in the altitude chamber by flight surgeons working at Department E5. We knew from these 'flights' that a fit young man was able to hold out for up to seven minutes without supplementary oxygen at an altitude of 7,500m (24,607ft) or one and a half minutes at 9,000m (29,529ft). At altitudes higher than that, without additional oxygen, he would lose control and suffocate almost immediately. In order to find out if and how the human body would adjust to higher altitudes, several groups, accompanied by doctors, were ordered to the Alps for two weeks, doing physical exercises with the doctors continuously checking us over. The tests that followed in the Rechlin altitude chamber, without oxygen at 25,000ft, showed no impairment of reaction or thinking abilities, even after one hour of 'flight', and the maximum time at altitudes of 30,000ft was extended from one and a half minutes to up to five minutes. However, this altitude 'acclimatisation' wore off after one to two weeks at normal altitude.

I have inadvertently experienced the effects of lack of oxygen in flight on two occasions. During one flight, I was wearing an oxygen mask at 6,000 metres (19, 685ft), testing new equipment. I was sitting in the rear seat, performing a test which involved taking instrument readings every two minutes and plotting the values on a chart. I had noted the first series of readings correctly, then started to enjoy the flight more and more and said to myself: 'Enjoy this beautiful flight! It is sufficient to take the readings every three minutes!' The world became friendlier by the minute, and the last thing I remember was making the decision to take the readings every five minutes. The pilot, as he told me later, looked back at me through the rear view mirror and saw that something was terribly wrong. I came to, after a dive from 6,000 down to 2,000m (19,685ft to 6,652ft), and wanted to continue to take readings. I realised, after glancing at the altimeter, that we were only at 2,000m and that my oxygen hose had become disconnected from the supply system. After landing, laying stretched out for half an hour on the conference table in my office, still wearing the winter flying suit, was sufficient to restore me to a normal condition.

Since that incident, I have always checked the oxygen hose connection at regular intervals when flying at high altitude. However, even this did not prevent a similar occurrence. Again, I was flying at an altitude of 6,000m., this time solo in a Ju 87. Checking the oxygen hose connection from time to time, I noticed that it had become disconnected again. I let go of the stick, the aircraft being nicely in trim, and reached for the two ends of the hose, trying to connect them. I was unable to manage it, and noticed that my ability to concentrate was fading rapidly, making it even more difficult to connect the hose. At least I was sufficiently 'compos mentis' to realise the need for immediate action! Holding both ends together with my right hand to keep a little oxygen flowing through the system, I pushed the stick forward with my left hand and established the aircraft in a shallow dive, watching the altimeter unwinding with great concentration. After levelling out at a lower altitude, I was able to re-connect the hose to the oxygen system without difficulty.

As far as I recall, this and other experiences of a similar nature resulted in the extension of the oxygen hose to allow movements of the head while wearing an oxygen mask and prevent the hose from disconnecting. On the other hand, the requirement for the hose to disconnect during a bale-out remained.

For flights above 12,000 up to 13,000 metres (39,371ft up to 42,651ft) breathing oxygen alone was insufficient, and pressurised cockpits and cabins were introduced for aircraft capable of reaching such altitudes. We therefore had to test the equipment for the air supply and pressure regulators of such cabins, which were required to maintain constant pressures of up to the equivalent of 6,000 to 8,000 metres (19,500 to 26,250ft. irrespective of the actual 'altitude'. I vividly recall two incidents which occurred during these tests. For flight testing we had a Ju 86 at our disposal, equipped with a diesel engine which enabled us to reach altitudes of

13,000 metres (42,651ft), quite unusual for that time. When flying so high, the sky above us showed a much darker hue than that seen at the altitudes with which we were more familiar. The temperature and climatic conditions in our cabin were excellent and that fact, coupled with the extreme altitude at which we were to work and fly, let us view events in a more relaxed manner, and to attach to many of them much less importance. If only we had not been at war!

With these feelings, comrade Stößel (who was later to crash) lit a cigarette; this was possible because the air in the cabin was continuously renewed and filtered and the smoke disappeared relatively quickly. This minor 'out of the norm' event turned our first real high altitude flight into something special – an almost solemn moment. The second incident concerned the area of responsibility of our flight doctors. There was to be a test to show how the human body would react to a sudden loss of pressure from an 'altitude' corresponding to approximately 2,000m (6,652ft) in the chamber to the very low pressure of 10,000m (32,809ft) – consistent with a sudden and unexpected rupture of the pressurised cabin. A small pressure chamber, holding only one person, had already been built onto the existing larger chamber for this purpose. The pressure in the main chamber was then lowered to the level consistent with the predetermined 'high altitude'. The small chamber had its own ambient temperature and pressure but, by means of an electromagnetically actuated flap between the two chambers, the pressure in the small chamber was suddenly dropped to the low pressure of the large one. Through viewing windows one was able to observe the 'volunteer' during the test. The sight of the subject, one of the strongest and fittest flight surgeons at Rechlin, at the moment of the sudden loss of pressure, was impressive, even frightening. I realised that the physical limit of human resilience had been reached. A further intensification could not exclude the dangers of side effects or actual physical damage. To illustrate the extent of the physical trauma involved, I observed that a balloon containing a small amount of air, which had been hanging limply inside the small chamber before the experiment, became almost fully inflated in an instant with the pressure drop!

A further example of technical advance and achievement was the development of the ejector seat, also touching the limit of human resilience. Due to the increasing speeds of aircraft, the development of the ejector seat became necessary in order to clear the tail of the aeroplane during bale-out. A further requirement, implemented later, was to guarantee the safe ejection and survival of the pilot should anything go wrong during take off. The first experiments and trials, with a compressed air cylinder connected to a seat, did not produce the required results, due to the small air ram diameter. Even telescopic rams were not able to produce the required ejection velocity. The compressed air was replaced by explosive cartridges and, with these, the required ejection speed could be achieved in a short distance with higher acceleration. It was then necessary to establish whether the human organism could withstand brief accelerations of up to 10g and more along the longitudinal axis of the body.

For this test, a seat with harness was mounted on an upward-tilted slide rail. With the aid of compressed air rams and then explosive cartridges, it was fired upward at different accelerations and smoothly decelerated towards the top. By filming each event, and by using time and distance markings, one was able to calculate the individual acceleration. From these trials, which were initially carried out using a dummy and only later tested with a volunteer, it was concluded that the upper limit of short-term vertical acceleration which the human body was able to withstand was around 20g. (The strain on the human body can readily be appreciated when considering the fact that, at the instant of firing the seat, a force of 20g is exerted on the body, and the average individual is pressed into the seat with a weight of 1,300kg (2,900lbs). The cheeks are pulled down with twenty times their weight, and the blood is heavier than iron at that moment.)

These few 'highlights' from the activities of the Rechlin Trials and Test site illustrate how new, important and interesting these duties were. After the War, the results of these experiments were disseminated worldwide and received grateful recognition, especially in civil aviation. This also proved that we, as college and university graduates, had made the right decision in choosing studies in aviation which led to new, interesting and progressive responsibilities and careers.

CHAPTER FIVE
Walter Baist
Kaltstart

Walter Baist recalls how the problem of the bitter cold was handled 50 years ago. For nearly ten years the so-called 'cold start procedure' played a dominant rôle in enabling quick engine starts, even in the lowest of winter temperatures. Nowadays it is almost completely unnecessary, thanks to the development of suitable winter grade oils and lubricants..

Dr.-Ing Walter Baist.

In the winter of 1934, the pilot was required to sit in the open cockpit of his Ar 64, Ar 65, He 45, He 46 or any of the predominantly open cockpit aircraft, virtually unprotected from the terrible cold. He was muffled in fur lined flying clothing from head to toe and, in this, was at least able to tolerate limited exposure. However, he would frequently be unable to get the engines of his aircraft started and running. The pilot who wanted to be ready to take off early the next morning had to ensure a warm hangar space for his machine the night before. However, the aeroplanes were large and the hangars far too small! The pilot who was not able to obtain hangar space had to rely on appliances designed to help thaw out the cold and frozen aircraft in order to get them to run. Hissing monsters (Kärcher devices) produced hot air by burning petrol, and blew it through a gigantic 'trunk' to the aircraft, nestling under cloth covers which had been spread over the wings and engines. Dressed up like this, the Ju 52 looked more like a grandmother than *Tante (Aunt) Ju'*, all wrapped in shawls, scarves and hoods as if she were undergoing a secret medical treatment. Despite all this, it was sometimes the case that the first engine could not be started until well after breakfast, and that lunch was being served in the Mess by the time numbers two and three were running smoothly.

Not only was starting the engines a problem, but also the run-up. This was performed to heat the oil to the required minimum temperature of 40°C (104°F). Valuable time was lost with engines having a small lubrication system (dry sump) and a large oil reservoir (eg the Ju 52, fitted with the BMW 132 engine). During short winter days it was sometimes not worth taking off, even after everything was at last running well – there was simply not enough daylight remaining to fly a sortie. This despite the enormous fuel consumption and the obvious lack of availability for a 'scramble'. The sceptics were doubtful if flying was really viable during extreme 'winter emergencies', especially when facing problems of this nature.

Times were not long past since a man had held a fuel-drenched cloth to the air intake, with a second man cranking the propeller and the pilot having to produce a strong spark with the hand-cranked inductor in order to start the engine – truly a team effort! In those days one had to drain the oil and/or the liquid coolant in the evening and return it after it had been heated up the next morning. Eventually it became possible to inject the volatile 'Fl. starting fuel' directly into the air intake, using a spray pump. With the aid of the Bosch-designed flywheel starter, it was possible to turn the engines sufficiently, even with temperatures at freezing point. However, it was still a familiar sight to see one or two men standing with one foot on the nose wheel and the other on the leading edge of the wing, cranking furiously on the starter, or standing on a foot-rest and clinging to a ladder, only to be blown off their shaky perches by the cold prop-wash. Eventually, the men were relieved of these rather dangerous jobs by the installation of the 'Bosch- Eclipse Starter'. This starter was electronically driven, although the facility to crank-start the engine manually was still maintained.

Replacement of the 'hissing monsters' began in 1935, when G. Reidenbach, Director of Trials at Rechlin, noticed an article in a Canadian newspaper stating that the Canadians were thinking of adding fuel to the lubricating oil in order to thin it down and make the engines run smoothly during cold weather. Reidenbach contacted the different companies producing aircraft engines, such as Daimler-Benz, BMW, Junkers and Argus, seeking their views on this idea. They all warned against it. To the best of their knowledge, fuel in the oil was worse than poison. For instance, when there was engine damage, the first thing to look for was fuel contamination in the oil. If this proved positive, no one thought any more about it. The diagnosis was clear: engine failure due to fuel in the oil, with resultant lack of viscosity. The only problem remaining was to find out how the fuel had got there.

Reidenbach, however, did not give up. He begged his colleagues, Wolfram Eisenlohr and his successor at Rechlin, Otto Cuno, further to investigate the Canadian claims. Eventually the problem was tackled in the summer of 1936, the first trials using the engine installed in an Ar 65, a glycol – cooled BMW VI straight 12 cylinder unit producing 750hp. Due to its floating crankshaft this engine was notoriously difficult to handle, not only during winter. With great care we began to add small amounts of fuel to the oil and, as time went on, more and more fuel was added. The engine was initially run up a few minutes before take-off. It didn't take long before the times from start-up to take-off were reduced. The pilot was barely able to take his eyes off the oil pressure and temperature indicators. Dr. Giessmann's 'combustible fuels and lubrication laboratory' was given a great deal of work in measuring viscosity. The engine shop had to dismantle a vast number of engines in order to take wear and tear measurements. But the BMW VI remained intact no matter how we treated it!

Helmut Schmachtenberg and Heinrich Lipp were seen at Rechlin dressed in fur flight suits and boots throughout the year. During winter they prepared the aircraft for cold start, and in summer they carried out their tests in the refrigeration chamber. This chamber measured 4 x 4 x 6 metres (13.5 x 13.5 x 21ft) and had been planned in 1936/37 to tackle the different problems of cold weather: it was completed in 1939, and was used almost exclusively to investigate cold start problems. The double doors were large enough to allow a lorry to be driven in, or for an Me 109 (without wings) or test engines mounted on trailers to be taken into the chamber. The real problems with low temperatures began only after several hours of cooling to temperatures lower than -10°C (14°F). Winter days when temperatures dropped that low were few and insufficient for fundamental studies at our latitudes. In the refrigeration chamber, which had a cooling performance of 100,000 cal/h (116KW) – equal to 290 household refrigerators – temperatures down to minus 45°C (-40°F) were achieved. At such low temperatures lubrication oil turns thicker than jelly and its viscosity increases dramatically. The trials in the refrigeration chamber proved that it was possible to start all aircraft engines down to +5°C (41°F) without assistance. 'Rotring' oil had a viscosity of 500°E equalling 3,800 cSt. To ensure sufficient engine start RPM at lower temperatures, fuel was added to dilute the oil to 500°E. This was achieved, using regular flight fuels (A3, B4, C3). Rotring Oil – Fuel mixtures reached a viscosity of 500°E at the following temperatures:

% additional fuel	0	5	7.5	10	15	20
500°E at temp.°C	+5	-5	-12	-18	-28	-39

In order not to complicate the procedure, three mixtures were eventually set, according to the outside air temperature range:

	+5° to -10°	-10° to -30°	colder than -30°
Outside air temp.			
% fuel	7.5	15	20

It was said that adding 1% of fuel had the same effect on the viscosity of the oil as an increase in temperature of 2.2°C (4°F). Initially, three potential dangers were identified:

First: The possibility of explosions within the crankshaft casing. This fear proved groundless. The mixture inside the casing was too rich, and far from the range of ignition.

Second: Engine wear might be too high. This was refuted by countless measurements during the cold start trials. It was, in fact, possible to prove a *reduction* of wear during cold starts.

Third: The oil could become too thin. This risk caused the greatest concern: it was found that the amount of fuel added was normally reduced to half after 15 minutes flight, through evaporation due to the temperature of the oil, and to a quarter after 30 minutes. After 1.5 to 2 hours it had evaporated completely. Aircraft fuel boils from 40°C to 180°C (104°F to 356°F): therefore the volatile elements evaporate quickly, leaving behind the lubricating oil, which has a much higher boiling point. The operating temperature of lubrication oil (average 90°C, 194°F) is reached within 15 minutes from cold start. The fuel which has been added to the oil is still half the quantity, and the relative viscosity of the lubricant is, at that time, lower than in normal operation.

An aircraft which had been 'treated' by adding fuel to the oil, was not merely available for a cold start, it *had* to be 'cold started'. Hitherto, the pilot had had to keep an eye on the oil temperature while taxiing out and running up the engine. With fuel introduced into the oil he no longer had to watch the oil temperature so closely, but had to keep his eyes glued to the oil pressure indicator. RPM needed to be increased in order to keep the oil pressure at maximum, but was not to be exceeded for fear of damaging the engine. This procedure produced very short starting and run-up times, of the order of only two to six minutes, depending on the type of aircraft. Even the third speculative 'danger' never led to engine failure. Either the risk was overestimated or the survival instinct of the pilots made them adhere strictly to *die Kaltstartvorschriften* (the cold start procedure).

The method of oil/fuel mixing was different with every type of aircraft. Those mainly flown in the east and north were given priority for fitting with a *Kaltstart-Mischanlage* (cold start mixing unit). The device itself consisted of an additional fuel line which led to a mixing valve and, from there, to the mixing nozzle and straight into the oil line. The injection of fuel into the oil, and the mixing of the two, was performed soon after landing, when the oil temperature had dropped to between 20° and 40°C (69°F-104°F). First, the duration of the flight was noted (to calculate the amount of fuel which would have evaporated from the oil) and the remaining oil level was measured with a dipstick. Based on these values, a time was taken from a mixing table and the mixing valve was opened for the specified time (normally between two and six minutes) in order to achieve the proper fuel/oil mixture. During this mixing process, the engine was run at 1,000 – 1,200rpm., continuing for a further few minutes after the closure of the mixing valve to ensure the diluted oil was turned over at least once, and circulated to all the parts requiring lubrication. During this time all regulators and controls lubricated by engine oil had to be moved to ensure they were supplied with the diluted oil. Lastly, the oil consumed by the engine during the flight was topped up from containers of pre-mixed oil and fuel. In this way, cold start preparations took less time compared to the days when the oil was re-filled and mixed with the engine running.

On older aircraft types, and on training and commercial 'planes, the mixing device was not installed. Mixing took place either by adding the required amount of fuel directly into the reservoir and stirring it with a purpose-made stick (if the design of the filler opening permitted) or by draining the remaining oil from the sump, mixing it with fuel in a drain pan, and returning it via the filler. Once refilled, or with the fuel having been added, the engine was run in order to turn the oil over at least once to lubricate all parts.

With these improvements, our experts were able to start all engines at temperatures as low as -35°C (- 31°F). When the mercury was even lower, the one remaining aid was the use of acetylene. Having a much broader ignition range when compared to petrol vapour it tended to help stimulate combustion and warm the cylinders. Initially, a small quantity of calcium carbide was placed on a wet tin lid close to the air intake, but with only limited success. Later, large amounts of acetylene, straight from a compressed gas cylinder, were directed into the inlet: however, the use of acetylene was unpopular with the 'troops' and was used only as a last resort, since it frequently caused backfires and explosions in the air intake, resulting in the bending of the regulators and damage to the control valves.

In tandem with the technical trials, commanding officers of active units and troops were being briefed and trained from early 1938. Heinz Fischer can still remember demonstrating a cold start on a He 45 in 1938 to a *'Ögemischten Schlapphut und*

49

Lametta Club (a floppy hat and gongs club – slang of the time for a group of officers). They not only showed very little interest, but also demonstrated brusque disapproval. Why waste all this energy? After all, temperatures had never limited the use of aircraft in any of the previous German 'campaigns', such as: the Spanish Civil War (17th April 1936 to 28th March 1939), the re-occupation of the Rhineland by German troops (March 1936), the annexation of Austria to Germany (13th March 1936) or even the take-over of the German areas of the Sudetenland (29th September 1938).

The situation soon became far more serious, and in March 1939 I was given orders to demonstrate the cold start method to a unit flying Me 109s at Bad Aibling. My orders came direct from Udet because, apparently, instructions had been issued to the unit but were being ignored. The welcome I received at the unit was rather frosty, and it was clear that at Bad Aibling everyone thought of the cold start procedure as a crack-pot idea created at Rechlin, which was to be introduced by one of these '*Schlapphut Fliegern*' (floppy hat flyers – boffins). The introductory lecture to all the pilots and technicians was conducted peacefully enough, as was the preparation of three Me 109's for the cold start. However, in the discussions which followed, both before and after lunch, feelings were running high and the commanding officer had to call for order several times. Not a single pilot volunteered for the flights planned in the afternoon, despite my having run up the engines on two of the aircraft immediately to full throttle after start-up, and taken off with the third straight from its parking position.

They remained unimpressed, but at least discussion that evening began more objectively. However, during the course of the evening, things degenerated back to their former inflexible position. This was perhaps partly due to the consumption and influence of alcohol but, whatever the reason, the rejection was most emphatic. The request I had made, for two pilots to perform a cold start take-off as a three ship formation with myself the next morning, was ignored. I expressed the view that I had done my duty: I had explained what cold start was all about, and demonstrated that it was safe. I said that I felt my mission had been completed, and that I would report its outcome to Berlin, and would probably be required to speak to Udet himself. The effect was electric: the *Kommandeur* stood up and called his pilots, in so many words, a bunch of cowards and volunteered himself for cold start the next morning. This proved successful, and after performing the cold start procedure the following day, I arranged a 'happy go lucky' dogfight with two of the most experienced pilots. Climbing, diving and banking above the beautifully sunny snow-capped Alps, and enjoying the pure exhilaration of flight was some small compensation to me for everything I'd had to put up with in that unit!

After leaving the squadron that very evening, I discovered why Udet had pressed so hard to introduce the cold start procedure to the unit at Bad Aibling: on 15th and 16th March 1939, German troops marched into Bohemia and Moravia to set up the *'Reichsprotektorat'*. I wondered if the *Kommandeur* at Bad Aibling had already had a secret order in the drawer of his desk?

Interest in cold start procedure grew, even at the highest level. During the visit by Hitler and Göring to Rechlin on 3rd July 1939 – even though it was summer – it was included in the demonstration programme. I had been tasked with this demonstration, and was to appear in an Me 109 coded IP+QS. Whilst someone else did all the explaining, Hitler walked up to the engine and felt the exhaust stubs to ensure that he was not being deceived. As soon as the engine fired, I opened the throttle to full power and took off at 12.00 hours according to schedule – straight from my dispersal point. It was said that I left a whirling mass of hats, caps and overcoats behind me. After a short flight I joined the circuit at the neighbouring Lärz airfield, flew a traffic circuit and touched down at 12.08 hours, thus conveniently removing myself from the hustle and bustle of the 'state visit' at Rechlin.

As good as all the demonstrations had been, and despite a few mishaps, the July 3rd visit brought more problems than recognition to Rechlin. The troubles which were later encountered in the front line nourished Hitler's suspicion of having been tricked at Rechlin. He was later to say that he should have taken into consideration the fact that we had been a well-trained team of engineers. For the extreme conditions at the front line, especially in Russia, his expectations should have been reduced by at least half.

The situation I had experienced at Bad Aibling repeated itself on a larger scale within the squadrons. The common reaction was: '...Have these chaps at Rechlin gone insane? Everyone knows that diluting the engine oil inevitably leads to engine damage. Why should the generals and experienced pilots now have confidence in this new method, about which the technical directors of the engine plants had been worried three years before? Should the crew chiefs now pour aviation fuel into the oil when they had previously been punished for such a heinous deed? Should the pilots risk life and limb for such a nonsense?'

In the first years of the war, most campaigns had taken place during the mild seasons of the year, or in warm climates. However, the necessity for cold start increased considerably after 22nd June 1941, when Germany declared war against Soviet Russia. In the winter of 1940/41, a fighter- bomber wing of He 111's was deployed from the Hamburg area to Stavanger, where the temperature was -15° to -20°C (5° to -4°F). Numerous engine seizures during this action led to the suspicion of sabotage. However, investigations showed that cold start procedure had not been employed, even though it was mandatory. On the occasion of an emergency landing by a Ju 88 from the meteorological squadron at Banak in Spitzbergen, a Ju 52 flew over to collect the crew. Due to the fact that cold start preparations had not been carried out when the '52's engines were shut down, they could not be turned over the next morning and, finally, a fire had to be lit below each of the motors to thaw them out.

Huppenbauer normally used a He 111 for his travels to Norway and Finland, but his regular aircraft was not equipped with a cold start mixing device, and the crew chief regularly had to prepare for cold start with a measuring pail and stirring spoon. Using this He 111, 'Huppes' was to fly *Generaloberst* Stumpff from Oslo to Stavanger. The General, being high up the ladder in his career, was not the least interested in cold start procedure. As Huppes recalls: '... as we taxied onto the runway, I asked the General sitting next to me, 'Everything okay?' He pointed out to me that the temperatures of the oil and cooling fluids were too low. I simply said, *'Kaltstart!'* and opened the throttles to take off power. From the corner of my eye I saw that my Commander had turned a little pale. After the uneventful return flight, he had personally gained faith in the cold start procedure.'

From 1940/41, colleagues from Rechlin were frequently en route to the front lines to help the troops by offering assistance in difficult technical situations, whenever and wherever they arose. My log book of that time shows a round trip with a Ju 52 from 23rd to 30th October 1941. The Ju 52 had been filled with experts from Rechlin and the routing of that journey was set via Baranowitschi – Smolensk – Chatalowka – Orscha – Reval – Szeschtschinskaja. We supervised the proper application of cold start procedures, and also had to take fuel samples from captured fuel storage tanks to check if the contents were suitable for use in *Luftwaffe* aircraft.

The *'Blitzkrieg Optimists'* were hoping to celebrate Christmas 1941 in the Kremlin, but the Russians were again helped by their strongest ally: just as in the war of 1813, when they were fighting Napoleon, *'Väterchen Frost'* (Little Father Frost) intervened. In December 1941, along the length of the new front line, the mercury fell to – 40°C (-40°F) and temperatures as low as – 50°C (-60°F) were recorded. Masses of snow fell from the skies and freezing winds drove across the steppe. What use were all the technical preparations? The relentless cold persisted and the dreams of the OKW (*Oberkommando der Wehrmacht* – Supreme Headquarters of the Armed Forces) turned to ice!

The *Luftwaffe* was better supplied with winter clothing than the majority of the Army and, thanks to cold start, it seems that 35% of the aircraft were operational at the time. But to what purpose? Mountains of snow covered wings and runways and, when refuelling was required, neither snow ploughs nor tankers nor other supply vehicles were able to move an inch. When ice and drifting snow obscured visibility, when the movements of ground troops literally grew stiff, nothing, no lorry, no weapon, no gun worked properly! No one had thought about winter operations! No one had taken precautions or made preparations for the ground vehicles. *After* things had gone wrong, everything and everyone was blamed. This included *Luftwaffe* ground crew for not preparing for cold start and applying the appropriate procedures. But it should be remembered that these men, for example, already half frozen, with empty stomachs and poorly clothed in temperatures of -40°C, often had to fight through the deep snow in order to reach a Ju 87 which had just landed, and would have to stand there for half an hour in the icy wind, intensified by the prop-wash, possibly under enemy fire, and prepare the aircraft for the next cold start... Devotion to duty in the extreme!

I could end my recollection at this point, if it were not for certain misleading accounts in post war literature which require challenge.

In the book **'The Blond Knight of Germany'**, by *R.F. Toliver and T.C. Constable, on* Page 79 we find the following:

The Germans were astonished in Russia when Red fighters swarmed over their airfields on sub-zero mornings, when they had been unable even to start their own aircraft. When Erich's squadron captured a Russian airman, he showed them with typical Soviet directness how the Red Air Force maintained its operational effectiveness at 40° below zero. The co-operative prisoner was proud of knowing something perhaps the Germans didn't know. He called for half a gallon of gasoline in a can, went over to one of the grounded Messerschmitts, and to the horror of the watching JG-52 personnel, poured the gasoline into the aircraft's sump. The Germans backed away twenty yards or more. The moment that *Dummkopf* turned on the ignition and attempted to start, there would be an explosion.

Apprehensive mechanics began cranking the motor by hand while a German pilot cringed down in the cockpit. After the gasoline was thoroughly mixed with the congealed oil, he turned on the ignition. The engine started. There was no explosion. The big Daimler-Benz burst into life and ran solidly. The Russian airman explained, through interpreting Germans, that the oil congealed at sub-zero temperatures and made it impossible for the starters to budge the engine. The gasoline liquefied the oil, and then evaporated as the engine warmed up. The only necessary precaution was to change the oil more often when using gasoline for sub-zero starting.

Erich also watched another captured Russian demonstrate a sub-zero starting gimmick. He tells the story in his own words:

'This prisoner called for a spare-parts tray. Again, there was a call for gasoline. While Bimmel and others watched, the Russian stalked over to a nearby Me 109 and set the tray on the ground underneath the engine compartment. He filled the tray to brimming with gasoline. He lit a match and sprang back. The gasoline vapour flared alight despite the sub-zero temperatures, and a wide tongue of flame licked at the underside of the fighter's opened engine compartment. For a full ten minutes the blaze continued. One of the mechanics said that the electrical system would be ruined – the insulation all burnt away – as the flames died down. The Russian simply said, 'Start it.' The instant smooth roar of the motor convinced everyone. Fighters could be started in sub-zero weather – once you knew how. We all felt indebted to the Red Air Force for this scheme, which helped us to get into the air to meet their early morning sorties...'

This report sounds fantastic, although Hartmann may have given the account of these incidents to his two American interviewers. However, the following may be assumed:

The first Russian, who poured petrol into the sump oil, knew this could be done. Shortly before his sudden death, G. Reidenbach said he had heard about the Russians possessing papers concerning cold start procedure. They appeared to be reprints of the initial graphic papers for the first cold start procedure we had produced at Rechlin, but in Cyrillic lettering. It will remain unknown if these instructions accidentally fell into Russian hands or if they were officially handed over during the co-operation phase of the Hitler- Stalin Pact, as were so many other papers.

The procedure used by the second Russian, lighting a small fire beneath the engine, only proves the ingenuity and the ability to improvise which is typical of these people. The staggering conclusion is that, as late as the winter of 1939/40, Hartmann's wing had neither heard of, nor followed, the orders given by highest headquarters concerning cold start preparations.

Similar reports were made by the 35 men from Rechlin who, under Milch's command, were supposed to give technical support to the troops during the disaster of Stalingrad: the orders for cold start preparations were followed by only 30% of the units. The most negative observations made, in Saporoshje, had been contained in the report by one of our colleagues. There he saw approximately a hundred sparkling new aircraft of all sizes and makes, fighters, bombers and transport aircraft, standing on the airfield. They had landed there for an intermediate stop before continuing to the front lines. Due to cold start preparations not having been carried out, the soldiers were unable to restart the aircraft.

In the book by David Irving and Erhard Milch 'The Tragedy of the German *Luftwaffe*', statements regarding cold start received some criticism. For example, referring to the aircraft at Stalingrad, it states that: 'Maintenance of the aircraft by units lying in the open was not possible because their commander was unable to provide his troops with the minimum of protection against the freezing cold...The demoralised crews did not make even the smallest of efforts to apply cold start procedure in order to start their engines and get them going.'

Theo Osterkamp (also in 'The Tragedy of the German *Luftwaffe*') replies: '...it is evident that cold start procedure was applied by all the units deployed in the Russian winter. Otherwise not a single Ju 52 would have taken off during that winter, especially at Stalingrad.'

The regrettably negative attitude of some units, as well as of their commanders, unfortunately persisted to the end. But there were many cases where cold start preparations were not possible, such as when an aircraft had landed with a damaged engine; or was lying on the other side of the airfield with a collapsed undercarriage; or when the crew chief had been killed or wounded while performing his duties...

Publisher's Note:

Whilst involved in the initial editing and design of this book, I was intrigued to read of the apparent ignorance of JG52 personnel regarding 'Kaltstart'. I reproduce here an extract from 'Spitfire On My Tail' which I co-wrote with Ulrich Steinhilper. Ulrich served with JG52 during the Battle of Britain, and what is even more curious is that his mechanic, Erwin Frey, went on to become Erich Hartmann's crew chief after Ulrich was shot down in October 1940.

Subsequent to the publishing of 'Spitfire On My Tail', and having read 'The Blond Knight of Germany', Ulrich twice telephoned Hartmann to discuss this apparent historical error. Hartmann was unwilling to discuss it, and on the first occasion closed by asking Ulrich who had been commander of JG 52 – Ulrich or himself?! On the second occasion he simply sent Ulrich a postcard which curtly told him not to get in touch again – Peter Osborne, 1998.

'From the middle of September there was a new procedure whilst our aircraft stood 'at readiness', which showed that supplies were being tightened up on the Channel Front. We didn't spot it at the time, but it was probably one of the first signs that High Command was beginning to accept that the battle was over and didn't want to waste any more supplies on it than absolutely necessary.

Normally, when we were at Stage 1 readiness, the ground crew started the aircraft up every hour to keep the engines warm. This was to keep the engine oil thin and the moving parts ready to go to full power for a scramble. The pilots sat close to the aircraft in deck-chairs, a scene identical to that of our counterparts who would be sitting a few miles north across the Channel. It was decided that this constant starting and warming up of engines was a waste of precious fuel, and so a technical directive came from the head of *Luftwaffe* Engineering. In future, as soon as the engine had been warmed up for the first time and the oil level had been checked, two litres of aviation grade petrol were to be poured into the engine to mix with the lubricating oil. Any shortfall on the oil level would then be topped up to just above normal. Then the engine was briefly run again to achieve a good mixture of oil and petrol throughout the lubrication circuit.

At first, we protested and asked if the HQ engineering section had finally lost its last tenuous grip on reality. Surely an oil/petrol mixture like this would result in vapour accumulating in the sump and under the pistons which would inevitably explode at some time? The theory was that the thinned-out mixture would provide efficient lubrication to run from cold to immediate full power, with the petroleum component of the mixture evaporating as the oil temperature rose to normal. It was with very mixed feelings that we tried it at first, and then only on training flights, never on a cross-Channel operation. But it soon became apparent that there were no adverse effects and it was accepted as routine. In a matter of weeks I had so completely forgotten about this procedure that I actually took one of my ground crew severely to task when I saw him pouring gasoline into the oil-filler; he reminded me that it was normal procedure. In those weeks at the end of September and the beginning of October, a few days seemed like a lifetime...'

CHAPTER SIX
Hans Dieterle
The Fastest Man in the World

In 1939, the Germans succeeded in winning the world speed record for the first time . This was achieved with an innovative Heinkel design, built in Germany. It was the talk of the whole aviation industry, and was to become headline news world wide. The most amazing thing about this peak of technical advancement was that it was to be repeated in just a few weeks. Approximately one month after the first record flight by the Heinkel, Messerschmitt surpassed its performance by a few kilometres per hour in their Me 209. What was even more remarkable was the fact that the first record set, using the Heinkel He 100, was soon to be forgotten – or at least ignored in the face of the Messerschmitt flight.

It was just bad luck for Heinkel that Messerschmitt had initiated a similar project, especially as the top speed of the Messerschmitt Me 209 was fractionally better – as can be read in the report following this introduction. Also, the Me 209 had a few fundamental advantages over the He 100, both as a production model and with regard to operational maintenance 'in the field'. It was considered a tremendous disadvantage by the powers-that-be that the mainplane of the He 100 was essentially one piece, rather than the port and starboard wings being detachable as required. The RLM (Reichsluftfahrt-Ministerium – Ministry of Aviation) therefore decided to go for the introduction of the Messerschmitt as the front line fighter. Heinkel's record-breaking aeroplane was not mentioned, and Hans Dieterle's report has almost been forgotten.

Dieterle was born, the youngest of nine, on 29th June 1915 in Rottweil am Neckar. He attended Grammar and High School, completed an apprenticeship as a fitter, then worked with the Hirth Motoren Werke (Hirth Motor Company). He had already begun flying gliders as a 15-year old and, by so doing, received free training for powered flight and acquired all the ratings available at the time. After completing his flight training he moved into the aviation section of the Hirth Motoren Werke, followed by another move into the construction and design offices. In the years 1936-37 he added to his knowledge by completing two semesters of studies at the Höhere Staatliche Maschinenbauschule (College of Mechanical Engineering) in Esslingen. From August 1937 onward he was test flying at the Ernst Heinkel Flugzeugwerke. Hans Dieterle, who had worked his way up from apprentice to technician and on as a pilot, proved to possess a wealth of knowledge and an instinctive feeling for aviation engineering. On 22nd November 1938, accompanied by Flugkapitän Nitschke, he conducted a flight in a twin engined aeroplane and set three international records: 1,000 Kilometres, (621.5 miles) carrying both 1,000 Kilograms, (2,200lbs) and 500 Kilograms, (1,100lbs) payload.

Hans Dieterle.

E rnst Heinkel, one of the most successful constructors of aircraft, designed and built his first aircraft in 1911 and then flew it himself. He had a lifetime fascination for fast aeroplanes, and in 1933 his He 70 *Blitz* (Lightning) caused a sensation. This elegant and aerodynamically refined machine was perfect down to the last detail: equipped with a 600hp engine, it reached the then tremendous speed of 350km/h (217.5mph). In 1937 the Heinkel company had grown to employ over 1,000 people, and in its aircraft factory they designed and built the remarkable He 100 as a prototype for a fighter aircraft. But, in producing this model, Heinkel had created the basis for a high speed aeroplane which was able to break the speed record of 709.2km/h (440.77mph), set by the Italian Francesco Angello. Remarkably, the He 100 had only undergone minor modifications for the record run!

The standard model of the He 100 was equipped with a fuel-injected, water-cooled, 12 cylinder Daimler-Benz engine which, at full boost, delivered a performance of just over 1,000hp. Using this severely time-limited output, and flying near ground level, the He100 reached a speed of about 550km/h (341.8mph). As a special refinement, it was then equipped with a surface area or condensation-cooling system. Installing this system meant that the drag produced by a conventional radiator could be eliminated and the speed further increased. The cooling liquid was under high pressure and, therefore, temperatures of 110°-130°C (230°-266°F) did not cause the water to boil. During its transition through the tightly riveted wing, the coolant lost its pressure and consequently boiled off to become steam. The airflow over the wing cooled the steam, which then condensed, returning to its liquid state, only to be fed back to the water jacket of the engine by a system of small pumps installed in the wings. Ingenious as this idea was, the cooling system proved unreliable and, despite long tests and trials, only worked with lots of luck and friendly persuasion. Nonetheless it provided an illustration of the innovative type of design which was Heinkel's trademark.

To prove the superior speed of this aircraft, Heinkel had set up the land speed record trial over a 100km (62.1 miles) closed circuit. The most favourable altitude for this trial was 4,500 metres (14, 764ft) where the engine still produced its full power, whilst the less dense air produced higher True Air Speeds (TAS). The day before the scheduled trial, General Udet came to pay a visit to Heinkel and, as an experienced and confident pilot, sat in the cockpit, took the controls and took off for a test flight. He flew the measured distance of 50km (31.1 miles) both ways and reached a speed of 635km/h (394.6mph). He had beaten the record by over 80km/h (49.7mph).

Ernst Heinkel's very special goal was to set the World Absolute Speed Record and, with his He 100, he had the machine with which he was able win the 'record of records' for his Company. The conditions set by the FAI (Fédération d'Aviation Internationale) required a near ground level altitude – below 75 metres (286.6ft) – and a distance of 3 kilometres (1.86 miles) to be flown twice in each direction. This regulation dated back to the first record flights, when an aircraft was considered to be flying very fast at 200km/h (124.3mph). However dangerous this regulation was, considering the advances of speed, it stood and had to be observed. The Italian Angello had set the record of 709.2km/h (440.68mph) in 1934, using a Macchi. He used a sea-plane, as did the Schneider Trophy winners, with the advantage that take-off and landing runs were, to all intents and purposes, unlimited on water. However, the floats created high levels of drag and this had to be compensated for by higher engine performance. Angello's aircraft had been fitted with two engines, mounted in tandem, and working together they produced a staggering 3,100hp. The small, sleek He 100, a land aircraft unencumbered with floats and bracing wires, and designed more like a fighter than a racing aircraft, was able to reach similar speeds with about a third of the power. In order to break Angello's record, the top speed of the standard He 100 had to be improved by more than 160km/h (100mph). This was achieved by adopting several different measures. Firstly, the drag of the aircraft was lessened by reducing the wing area from 14.6 to 11 square metres (157 to 118.4 square feet). Secondly, a very sleek cockpit and canopy were designed and built, causing the forward vision of the pilot to be severely reduced. In order further to reduce the enemy of speed – parasite drag – rough parts on the fuselage and wings were smoothed, using lightweight filler, and finally applying a high polish to the whole of the aircraft. Thirdly, the engine specialists had super-charged the engine up to 1.8 ata and 'tickled' the standard 1,000hp up to approximately 1,800hp by increasing the top end rpm. Boosting the normal filling capacity of the individual cylinder by use of blowers was common practice in Germany at that time, even in the motor car industry. Normally this 'improvement' was for short term use and usually only up to 1.3 ata. This stress, combined with the increased performance, led to additional demand on the cranks and rods, and failure was common if the boost was protracted. An increase of up to 3,000rpm on an engine with a cylinder volume of 2.5 litres (152.5 cubic inches) required a heavier piston as well as an increase in strength and mass of the other main mechanical parts. Another consideration was the high thermal force of a well boosted engine, which had to be mastered at the same time if the engine were not to suffer catastrophic failure. This was achieved using special fuels which, on the one hand, had the property of absorbing the engine heat, whilst on the other were able to take the high compression without self-igniting or detonating. Special spark plugs were required due to the high heat values (very 'cold' plugs) which, at low power settings, quickly became fouled. It was, therefore, understandable that an engine so extremely stressed could not be guaranteed longevity – the manufacturer thought approximately half an hour...! Lastly, the aircraft was fitted with a special propeller. It was highly effective at high speeds, but had a poor performance on take-off. Calculations showed that this race version of the He 100 was likely to be faster than Angello's aircraft. According to the rules of the FAI, the speed of the previous holder of the record had to be exceeded by at least 8km/h (4.97mph).

Heinkel had the third prototype of the He 100 built precisely as described above. This V3 was to win the record for the Company. With all these changes, the aircraft had become very difficult to handle and had to be flown with kid gloves. At the time I was a very young Works pilot with Heinkel, and it was an honour for me when I learned that I was to perform the initial flight tests. The chief pilot of the Heinkel Works was to fly the final preparation and the record run. Sadly, this record run was never made. On the last preparation flight in September 1938, one of the undercarriage legs would not fully retract after take-off nor fully extend for landing. The cause of this disaster was never found. When the engine eventually stopped, the pilot was forced to bale-out and save himself by parachute.

Professor Heinkel was shocked by the loss of his favourite aircraft, but he never gave up on his plans and had the He 100 V8 version built as a new record breaker. Rather surprisingly, he nominated me as the pilot for the intended record run. I was

The He 100 V8.

only 23 years 'young', but had the proven ability to control fast aircraft, even in difficult situations. At the end of February 1939, the V8 was ready to fly. The record trials were moved to Oranienburg, a subsidiary airfield of the Heinkel aircraft company. The available runway at this airfield was much longer and the entire team, about 25 men, was able to pursue its preparations in the peace and tranquillity of this field, remote from the hubbub of the main Works.

As mentioned earlier, a measured test track of 3 kilometres (1.86 miles), with half a kilometre (546.8 yards) of overrun at either end, had to be flown twice each way. I selected a suitable 'racetrack' along a railway, practising as often as possible by flying a standard He 100 which was at my disposal solely for this purpose. After each run I throttled the engine back and took a bearing on the turn point, approximately 25km (15.5 miles) away and flying at a height of 400 metres (1, 312ft). From this point I aimed for the test track: at full throttle I pushed the aircraft down to below 75 metres (246ft). It was very important to memorise the route and track due to the reduced forward visibility from the scaled down cockpit and canopy of the race version.

The V8 was 'broken in' with a standard engine and any necessary changes or modifications were made. To minimise the risk of losing another aircraft, all non-essential flights were avoided and, immediately after the installation of the racing engine, the record trial was tackled. Flying towards the racetrack, I was forced to break off the run because the engine was vibrating strongly and full thrust could not be achieved. The fuel pump proved unable to supply the engine with the large amount of fuel required for full power. The mechanics had overlooked the fact that the modified engine was very 'thirsty' when full throttle was required. The specific fuel consumption was indeed extremely high, equal to approximately 500 grams hp/h (1.1lbshp/h).

Following the installation of a more efficient fuel pump, the second trial run was also a failure. I had made two passes over the 'racetrack' when I noticed a high oil temperature, accompanied by unacceptably low oil pressure, forcing me to land. This He 100 was not equipped with a conventional oil cooler to avoid aerodynamic drag. The hot oil was fed into a heat exchanger which had been installed in the fuselage behind the pilot's seat. This heat exchanger was cooled by methyl alcohol, which has a relatively low vaporisation temperature. When the oil reached the exchanger and a temperature of 65°C (149°F) was exceeded, the methyl alcohol vaporised, thereby extracting heat from the oil by the process of latent heat, and cooling it down, in a process similar to the technique of feeding vaporised coolants into the wings to condense. Vaporised alcohol was piped to the vertical fin, cooled and condensed to liquid methyl alcohol, and again fed back to the heat exchanger using small pumps. It was no surprise, given the abnormally high volume of heat developed by this special engine, that problems with this innovative cooling system manifested themselves.

The two legs of the record attempt and some ground running added up to about half an hour. The maker's warranty had expired and we were left with the question: 'Should I not, for the sake of my unbroken limbs, resign from this whole thing?' From then on the danger of the engine blowing up in flight would be ever present. For me, however, the enthusiastic pilot, there was not one shred of doubt in my mind. On the contrary, the reputation of the Company was in my hands and the record within my reach, which called for the subordination of all personal considerations. Furthermore, we had gained assurance, through the data taken during the unsuccessful test run, that the He 100 V8 had enough speed to exceed Angello's record.

On 30th March 1939 the weather was suitable, and I decided to go for a further trial run. There was no such thing as a simple take-off, due to the fact that extensive preparations were required for each flight. The 'Prima Donna' was towed to her take-off position, facing into wind, and started and run up using normal spark plugs. After reaching the operating temperatures and pressures, the engine was shut down and specialists from the engine shop took out the normal (hot) spark plugs and exchanged them as quickly as possible with the (cold) racing plugs. Everything had to be done very quickly, because we didn't want the engine to cool down. In the meantime, I climbed into the pilot's seat and was strapped in and, as the last mechanic jumped away from the engine, I restarted. Because of the sensitivity of the spark plugs to fouling we had to maintain high throttle settings. Even so the engine ran very rough, and normal checks by the pilot were impossible. The engineers from the engine company checked the colour of the flames from the exhaust stubs of the 12 cylinders and, as soon as they were satisfied, the chocks were pulled away and the machine started rolling. Due to the flat pitched propeller, acceleration was pathetic. With the tail dragging on the ground, it was rather difficult to pick up speed for lift-off. In order to make it easier for me to maintain the centreline, a large coloured flag was waved at the end of the runway to show me the way.

After safely lifting off, I set course toward the racetrack with the firm intention of risking a trifle more than usual. Within the thirteen minutes between take-off and landing, I sped along the 'racetrack' four times, pushing the throttle fully forward each time. I was not as fastidious in checking the oil pressure and temperature as I had been before. The safe landing, also a requirement, was performed without a hitch. I should mention that the landing characteristics of this race version of the He 100 were something of a challenge too! Near stalling speed, the little hussy was prone abruptly to drop one wing and spin without any warning.

The analysis of the times for the four runs produced an average speed of 746.6km/h (463.92mph) and I had become 'The Fastest Man In The World' at least for the moment. It is well known that aircraft fly faster at higher altitudes than they do close to the ground. This is due to the fact that the air is thinner and the drag therefore lower. A prerequisite is that the engine must not lose power with increased altitude, and this is

Jubilant reception following the Record Flight.

overcome with positive pressure induction (blowers). Normally, when reference is made to the top speed of an aircraft, it actually means the speed reached at the most suitable altitude. A speed of 746km/h (463.5mph) reached at 50 metres (164ft) above sea level is approximately equal to a speed of 920km/h (571.7mph) at 6,000 metres (19,685ft). This is, perhaps, much more impressive and should be mentioned here in order fully to appreciate the success achieved at that time.

Publisher's Note: *A further increase in the True Air Speed would most probably not have been possible. As Fritz Schäfer, who was also a test pilot with Heinkel, recalls and reports in Chapter Ten, Hans Dieterle told him at the time that he had to throttle back on the top speed by a few kilometres per hour because the He 100 showed the tendency to go 'nose down'. This effect was clearly identified later, with the advent of jet propelled aircraft, as an aerodynamic phenomenon which occurs when approaching the speed of sound. English aviation terminology: 'The Nose Down Effect'*

This achievement was played down by the government in its official reports. It wanted to give the impression that the record had been achieved by a production model. This was also the reason why the *Reichsluftfahrt-Ministerium* (RLM) only mentioned the He 112 U (a well-known 'standard' aircraft) in their official bulletins. On the other hand, the RLM went to great lengths to support Messerschmitt in order to win the absolute world speed record for Germany. For this purpose, Messerschmitt designed and built the Me 209, and fitted it with the Daimler – Benz record engine. Four weeks later, Fritz Wendel reached a speed of 755.1km/h (469.2mph) over a three kilometre course near Augsburg. He had needed only to achieve an additional 8km/h (4.97mph) to exceed the record I had set on 30th March 1939 and to become the new record holder.

This best performance of a Messerschmitt aircraft had been achieved under the same difficult circumstances as for our He 100. Mind you, the altitude advantage of the higher airfield at Augsburg (500 metres (1,640ft) Above Mean Sea Level, compared to 50 metres (164ft) AMSL at Oranienburg) gave Wendel the edge. The altitude difference of 450 metres (1,476ft) (assuming the same engine performance) translates to a speed improvement of 13km/h (8.08mph) due to the lower pressure altitude. In other words, the Heinkel aircraft would, if flown on the Augsburg course, have reached a speed of

757km/h (470.4mph) instead of 746km/h (463.5mph) and could not have been beaten by the Messerschmitt. In recognition of this state of affairs, Heinkel began preparations to move the flight facility to the south of Germany, to higher ground, and in this way win back the record.

However, the RLM was not kindly disposed towards this intention. The impressive fact that two companies in Germany were independently able to produce aircraft with similar top speeds was self-evident. This was taken for granted, and no further efforts seemed necessary: it was felt that the point had been made. Moreover, war was just around the corner.

The Messerschmitt aircraft was named in the Press as the Me 109 R, even though it was a specially designed machine, built solely for this event. This was again intended to foster the belief that the record run had been performed by a standard *Luftwaffe* fighter.

The war was to expedite the development of jet aircraft, which had the advantage over those which were propeller driven. The propeller loses its effectiveness in direct proportion to the increase in speed. In fact, it becomes such a poor means of propulsion at high speed that the most radical increases in output power from the engine achieve very little increased speed. This fact was the reason why Wendel's record flight was left unchallenged for such a long time.

Despite all the circumstances previously described, and long after World War II, the American Daryl Greenmayer made it his goal to improve the world speed record for piston-engined aircraft. For this purpose, he modified a Grumman Bearcat which he had acquired as war surplus. In the summer of 1969, Greenmayer achieved the record speed of 870km/h (540.60mph) at Edwards Air Force Base in California. Through this achievement, he became the proud owner of the beautiful trophy donated by the FAI. I am convinced that his preparations for this run were as extensive and exhausting as they had been for Wendel and myself, but it is not for me to judge if the risk of flying was as high as it had been on our flights.

Sadly, my He 100 V8 became a victim of war. It had been displayed in the *Deutsche Museum* in Munich, and was destroyed during a bombing raid on the city. What a shame. Looking at that aircraft was pure aesthetic joy. It epitomised the high standing of German aviation, and the abilities of the constructors and designers of aircraft of that epoch.

CHAPTER SEVEN

Heinrich Beauvais

My Experiences During Trials of the Me 109
and Other Types

In the Thirties and Forties, it was said that Dipl. Ing. (Doctor of Engineering) Heinrich Beauvais was the safest, yet the most critical and discerning examiner of military aircraft. His meticulous evaluations did not miss even the smallest faults in any of the new aircraft he checked. In the years of the expansion of German military aviation, he flight-checked hundreds of aircraft. We, the less experienced flyers, looked upon him as a 'Judge of the Inquisition'. His infallible instinct, his talent for flying and his unique expert knowledge led him to identify each and every advantage of a flying machine. It also enabled him ruthlessly to diagnose any fault, however major or minor.

For a long time his judgement was taken as if it were the 'word of the Pope'. However, he was also forced to accept doubts as to his infallibility. At times, his natural self-confidence seemed a little too pedantic, sometimes even bureaucratic, especially when he had yet again uncovered a fault or dangerous flight characteristic. Although he was expected, especially during wartime, to expedite the examination and certification of aircraft, he never wavered from his duty, even though the holdups caused increased production costs and delayed the arrival in service of new and innovative aircraft.

Heinrich Beauvais in the Me 108 'Taifun'.

68

General observations on the 109

My very first impression of the Me 109 was Knötzsch's 'headstand' upon his arrival at Rechlin. Following touch-down, his undercarriage collapsed and the aircraft stood straight up on its nose, hesitated, and then decided to fall back onto its belly rather than completely nose-over. Fortunately, nobody was injured on that October day in 1935.

At Rechlin, we heard very little about the evaluations which were performed at Travemünde. These trials included the demonstration of the Me 109 to the public by Messerschmitt pilots, as well as several comparison flights made with its main competitors. It was not until 1937 that we took over the continuation of trials at Rechlin.

My first flight in the Me 109 (Serial number 884, Reg.: D-IXZA) was a comparison flight, a Me 109 against a He 51. My flight experience at that point in time included the B-1 licence and all type ratings up to the He 112; on that day, 14th April 1937, Thoenes was my 'opponent'. My last flight in the aircraft type (actually a Buchon) was in Seville, Spain in 1956. It was fitted with a license-built Merlin engine – incredibly there had been two decades between the flights.

The flight characteristics and performance of the Me 109 were mostly quite satisfactory, although some pilots disliked the narrow undercarriage and the large pitch changes during approach and landing. With the steady increase of the wing loading, the demands on the pilot also increased. Attempts to improve the roll rate of approximately 5 seconds per full aileron roll, compared to the 4 seconds of the Fw 190, had never ceased. I was the one to re-test and evaluate nearly all new series productions, as well as the odd trial versions (e.g. V – tail). The turning performance was never systematically flight tested and I am able to recall only one set of figures: 12 seconds for a full 360° turn, and that was probably on a Me 109 C.

During acceleration trials, the Me 109, flying at maximum power, was nearly able to keep up with the Do 335 but, as soon as the top speed was approached, the Do 335 pulled steadily away, as was demonstrated at Mengen in early May 1944. With snow on the ground, or lack of attention by the pilot during take-off, the tips of the propeller were often bent. These bent ends were then simply cut off. Loss of performance was negligible.

Later in the war, additional tests were performed to develop an Me 109 with the capability of chasing and catching a De

Havilland Mosquito. The109 was completely stripped down to the minimum of equipment, and only an engine mounted gun. The engine was tuned to develop higher revs, and during one of these trials, I reached 10,000 metres (32,809ft) in only ten minutes. I climbed at an average of 16.7 metres/sec. (3,287ft/min.) which was normally only possible up to an altitude of 6,000 metres (19,685ft) – full throttle altitude.

Diving

During each development of an aircraft, the designers attempt to achieve a wider range in the centre of gravity. The designers at Messerschmitt believed they had achieved this with a new elevator and Flettner Tab (trim tab). I did not quite share this opinion: however, I was willing to make a test flight. After take-off from Augsburg on this particular flight, I saw a parachute some distance ahead and wondered what type of cargo-dropping trial this could be. On closer inspection and watching its descent to the ground, I saw a man hanging from the parachute. I considered landing and going to his aid, but saw it was not necessary, since help was on its way from a nearby anti-aircraft battery. Later, after having landed myself, I learned it was Wendel who had baled out from an Me 109T.

Continuing with the test, I climbed to an altitude of 6,000m and, going into a dive, noted that careful movements of the elevator showed nothing unusual. I then encountered an area of turbulence, and the aircraft showed a marked tendency to remain in the vertical. The indicated airspeed was about 650km/h (403.8mph) and I had to pull fairly hard on the stick until any perceptible change was evident. Then the change became uncomfortably violent: I was pressed into the seat in a way which led me to expect that the aircraft would begin to break up. The typical 'bath tub effect', as I called it, had begun. You might ask where this comparison comes from. Just imagine a bath tub full of water, one end resting on a lever, the other end on the floor. In order to balance the tub, you must exert considerable effort and use a fair amount of strength. When you finally manage to balance the tub, the water shoots up to the other end. This is exactly what the aircraft did, in that there was very little initial response to the control input, and then a sudden and violent over-response. I was able gradually to reduce the oscillations and, most importantly, to reduce the speed and pull out of the vertical dive. Afterwards, back on the ground, a crack in the main mounting of the wing was detected! It appeared possible that I had gone through the same area of turbulence which had caused Wendel's accident. (This must have been 3rd April 1941). The 'improvement' to the elevator proved to be of no use whatsoever.

Stalling

The stall characteristics of the 109, up to and including the 109 E, had been classed as satisfactory. The tendency to drop a wing during landing was not easily analysed. Did 'crabbing' or

The instrument panel of the Me 109 E-3/B (1939).

side-slipping or using the rudder too robustly cause this to happen? Or did pilots landing 'crabwise' (side-slipping) flip over the wheel and dig the wing in due to the narrow undercarriage? What effect did misjudgement of landing attitude have? What effect on overall orientation was there with the continual changes in yaw affecting the reference points on the canopy rail, as well as the constant changes of pitch affecting the use of the runway as a fixed reference point? In any event, touching the wing tips on the ground when landing usually caused only minor damage without further consequences for anyone. I am unable to recall the stall characteristics of the 109 with the (leading edge) slats retracted but, at the beginning of the trials, the slats were released when the flaps were lowered. When the slats then automatically extended at low speeds, the ailerons briefly, but suddenly, deflected. In order to prevent this, the aircraft had to be 'broken in' in order to smooth out the slat movement. It was also essential, through careful maintenance, to keep them moving freely and smoothly. When the Project Office proposed clipping the wings to increase the speed of the aircraft (Woldemar Voigt's idea), effectively shortening the wingspan and squaring off the wing tips, the aircraft frequently flipped over with great ease. Although I do not recall all the methods attempted to cure this phenomenon, I remember that, throughout 1938, I paid numerous visits to Augsburg, but without any perceptible final solution to the problem. My colleague, Liebe, was also involved because he was testing 'his' boundary layer control and, with these control devices, the aircraft 'flipped' a littler later and at lower airspeed. Generally, the flight controls were quite satisfactory: the elevator deflection was adequate to overcome Ca max, the ailerons and, especially, the rudder, were sufficiently effective to control and stop dropping of the wing and nose diving. However, the onset of wing-drop with shorter wings was far too abrupt and violent to be controlled, even though it could be proved that the controls themselves were, theoretically, capable of doing so.

Finally I suggested either a return to the old wing or, at least, testing different wing-tips. The engineers at Augsburg initially refused to co-operate but, eventually, decided on a 'new' wing-tip' – in fact the type which had already been well established. It proved its efficiency, and that was it! No one seemed interested in optimising the wing, and the front-line pilots did not complain about the stall characteristics of the Me 109 F, nor of its successors.

Plenty of G

In the early days of the Me 109, many bent wings were brought to Rechlin. Then, after some time, no more arrived. Had the troops learned? Or had everyone grown used to bending wings? I do not know. Later, during the war, the damage increased again. Späte writes:..'*In at least three cases I had returned home with damage to the wings of my Me 109, due to my own fault in having failed to observe the speed and G limits in air combat...*' There would never be a totally safe way of avoiding over-stressing the aircraft, either through strengthening the airframe or by improving the flight controls and wing loading. It all boiled down to a compromise of strength, sturdiness and flight performance of the aircraft, i.e. purely tactical requirements. Finally, agreement was reached on the standard 'n' safety at 7. During comparison of the Me 109 with the new Fw 190 by Gollob at Rechlin 1941, he did not believe that the aircraft 'bucked' at about 400km/h (248.5mph), because it had stalled in the turn. The speed limit at which Ca max was reached, or a high speed stall was achieved, had not been researched mathematically or experimentally, although different accelerometers and other means of measuring acceleration (with and without drag pointers, including the DVL *Ritzgeräte*) had been installed and tested. But limitations were never systematically evaluated and, for instance, I can remember it being difficult to maintain 5g in a spiral dive. However, high g loads were easily achieved for short periods of time.

Spinning

Dr. Wurster had demonstrated the spin with the 109 V 1 at Travemünde (No one from Rechlin was in attendance). Geike reported: *'After slowing the aircraft down, using idle power and then stalling, the 109 performed one turn in a steep spin, the next in a flat spin, alternating thereafter. After 10 to 12 turns, the aircraft was put into a dive by pushing the stick fully forward.'* In regard to this I must say: The pendulum effect of the nose was also observed on other types of aircraft: (e.g. the Do 27 and the Jet Provost). It was either more or less pronounced on all types of aircraft. The only point to be made is this: The periodic changes in pitch were not in line with the number of turns. It seemed very unusual to stop the spin by pushing forward instead of using rudder, even by the standards of that time.

When the Me 109 came to Rechlin, the question was: How would it spin after the improved slats had been installed? The answer to this question was deferred. The danger of an inadvertent spin seemed slight, and no one had requested the spin for tactical reasons. Fairly late (in about 1943) Karle Baur performed spin trials (with the F or possibly the G). As far as I can remember, the sink rate during the spin was tremendous and the pendulum effect was still present. I do not believe that the periodic changes in pitch had anything to do with the number of turns. The amplitude of the pendulum depends on the type of entry into the spin (dynamics of stall entry). Stopping the spin was quickly and easily achieved with the 109 by using the usual recovery procedure of reducing power and applying 'opposite' rudder.

Flight controls

One would have liked to have more effective ailerons, as well as lower control forces, at high speeds. I do not remember all the different methods tried to improve this, but the following two are still clear in my mind. One was designed by Blohm & Voss, adding a Flettner trim tab which resulted in a reduction of control forces: however, performance was not as smooth and effectiveness had not improved at all. A later form was the *'Keulenquerruder'* (a shape of aileron tested at Memmingen in 1944) which had seemed promising, but had never been introduced. The rudder had no trim: it was 'ironed out' especially for the dive and produced fairly high aerodynamic forces during the climb. Nevertheless, it seemed the best of compromises: a spring to counteract the strong forces during the climb was considered, but never incorporated.

Take-off and Landing

A powerful engine, in conjunction with a large propeller, required the smooth application of power and rudder in order to keep the aircraft straight after brake release. Lifting the tail created no problem, since it occurred almost instantly and was easily controlled with the very effective rudder. Timidity during control input was not required, and the demand on the pilot was not too high, provided there was good visibility. A statistical analysis of take-off accidents revealed that the pilots had not been given sufficient training during their conversion to the aircraft. In order to reduce work load on pilots flying in reduced visibility conditions, a 'course steering' mode was installed in some of the Me 109's. This meant more time and expense, as well as a higher susceptibility to failure and possible mistakes: during one of the first trials at Lärz near Rechlin, I experienced this. Having performed the preparations required – i.e. running-up of the gyro etc. – I started my take-off roll on the grass next to the runway. The aircraft did not roll in a straight line, but began to veer towards the runway. On the edge of the concrete, the aircraft tipped over the wheel towards the left wing tip but, in order not to damage the airframe, I did not correct the heading or reduce the power. I lifted off easily by pulling back on the stick, avoiding slip as much as possible. Wüst, my colleague, explained to me later that I had not given the gyro sufficient time to run up to reach the required rpm. However, I had maintained all the limits and performed all my checks properly. There had been only minor damage to the wing tip and the propeller tips. The imbalance of the prop was hardly noticeable, and Wüst was able to fly back to Werneuchen without problems.

To determine whether re-trimming was required during an overshoot, we attempted to take-off with full nose-up trim: it proved possible, but not very comfortable. The effectiveness of the tailplane was adequate, but one had to push the stick fairly hard into an uncomfortable fully forward position. In order to reduce the nose-high attitude during landing, a higher tailwheel was proposed and designed. However, in my view this was not to be recommended because the aircraft tended to bounce on landing in its new 'three point attitude', and was difficult to control. A landing at full Ca max, where the high tailwheel touched down first and absorbed the initial shock, produced a rapid pitch-down movement. This landing technique, coupled with the extended tailwheel, was another I could not recommend.

'Double Rider' and 'Country Bumpkin'
by Prof. Dr. Madelung

The *'Doppelreiter'* (Double Rider) consisted of two high, narrow gondolas, one mounted on top of each wing. As far as I remember, they were large enough for a man to sit in. The *'Wurzelsepp'* (Country Bumpkin) was a kind of oversized fillet, to be mounted on the wing. I believe it was only to be put on one wing, and was intended to carry various loads, eg. fuel. Whether it was long enough for a man to lie in, I am unable to recall. However, it hardly influenced the aerodynamic properties of the Me 109. Performance, or loss of it, was not investigated, but the speed, compared to a 'clean' aircraft, showed remarkably little difference.

Double Seater

The two seat variant did not offer anything special, except shorter endurance and poor visibility from the rear seat. However, it was most interesting to observe the vast differences in technique, as well as the large and small variations in performance, of pilots of all ages and stages. This had little to do with the relationship of instructor and student, and was an indication of how unsuited the requirements of flying were (and still are) to over-rigidly defined rules and procedures.

Night Flights

On one occasion we had to establish whether a 109, flying alongside the landing light beam of a He 111, could be detected and, if so, at what point. In order to perform this test, I was required to approach from above, push the nose

Bf 109 G-2/R Trial version with 500kg bomb and detachable tail wheel.
Flown by Beauvais on 30th June, 1942, at Rechlin.

down to accelerate, and then pull the fighter up into the beam of the light. I had done exactly this, flying at a speed of approximately 650km/h (403.9mph), when suddenly a Fi 156 'Storch' appeared next to me. After landing, I complained bitterly about the 'near miss' and roundly cursed the idiot who, without giving notice, had flown into the test area. I was directed towards a group of gentlemen standing in the dark, and saw that *General* Udet was among them. He asked: 'Are you the pilot of the 109?' 'Yes, *General*,' I replied. 'I did have my navigation lights on; I believe you saw them?' said Udet. 'Yes, *General!*' (I kept the supplementary remark to myself, but it would have been something like: 'But only after it was too late to avoid you, and who in the world would have been expecting anything of the kind?').

Point Landing

Once, during a climb, at approximately 4,000 metres (13,123ft), the engine suddenly stopped. Not a single spark, no splutter, nothing of that sort. I initially turned onto my reciprocal heading, not knowing if I would be able to reach Rechlin in the glide. At about 2,500 metres (8,202ft) I saw, through a hole in the clouds, what I believed to be another airfield – although I didn't recognise it. I noted the heading, altitude and time, hoping to be able to reach the hole in the clouds through which I had previously climbed, and expected to see the airfield from there. This I achieved and, having descended further, I was able to make out a fishbone pattern on a field, obviously drainage ditches, but at what stage of progress? Were the ditches still open? Were the lines soft and muddy? Was there hard, solid ground? I selected a diagonal path. Trusting the narrow gauge of the Me 109, I decided to land on this field, and lowered the undercarriage. It was rather exciting but all went well, and it appeared to me that a landing along the field would have been possible. On the edge of this airfield I found a construction workers' hut, from which I was able to call Rechlin. After a short while, our master mechanic Francke (nicknamed 'Flammeri' – Flame) arrived with his team. The first thing he wanted to do was to start the engine, which obligingly turned over, saving the effort of starting it manually. If, after a long glide with the engine turning, the engine did not 'move', any attempt to start it would be useless. Later it was discovered that the gear of the camshaft drive had failed. With this type of engine failure, there can be no more power.

The scene of this little incident was the Wittstock Airfield which, at the time, was indeed still under construction. Luck? Yes, but you have to make something of it!

Firing

I cannot remember ever firing the aircraft's guns air-to-air at Rechlin, but I have clear memories of live firing at Tarnewitz. Judging the firing position in relation to the target, especially over the sea, required concentration and practice. In the course of time, all groups of weapons were tried and tested, some of them being centre-mounted and the rest wing-mounted. They were all of varying size and calibre – and markedly different in operation. When the light was right it was actually possible to see the 30 mm (1.18ins) shells in flight.

A firing exercise with a difference was the demonstration of air-to-ground gunnery at Rechlin with a railway locomotive as a target. The engine had been parked between the southern and western hangars, and was under a full head of steam. The footplate had been covered, using heavy gauge steel plates to protect the engineer and fireman (had they been aboard). I was asked to first hit the boiler and then the cabin and, for practice, was given a Russian T 34 tank on Range C. Firing on the tank proved to be more dangerous than expected, because of the ricochets from the heavy armour. The approach for the exercise on the loco took me straight overhead the spectators (among them representatives of the *Reichsbahn* – German state railway). Because of this the guns could only be cocked very late, leaving very little time for aiming, but the test went as planned. The engine looked a very sorry sight after the attack, with the steel plates and the boiler smoothly penetrated by 15 mm armour-piercing cannon shells.

Engine Trials

I was tasked to perform the initial trials on the Bf 109, fitted with the DB 601 engine, at Augsburg. Lengthy running of the engine on the ground caused it to overheat, which was only to be expected, and although it blew off steam in large quantities, there was relatively little water loss. I saw to it that the problem was solved, working together with *Herr* Assam from Messerschmitt and *Herr* Birk from Daimler Benz. After several trials, Birk succeeded in finding a solution but, in the meantime, the Me 109 under test had 'steamed off' on numerous occasions. Dr. Wurster, observing this from his hangar, judged it an unnecessary running-up of engines and a waste of money. For decades he talked about it as the 'biggest lining of pockets' ever. Not until the 70's was he to be convinced of the necessity of these trials. Rechlin also received reports of the 'unreasonable treatment' of the engine, and Francke continued his reproaches, but eventually gave up.

Later, an Me 109 (I think it was an F) was assessed because it had been reported that the oil pressure dropped too quickly during inverted flight. To check the effectiveness of the remedy, I rolled the aircraft on its back and attempted to observe the oil pressure. All I saw were little stars, and I was left wondering why I felt so horrible; had I had such a rough night in the sleeper, travelling from Berlin to Augsburg? On landing, it was found that the injection fluid, containing ether, had leaked when I rolled the aircraft on its back. The oxygen mask had absorbed the smell, but had not prevented the ether from affecting me.

The Canopy Blows Off

After take-off, at a height of 15 metres (50ft), the canopy opened, was torn off by the slipstream and damaged the horizontal stabiliser in passing. It had, I thought, been tightly locked, but the safety pin had probably not engaged correctly. The usual shaking of the handle and 'rattling the cage' had not exposed the potential problem. As far as I can remember, the stabiliser control tab was bent downward and the outer section of the right stabiliser had come loose. I wanted to avoid further damage or tearing off of the loose parts; damage of this nature was not easy to handle and the aircraft would not be easily controlled. At least I was still flying, and it therefore seemed best to make as few changes as possible and return towards the aerodrome. Very carefully, I reduced power and commenced my descent, flying a very wide circuit. I left the undercarriage and flaps where they were, in take-off position and, in this configuration, I flew close to the ground, reduced power, and smoothly pulled back on the stick. The aircraft behaved well, and I made a smooth landing.

The Countryside Above the Canopy

It was a beautiful day, but rather hazy. During a climb, I lost visual contact with the ground prior to reaching the aircraft's operational ceiling. I quickly made a few notes and un-caged the artificial horizon. Although the indication was correct, the aircraft started to 'murmur' and the indicated airspeed increased. I thought that, most probably, I had un-caged the horizon a fraction too late and looked round anxiously, eventually spotting a small river in hazy countryside, just to the right and *above* me! At first I thought it to be a mirror image: according to my senses and instincts it just could not be the ground, and I couldn't be flying virtually inverted. However, it seemed prudent to roll the aircraft out parallel to this image. Slowly the roaring decreased as the airspeed bled away back to normal. It took quite a long time to rid myself of the feeling that I was still flying upside down.

Me 209 (V4)

The Me 209 (V1 – V3) was an attempt to clear the way for an attempt on the Absolute World Speed Record. The military version evolved from the aircraft commonly known as the V4. It was redesigned with larger wings, leading edge slats and weapons. The aircraft, coded D-IRND, was flown on 3 June 1939 by a colleague and myself at Augsburg.

Me 109 G-6.

The *'Fischschwanz'* (Fishtail), as we called it, required less rudder on take-off than the 109, and I remember no difficulties during the flight. I recall that we definitely tried to stall, but had no reason to explore spin characteristics. Landing, however, was quite exciting – for one thing, visibility from the cockpit was worse than from the Me 109, and judging one's height above ground was not easy. After touchdown, it was hard to maintain direction and keep the aircraft heading down the runway, as it was rather 'touchy' when passing over bumps in the runway's surface, and bounced considerably. A wide undercarriage is not always the solution to all problems!

Kens/Nowarra wrote:

'The re-commencement of flying by the *'Luftwaffen – Erprobungsstelle'* (Luftwaffe Trial Centre) proved this aircraft too difficult to fly for the conventionally trained pilot. It could not be operated from front line airstrips. With the incorporation of a standard cooling system, the advantage in performance over the Me 109 had diminished, and the development was eventually stopped.'

I can confirm that. From then on the flying programme was performed by the pilots of the *E-Stelle* (Trial Centre) at Messerschmitt's own site, and not the *E-Stelle* itself. The V4 was also at Rechlin, but only for a demonstration for Hitler; I also flew it there. The continuation of the test programme at Augsburg had its own repercussions: one of my colleagues had rounded-out too high during landing, and had slightly damaged the aircraft. One of the bureaucrats in administration, not knowing the difficulties of this aircraft, regarded this as a criminal act and discontinued my flying pay for a period of time Although it had not been my fault, I was blamed. However, I had no wish to argue with these *'Sesselpupern'* (seat-warmers / armchair aviators), and left it at that…

CHAPTER EIGHT

Lukas Schmid

When the 109 Put its Ears Back

When you are in the flying business, and amongst fliers, you will sometimes meet the type of person who is best characterised with the words: 'Stand back everyone; Here I come; Look at me, I am a daredevil!' Lukas Schmid was exactly the opposite. Even though he was a most daring Test Pilot, who took the greatest of risks on many of his flights, he performed his duties with the coolest of heads. He was one of those men who were driven from their drawing board to the airstrip by their love of flying. It was not his style to make much of his deeds. If the two of us had not endlessly chatted and relived his experiences with the Me 109, this report would probably never have been written.

Lukas Schmid – four decades later.

A long table stood right by the window in the office of the test department, and from it you had a good view of the airfield and also of the Messerschmitt factory at Augsburg-Haunstetten. The seat at the centre was reserved for Karle Baur, the head of flight and trial operations and, when he was not flying, Fritz Wendel sat next to him. The seat was naturally unoccupied when he was out on the Leipheim airstrip, or visiting Lechfeld, or when his advice was required by the front-line-troops. The third seat was mine – the *'Dogsbody'*, so to speak.

Karle Baur arranged the allocation of the forthcoming trial flights which had been requested by the design office, or any other authorised department. In the briefing, his opinion and points of view were the factors which were the most valued and decided how the task was to be tackled. Everyone respected his experience and ability and he usually undertook the initial flights himself. Things were much the same for Fritz Wendel. It is now common knowledge that he had been tasked with the world record flight in the Me 209.

Generally, after the first series of tests on a prototype had been completed by the Chief Pilot, and all involved were satisfied, the full programme began, involving countless take-offs, test flights and landings – usually followed by more individual trials and tests. If modifications were made to the aircraft, eg. the air supply to the water or oil cooler, or the engine air intake, a test flight was required. The operation of navigational instruments, and the range of radio navigation stations, had to be tested and checked. Even though the *Luftwaffe* had its own trial and test centres for such operations, the initial trial had to be performed at the factory. Detailed work of this nature exceeded by far the work capacity and available time of a Chief Pilot, and many of these more mundane tasks were therefore handed to the *'Dogsbody'* – me.

After the beginning of World War II, time was pressing. Pilots from the forces were posted in to work with us: Herlizius, Ostertag, Schmidt, Auffermann, Tesch, Olzmann, Gutsche, to mention just a few. For several weeks, pilots from Rechlin and other test centres were also posted in to help carry out urgent or special flights.

When, in June 1938, I had finished my training as a military pilot at Oberwiesenfeld, I was hired by Messerschmitt to work as group leader. One of my very first jobs was to help develop the variable pitch propeller for the Me 108. The same propeller was then re-designed to fit the Me 109. After only a few flights, performed by Karle Baur and Fritz Wendel, this new propeller had proven itself, but the head supervisor of the design office demanded a long term test of 500 flight hours.

'I am burdened with testing the Me 261, the Me 321 and the *Gigant* (Giant)', Karle Baur protested during the briefing. '...And on top of that, all this paperwork is being thrown onto my desk every day! You have to do that', he said emphatically to Fritz Wendel: he, in turn, declared that he was under similar pressure and therefore I was the one 'selected' to do it. So I, with two other pilots with whom I had trained earlier, flew the 500 hour trial. As usual, we found various crucial items requiring change and improvement.

Incidentally, I had worked in the design office of the *Bayerische Flugzeugwerke Messerschmitt* in Augsburg from October 1934. Among other things, I had worked on the design of the wings for the Me 109, the Me 110 and the Me 210 (on the drawing board). I have to admit that producing blueprints for seat adjusters, or the reinforcement of a stringer in the area of the undercarriage bay, soon meant as little to me as did the drawing board at which I sat. I just had to get out! Then, in 1937, I found a way, and grasped the opportunity for flying training. With immense pleasure I left the drawing board, pencil, eraser and ink-pen and went off to learn to fly: I was actually going to pilot one of these machines of which, up to now, I had only been able to draw parts. In the winter of 1942 I was sitting at my desk when Caroli, the trial manager of Messerschmitt, walked in and dropped a few papers on Karle Baur's desk. Right on top I saw an instruction for internal use only, from Professor Messerschmitt himself: he was well known to everyone in the factory, and not only by his physical size. I was very curious to have a glimpse of the top page, personally signed by *'Mtt'*. As I recall, the instruction briefly said: 'The top dive speed of the Me 109 G is to be flight tested.'

Shortly thereafter Karle Baur came in. He read the paper signed by *'Mtt'*, shook his head and muttered something like: 'That's all I needed!' Later Fritz Wendel walked in, read the Professor's instruction and firmly said: 'Without me! The work on the 262 is at a crucial stage and is taking up all my time. And all the other things on top of that! That can be done by whoever pleases, but not Fritz Wendel!'

I knew very well what the edict from the head of the company was based upon. Only a few days earlier, Caroli had presented us with an official paper to read. The paper had been marked confidential and stated: '...the troops have recorded more than twenty fatal accidents involving the Me109 *'Gustav'* within the last two months'. All had been preceded by dives from high altitudes. During the Battle of Britain the Me 109 *'Emil'* had revealed certain unpleasant characteristics during the dive which had caused complaints. In air combat the Me 109E was supposedly able to out-climb the Hurricane (as well as the Spitfire, with a bit of luck). Or, depending on the situation, dive away from either, having first executed a full forward bunt. Presumably, in the heat of battle, the recommended top speed had been exceeded. It is interesting to read the notes taken by Rechlin's leading test pilot, *Dipl. Ing.* Heinrich Beauvais, regarding these complaints:

'In October 1935, in Travemünde, Dr. Wurster (*Bayerische Flugzeugwerke / Messerschmitt*) demonstrated the Bf 109 V1 fitted with a Rolls-Royce Kestrel engine. He also performed several dives of longer duration. I have no knowledge of the speeds and altitudes at which these trials were performed. Dr. Kurt Jodlbauer's attempt to demonstrate a dive with the 109 (fitted with a Jumo 210 engine), on 17th July 1937 at Rechlin, ended with a vertical impact on the Müritz. As far as I can remember, Jodlbauer had wanted to dive from 5,000 metres (16,404ft). The day before, I had suggested he go at it step by step; unfortunately he thought such caution unnecessary. He only said: "Watch, my dear boy...!" A few years ago, Dr. Wurster told me that he had earlier suggested to Jodlbauer that he should not attempt to trim the aircraft during the dive.

In 1940/41 the *Luftwaffe* reported problems with the Bf 109 E (DB601) in the dive during an operation over England. The 109 was able to dive away from a Spitfire and to outrun her. We had limited the speed to 750km/h (466mph) 'on the deck' (the indicated air speed fell due to air density reducing with increasing altitude). Obviously these values were well exceeded during aerial combat, but there were no more explicit details to be found. Rechlin was ordered by the RLM (*Reichs-Luftfahrt-Ministerium*) to examine the behaviour of the Bf 109 E during the dive.

In my first trial I intended to perform a straight dive from an altitude of 9,000 metres (29,528ft) and at a speed of 750km/h (466mph). This speed was to be reached at about 6,000 metres (19,685ft) and was rather higher than normally permitted. I went into the dive, performing a half roll, and attempted to recover at an indicated air speed (IAS) of 750km/h (466mph). A small frozen lake – I think it was in January – did not want to move out of view. I said to myself – 'Jodlbauer case'. Despite all my reservations about the stability of the flight controls, I decided to pull with all my strength. If this had no effect, I was going to try recovery using the elevator trim. The exertion proved sufficient: At an altitude of approximately 4,000 metres (13,124ft) the 109 was flying level again.

I am not able to recall at what altitude and by how much the 750km/h (466mph) mark was exceeded. Following this experience, such trials were prohibited, especially for me. We intended to find out more about the phenomenon, partly by comparing Jodlbauer's accident report with experiments in the wind tunnel. It was also our intention to perform more trials following the installation of safety features such as an ejector seat and air brakes.'

In June 1941 Ernst Udet expressed his worries about the Me 109 to Professor Willy Messerschmitt. The Professor explained the situation in two letters: the first stated, 'The deformation and breaking of the wings of the 109, as well as the dismantling of the empennage on the 210, can be put down to the fact that there is uncertainty about the load distribution on the wings and empennage at high speeds. As far as I know, all accidents occurred at speeds considerably higher than 850km/h (528.2mph). (Today we are aware of the fact that the distribution of aerodynamic load at high speed is dramatically different to that at low speed). We are still far from drawing satisfactory conclusions. However, we completely lack knowledge of the effect of rudder inputs during high speed. By measuring the load factor during dive recoveries and repeated load trials, we learned that the aircraft would not be damaged, if and when the speed – as well as the 'g' limit – was adhered to. To fully reveal the mystery of these accidents, exhaustive tests, measurements and readings must be taken in high speed wind tunnels. The 'g' loading during air combat needs to be verified in practical tests and flights.'

In his second letter he wrote: 'I could make life so much easier for myself by building aeroplanes which conform to common knowledge and limits. Needless to say, nothing much would change. The words 'common knowledge' reflect the fact that these aircraft are in no way superior to others. I could also sit and wait until all the possibilities of science are exhausted, then start building a completely new aircraft as is often done in the technical line of work. Then I would have to wait further until a series of wind tunnels are operational and conclusive tests have been performed, and until thorough readings of today's high speed aircraft have been taken by the front line troops. Surely you will agree with me that this responsibility is not to be borne, and that the loss of time could never be made up. So we are forced to take risks and to build aircraft which venture into the unknown. By doing this, we will and must learn from the bitter losses of lives and material. It goes without saying that the greatest care needs to be taken and all risks avoided in performing these trials and tests. Who is to set himself up in judgement and later declare: You should have known better?'

The troops were correct in complaining to the Fighter General. The general staff had previously complained to the *Reichsluftfahrt-Ministerium*, who then sent orders to Rechlin to look into the situation. When the problem in question proved to be something unknown which could not be easily 're-flown', but which required systematic and fully realistic trials and tests, the decision was made – and with good reason – that this was the duty of the manufacturers. They were the ones who sold the aircraft to the Ministry. Their test pilots should fly at and beyond the limits before the authorities conducted further checks. The manufacturers' pilots were well paid for their jobs.

Karle Baur was left 'holding the baby'. Somehow I had the feeling that, sooner or later, it would end up in my lap. Because of this, I continuously kept my ears open whenever the subject 'High Speed Dive of the Me 109'came up. For example there was Berbohm, the structural engineer. His statements about how much stress the fuselage, wings and tail of the 109 could take, and at what point the whole thing would begin to shake and break, were of great importance to me. I also maintained close contact with Zeiler and Kalinowski from the flight test department. It was from them that I learned about the Me 109 F, *Werk Nummer* 9228, which had been fitted with the wing assembly of the Me 109 G and which was intended for use in the dive trials. In this configuration, the aircraft had previously been flown by the DVL to measure pressure distribution on the airframe. The internal orders for the flight tests were registered under Nr.109 05 E 43 and briefly said: 'First: Investigation and clearing of accidents. Over-correction of the aileron and insufficient effect of the

Me 109 F (trial version) Coded: PH+ BE).

elevator at higher Mach numbers. Second: Proof of stability of the Me 109 *Wk. Nr.* 9228 at high Mach numbers.'

'What can you do for the safety of the pilot who has to perform this task?' I asked Kalinowski. 'Everything possible', he muttered. It seemed more important to him to prevent the landing gear from being sucked out during the high speed dive. During steep dives, suction acted not only on the top surface, but also under the wing. During horizontal flight and at medium speed ranges, only excess pressure and a ram air stream were to be expected. (Later the dive and high speed trials for the Me 163 proved that the flaps were drawn out with a force of up to 500kp (1,106.2lbs)).

I persisted: 'What else can you do for the pilot if and when he has to take to his parachute at speeds greater than 800km/h (497.1mph)? He will most probably not be able to get out of the aircraft due to the high wind forces; even if he succeeds in clearing the aircraft, the air stream will tear his ears off or his eyes out!' Kalinowski did not get worked up at all by such pessimism. 'First of all,'he explained to me, 'a catapult seat is being installed in 9228. Something absolutely new which has been developed by Heinkel. The pilot is ejected with the seat when the situation gets dicey. A protective shield is pulled in front of his face. One should not wait too long before ejecting. Not until it is too late, as Jodlbauer did.' Then Zeiler added, 'The aileron is limited to 50 per cent of its maximum deflection. Hopefully that will stabilise the aileron at high Mach numbers'.

On 5th January 1943, one of the flight orders landing on my desk, nicely typed on the usual form, read: 'Test flight – Me 109 – *Werk Nummer* 9228'. The alterations and

Professor Willy Messerschmitt in 1973.

modifications had been completed. Now an in-flight test had to confirm that the aircraft, with all its new installations and fittings such as modified hydraulics, variable pitch propeller, electrical system, different instruments and gauges to register forces applied under test etc., was in trim and 'cleared' for the trials to follow. Such flights were often my responsibility. As usual, everything was taken care of within only two flights, each lasting approximately 15 minutes. A fortnight later, there were two more flights, for calibration of the airspeed indication system and a trial for the newly installed robot camera. This was installed close to the head of the pilot, at the back of the cockpit, facing forward, and would automatically take pictures of the instruments during the dive. (Recorders for such data, common in flight testing today, were few and far between at that time.)

One morning at the end of the month, during briefing on the day's test flights, Karle Baur looked at me and casually remarked: 'You have performed the test flight on 9228; it would be best if you were to take over the trials for the dive. You have hundreds of hours on the 109; you are the most experienced on that bird.' Now I really was left 'holding the baby', but I have to admit I was not too indignant about it. It was almost a feeling of satisfaction which came over me. Tasks which contained a certain risk appealed to me. Something had to be looked into and tested which was of great importance for the Messerschmitt Aircraft Company. For many pilots in the front lines, this trial was vital. Hundreds, even thousands, waited for the results of this trial series. During their daily service at the front with their Me 109, the fighter pilots were in mortal danger during dog

89

fights. Countless pilots had lost their lives. For a few weeks I was to confront the deadly risk which comes with flying to unexplored aerodynamic limits.

At that time, I had been married for six months and my wife was expecting a baby. However, this was not to hold me back in any way. We were right in the middle of a terrible war, and all personal considerations had to be put aside. Nevertheless, I had decided not to do anything ill-considered: I wanted to tackle this trial properly and proceed in small, clearly defined steps in order not to risk any dangers through carelessness. This was to be my policy during the following days and weeks.

Nearly the whole of January had passed working on 9228 which, incidentally, carried the codes **TH + TF**. The construction and design office, as well as the trial management, were well aware of the fact that these dives would take me to limits which had never been safely reached by any previous flier. The trial preparations were performed taking the utmost care. No one wanted to expose himself to even the slightest blame if anything were to go wrong. On 28th January I performed a 20 minute calibration flight to ensure proper operation of the flight instruments. On 29th January, at 10.35 a.m., I took off for the first flight in the 'maximum dive speed' programme. After only twenty-three minutes I landed: I had climbed to an altitude of about 7,500 metres (24,607ft) before realising that the elevator trim was not working properly. Nevertheless, I began my dive. Performing a half roll, I turned the aircraft on its back, reduced the power to idle and pulled it into a 60 to 70 degree dive. Mother Earth moved towards me with increasing speed. Initially, I had to push hard on the stick, but it was not long before the longitudinal pressures changed. Going through about 650km/h (403.9mph), the aircraft tended to enter a steeper dive. I had to pull back harder and harder, and attempted to reduce the forces by using trim. It was not possible. The trim was completely jammed. Finally, using both hands, I pulled back on the stick and recovered the dive. The workshop checked the trim system after my report. No fault was found. During the approach for landing I had already found the trim working properly again.

That afternoon I sat in the aircraft again and, just as a few hours before, reached the starting altitude of 8,000 metres (26,247ft) after fifteen minutes. Again the elevator trim jammed, again the trim wheel seemed to be stuck in the dive.

Since I had extended the dive by a few seconds, it required a pull with both hands and great effort to bring the aircraft back to level flight. I had performed the dive towards the airfield, so that it took only minutes for me to land and taxi to the workshop hangar. This time the trim was still jammed when I reduced power for the approach and to lower the undercarriage and flaps.

To put it mildly, I was annoyed. Annoyed at the fact that the workshop had handed the plane over to me with the trim not working properly. Climbing out of the cockpit, I made a few remarks to this effect. The eagle-eyed mechanics inspected the tail section, opening all hand-holds and access panels to have a better view of the trim spindle. But, no matter how carefully they looked and how much they turned the trim mechanism, no fault could be found. They asked me to climb back into the seat and try the trim. I was pretty surprised when I found it working smoothly again. Well then, refuel for another take-off! Just under an hour later, 9228 and I were airborne again.

No one had reproached me but, somehow, I had the feeling that they did not believe my report of the trim being jammed. I climbed above 8,000 metres (26,247ft) and this time I found it almost impossible to move the trim. Nevertheless, I rolled the aircraft into the dive, just a little steeper than before. Again I delayed the recovery for one or two seconds longer than in the previous trial. I had no time to think about whether this was too big a step for this stage of the trial. I only remember the same thought coming into my mind as Heinrich Beauvais, the Rechlin test pilot, had had in a similar situation: 'Jodlbauer case...?' 'Vertical impact with the ground...?' Recovery was only achieved by using brute force. What luck that I had intentionally set the initial altitudes for these flights so that the profiles were normally to be completed at 3,000 metres (9,843ft) above ground level! In this case, I had descended to 1,500 metres (4,921ft) before I was able to recover and resume level flight.

The mood I was in, taxiing back to the hangar, can easily be imagined. To my surprise, I was greeted not with scepticism, but with the assurance that they had thought about the problem and had already found a possible solution. The jammed trim of this flight matched the technicians' theory, in that although the trim spindle was well lubricated, the lubricant was not 'cold-resistant'. On this January day the temperature at 7,000 metres (24,607ft) was probably -40° Celsius (-40°F). This had caused the lubricant to congeal and effectively jam the trim spindle.

On 30th January I made my fourth test flight after the trim spindle had been lubricated with low temperature grease. To my surprise, the elevator trim worked smoothly from take-off to landing, even though I had climbed to 9,000 metres (29,528ft), where the temperatures were Arctic. Even in the dive the trim moved willingly in all directions. A fifth flight, one hour later, proved that a very important cause of the fault had been discovered. The optimists among us expressed delight that the entire problem had been solved: I was not so convinced.

Flights six to ten, which I performed in thoughtful mood, proved my caution justified. Despite – or because of – the smooth operation of the trim, it was difficult to find its proper setting for the onset of the dive. When changing the trim during the dive particular care was needed, because the smallest of changes caused large and unexpected changes in pitch, especially when running the engine at a manifold pressure of 4"hg (34psi). It also proved very helpful to set the limit of the elevator at 1° 45'. It was very difficult to set this position in flight without an automatic stop.

This refitting made it necessary to delay the trials of 9228 for ten days. During this time I flew other trials, such as the V-tail Me 109, works flight with the Me 210, performance measurements on the Me 309, single engine and radiator test flights with the Me 110 – just about a complete cross-section of the whole manufacturing trials programme. However, starting again on 17th February, a daily Me 109 'maximum dive speed' trial was to be flown. Very carefully, I increased the speeds during the dive, thus increasing the load factor during recovery. At indicated air speeds of more than 650km/h (403.9mph), instability along the lateral axis occurred. This meant that I was suddenly required to push instead of pull on the stick. Uncontrolled movements around the yaw axis also developed, putting the aircraft into a tumbling motion. This happened especially during flight fifteen on 18th February, when I performed a dive using full throttle for the first time. Due to the pitching up moment of the engine I was only able to reach a dive angle of 60 degrees. During the recovery I blacked out due to the high 'g' loads, and I was worried that the wings or wing mountings had been damaged because of ominous cracking sounds.

After I had put in my report, we had a very exciting debriefing. Berbohm, the structural engineer, pushed his slide-rule back and forth, and then announced: 'From now on I will not take responsibility. At 5,000 – 6,000 metres (16,405 – 19,685ft) the indicated air speed is approaching a true air speed of 800km/h (497.1mph)'. 750km/h (466mph) was the limit to which the calculations would guarantee stability for the Me 109. In excess of that, he was not able to guarantee the structural strength of the aircraft.

I believe there was a dispute as to whether the true air speed or the indicated air speed was decisive. In the end, the Head of Flight Quality took a firm stand. He thought it unfitting and unnecessary to frighten the pilot. Turning to me, he said: 'You have to make your own decisions about these trials. It is up to you to make up your mind and decide if you wish to continue with them' 'Be assured,' I replied, 'in my opinion, I am taking all sensible precautions and I will continue the trials. In doing so, I will take full responsibility.'

The crucial factor in my decision was the previously mentioned report by Caroli, concerning the twenty fatal accidents in the *Luftwaffe* over a short period of time. I felt committed to help our fighter comrades at the Front. Above all, it was of the utmost importance to my Company that the tens of thousands of Me 109's produced up to this point maintained their good reputation, and that the superior fighting power of the aircraft was not lost.

The elevator of 9228 was fitted with a larger fixed trim tab which made it possible to reach dive angles of more than 60 degrees and increase the indicated airspeed to 700km/h (435mph). From then on, each and every flight was a strain on the nerves. The time between take-off and landing was only about half an hour, but I climbed out of my seat bathed in sweat. As mentioned before, it was a considerable risk to use the trim towards the end of the dive, approaching maximum speed. A bit too much always resulted in pitch changes which were hard to counteract. More than once, I waited fearfully for the aircraft to break into pieces, with me in it. Five flights later, I was at least able to define the forces which occurred on the stick (see graphic next page).

To achieve these values I finally climbed to an initial altitude of 10,000 metres (32,809ft). I reached a final speed of 700km/h (435mph) in the dive (ram air pressure indication) and had to deal with stick forces which no one could expect a pilot in aerial combat or the regular line of duty to handle. Furthermore, the

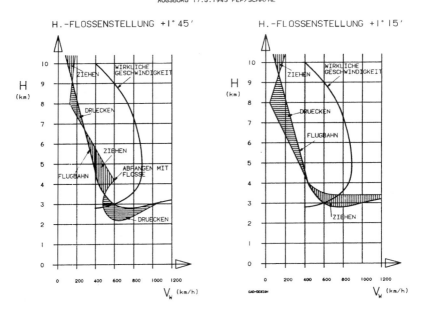

HOEHENRUDER-KRAFTVERLAUF

GROESSENORDNUNGSMAESSIG UEBER DER FLUGBAHN BEIM STURZFLUG AUFGETRAGEN

AUGSBURG 17.3.1943 FEP/SCHM/HE

Diagrammatic representation of elevator pressures.

stress on the airframe was far beyond all that it could have been reasonably expected to take. In addition, there was a further unexplained phenomenon: 9228 oscillated around the longitudinal axis. The swaying and tumbling movements observed at the beginning of the dive degenerated into a progressively rolling momentum, which was barely controllable with increasing speed. My ultimate objective in these flights was to find a means of reducing the forces acting on the stick to a tolerable minimum. This required finding a position for the elevator trim which could be maintained, without adjustment, throughout the dive and recovery. This position had been found by dive trial number twenty-two, on 26th February 1943. I remember the date, because I performed an emergency landing on that day. An engine malfunction forced me to land on the Lechfeld. After changing the spark plugs I returned to Augsburg the same day.

The next four flights followed with a trim setting of 1° 15'. The course of pressures on the elevator control can be seen in the graph entitled *Höhenruder – Kraftverlauf'* (elevator-pressures). With this trim setting, one had to overcome high forces by pushing forward on the stick during the start of the dive. These forces reduced to zero at the recovery point of the dive. By pulling smoothly but firmly, the aircraft recovered safely. During these dives I was able to increase the indicated air speed to more than 700km/h (435mph), but only to a point beyond which a further increase did not seem feasible.

As mentioned above, I had increased the initial altitude for the dives to 10,000 metres (32,809ft), which enabled me to reach maximum speed at an altitude well above 5,000 metres (16,405ft). As a result, I reached more than Mach 0.8, i.e. in excess of 900km/h (559.2mph) true airspeed. Whenever this speed was reached, the aircraft started the rolling motions previously described, giving me the jitters every time. I was travelling at a speed nearly 200km/h (125mph) faster than Fritz Wendel during his (horizontal) record flight with the Me 209. This phenomenon is best described thus: The aircraft would begin to bank slightly to the right, which I was able to counteract using aileron. Without prior warning, the forces reduced and suddenly reversed. The roll to the left then had to be counteracted. Just as I had it under control, it flipped to the other side again. These pendulum type movements continued until the speed had been reduced during recovery. If aileron deflection had not been limited to half the value of normal travel, the overcompensation of the ailerons could have cost me my neck. By modifying the ailerons, Messerschmitt was able to reduce the phenomenon to a tolerable minimum.

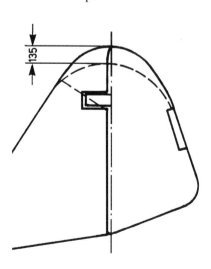

Modifications to the rudder.

On 16th March, I made my twenty-sixth, twenty-seventh and twenty-eighth dives with the Me 109G *Wk. Nr.*9228. In my final report I declared the task completed, and summed up as follows: 'Achieved maximum values with an initial altitude of 10.7 Km (35,106ft) above sea level and an in-flight weight of 2,900kg (6,380lbs). The dive was initiated by rolling in at a speed of Va = 240km/h (149.1mph). The elevator trim was set to +1° 15' and the engine performance at 100 per cent. The dive angle was approximately 70°-80° (reported by the pilot) maximum indicated air speed: Va max = 737km/h (459mph) at 4.5km (14,764ft) altitude. Maximum true air speed reached, Vw max = 906km/h (563mph) at 5.8km (19,029ft) altitude. Maximum Mach number reached: M max = 0.805 at 7.0km (22,966ft) altitude.'

The workshop planned to refit 9228 for the next trial, that day. The fuselage was to be fitted with a wooden empennage instead of that made of aluminium. Dear old 9228 had served me well and truly during the one and a half months of the dive trials, and had withstood all manner of tortures. However, there was a visiting *Luftwaffe Leutnant*, wearing the Knight's Cross, who, after spending some time in the hospital, had the desire to fly a Me 109 again. He was given 9228 and I happened to see his take-off, probably one of the worst in the *Leutnant's* career, which took a lot out of the landing gear. This take-off was reason enough for me to watch his landing. He finished his landing by rounding out 'five storeys high', and touched down accordingly. The undercarriage proved the quality of its sturdy construction and withstood this coarse treatment.

Due to a clerical error, trials management requested a further dive trial with 9228. My final report had probably not yet been distributed to all the desks. I refused to take off before the undercarriage had undergone thorough inspection and a heated debate developed. I won the day and did not fly 9228. Only when, two days later, they presented the aircraft to me with the wooden empennage did I make the planned stability test flight, during which I dived, accelerated and reached a true air speed of 805km/h (500.2mph). I pulled out of the dive with 6g. This concluded the stability test for the wooden construction. At the end of the month a bonus of 3,000 marks was transferred to my bank account for this flight only. Not a penny was paid for the whole of the dive trial because, it was alleged, I had been too 'pussy footed!' I never lodged a complaint. At the time you could not buy much for your money anyway. Some time later it was suggested to Professor Messerschmitt that all works pilots were to be urged to be as inconsiderate of their personal safety, while performing their duties, as were the front line *Luftwaffe* pilots. His reply was, 'We can definitely exclude Lukas Schmid from this exhortation. He flew the dive trials'.

CHAPTER NINE
Hanna Reitsch
My Crash in the Me 163 Rocket Fighter

Hanna Reitsch is very well known throughout the flying world and does not require a special introduction. Nevertheless, do allow me a few words to characterise Hanna as a test pilot.

Hanna and I were colleagues for a long time, working at the DFS. I even knew her from the start, when she began glider flying, and I was there when, in 1932, she qualified for her glider licence at Grunau . Unlike us, the 'common flight students' who had to land after five minutes, Wolf Hirth gave Hanna permission to stay in the air for five hours. That was a world record there and then. When, later – more by accident than intention- she reached 2,800 metres (9,187ft) flying in cloud, she achieved another world record. She also flew distance and, again, set a world record for women pilots, although other male colleagues had flown much further.

An infallible flying instinct, as well as natural ambition, enabled her to perform extraordinary feats of airmanship, and to remain always at the top of her profession. Originally, she had envisaged a completely different life. When, in the early thirties at Stettin-Altdamm, she had made her check flight for piston engine aircraft, her course colleague, Hermann Nein (later to become a Captain with Lufthansa) had asked her: 'What are you going to do when they hand you your licence? Are you going to continue training to become a professional pilot?' 'Heaven forbid!' Hanna had replied. After completing the course she intended to return home and take a splendid vacation. Then – purely out of interest – she would study medicine for a few semesters and, later, get married and have six children.

This was not just idle chatter either; it corresponded completely to her very feminine nature, largely based on emotions. Later on, she took part in competitions, putting even male competitors in the shade, which soon made it difficult for her to find a partner of similar outlook and temperament. She was denied married bliss, as well as the intended six children. It seems almost that the aircraft which carried her into the air became substitutes for the children she never had. When she flew a trial with a new aircraft, she did it with the depth of female emotion given her by Mother Nature. She 'lived' the flight and grew to be as one with the plane, just as a mother does with her child.

In placing Hanna's report – with her description of how she crashed in a Me 163 during a factory trial flight – in this section of the book, I intend to demonstrate how a woman flies an aeroplane. Hanna did not critically and analytically 'dissect' the aircraft, but lived the flight with all her feelings and emotional intensity. The report also shows how much energy was within this small lady. This, and her willpower, enabled her to achieve great performance.

Hanna Reitsch climbing into the cockpit of an Me 163 A.

Those who had the opportunity to fly the rocket aircraft during the war believed it to be part of a fairy tale. One took off into the skies, flames roaring out of the engine and climbing at an enormously steep angle, unable to see anything but the sky above. It seemed unreal to be sitting in the aircraft, firmly secured to the ground, when the infernal, flame-emitting noise began around you. Through the canopy I was able to see the people moving back, frightened, their mouths wide open and their hands over their ears, while I was trying to get used to the continuous detonations the aircraft had to withstand. I felt as if I were being subjected to the elemental forces, and all Hell was breaking loose. It was beyond belief to me that mankind would ever be able to control this energy.

Nevertheless, I was now sitting in the cockpit of this aircraft, becoming accustomed to the noise while the engine was tested. The noise did not frighten me, and did not impair my ability for a single second to make cool, calm and collected decisions about the tasks I had to perform. After becoming airborne, the smallest of mistakes could jeopardise the aircraft and, at the same time, mean loss of life – my life! I could feel the mounting tension and expectation at the approach of my first take-off. I felt the tension all the way to my fingertips while my mind systematically worked through the preparations for take-off.

In October 1942 I flew the Rocket Aircraft Me 163 'a' and 'b' with the Messerschmitt Company at Augsburg. It was a tail-less aircraft, propelled by a rocket engine, which was the result of years of research by Dr. Alexander Lippisch and his test pilot *Kapitän* Heini Dittmar at Darmstadt: this research was to be completed with the Messerschmitt Aircraft Company. The Me 163, which was propelled by the Walter-Rocket, had proved very reliable, and had been developed as a combat aircraft to be used during the war. The Me 163 b was the new Mark and was intended for use as an interceptor. She was to split up enemy bomber formations in order to make them easier targets, then shoot them down individually.

The Walter-Rocket was a liquid propulsion rocket. Highly concentrated hydrogen peroxide (designated '*T-Stoff*') and a special fuel ('*C-Stoff*') were burned in a combustion chamber at 1,800°C (3,272°F). The two elements of the fuel were fed into the tail section, to the combustion chamber, in a predetermined ratio. This was done through a pipe system, using a pressure of 285 psi. There they were mixed by twelve spray jets, and left the tailpipe as a tongue of flame, producing a thrust of approximately 4,500hp. When *C-Stoff* and *T-Stoff* are mixed, immediate decay results, making a source of ignition unnecessary. The pressure of this blast was so strong that one could feel the vibrations on the body at about 100 metres (328ft) behind the aircraft.

Shortly after lift-off the rocket aircraft reached a speed of approximately 350-400kph (217 to 249mph) and, at an altitude of just 8-10 metres (26 to 33ft), the dolly type undercarriage had to be jettisoned because it produced too much drag and could not be retracted due to lack of space. Release of the dolly at too low an altitude could result in dire consequences. Under certain circumstances it could bounce back and hit the lower part of the rear fuselage where the tanks containing the explosive fuels were located. Damage to this part of the aircraft could result in the leakage and mixing of the fuels with disastrous results. After dropping the gear, the aircraft accelerated to 800kph (497mph) within only a few seconds, and with this speed one could achieve a climb angle of sixty to seventy degrees and reach 10,000 metres (32,809ft) within one and a half minutes!

The aircraft possessed flying qualities which I had never experienced, before or since, in any other plane. Flight endurance was very short, due to the extremely high fuel consumption. Two thousand litres of fuel – the maximum to be carried in this small aircraft – gave a powered flight time of approximately five to six minutes. During take-off and landing the Me 163 required the pilot's undivided attention. Several flights in a towed aircraft with no power were required for introductory training. In order to land, abilities in aiming as well as estimating distances were required. One landed without the aid of the engine, just as in a glider, because all fuel had been used during the short flight. At landing speeds of 230-240kph (142-150mph), a precision 'point' landing was not a simple task to perform.

The first flights of the Me 163 b series aircraft were performed by my comrades Reinhard Opitz and Wolfgang Späte, as well as myself. We were operating from the field at Obertraubling, near Augsburg. Heini Dittmar was the man who had flown all the initial tests and trials of this aircraft but he was in hospital at that time with a spinal injury sustained during the trials. (He was the first pilot to have reached and exceeded a speed of 1,000 kilometres an hour (621.38mph)). Initially we 'flew' without an engine, and I was to make my fifth flight of the day. The twin engine Me 110, which was to tow me, taxied across the airstrip, the towline became taut and a few minutes later the Me 163 lifted off. At a height of about 8 metres I tried to jettison the undercarriage by pulling a handle in the cockpit, but noticed that, this time, something was terribly wrong. A humming vibration engulfed the whole of the aeroplane. It felt as if it were caused by strong turbulence underneath the aircraft. At the same time I saw red flares being fired from the ground: *Achtung! Gefahr!* (Attention! Danger!) I tried to establish contact with the tow-aircraft via my throat microphone, but it had failed. Instead, I saw the observer in the machine gunner's position wildly waving a white cloth, while at the same time the Me 110 towing me began to continuously lower and raise its landing gear. Now I knew for sure that something was wrong with my undercarriage. The Me 110 towed me around the

An Me 163 B. This particular aircraft was returned to Germany from Britain after the War. Shown here following a complete refurbishment to display condition.

airfield in several large circuits. I had only one wish: To be towed up to a safe altitude where I would be able, after having been released from the tow rope, to check if the aircraft was still controllable. Since I did not release the tow rope, the pilot in the Me 110 soon realised my intentions and dragged me to an altitude of 3,500 metres (11,500ft), just below the cloud base. There I released the tow rope.

I tried to jettison the undercarriage by making high 'g' turns and pulling out of short, high speed dives, but to no avail. The incessant vibrations proved to me that I had not been successful. All there was left to do now was to check if the aircraft was fully controllable at all attitudes, or if the jammed undercarriage impeded any of the controls. No pilot would ever give up such a valuable aircraft and abandon it by parachute, as long as there was even the slightest chance of bringing it back to the ground in one piece. Where and how the ill-fated undercarriage was hanging under the fuselage, I could not imagine. The question remained, would the gear tear open the fuselage upon landing? I could only trust my luck. I was confident that I would be able to take the aircraft back to the ground in one piece, but I was to be proved wrong.

I arrived at the boundary of the landing field, just as I had planned, with an altitude reserve of approximately 80 metres

(263ft). My intention was to lose this altitude quickly by side-slipping towards the touchdown point (side-slipping, or yawing the aircraft using cross controls – e.g right aileron and left rudder – causes extreme drag and a consequent rapid loss in altitude). Suddenly, I noticed that, despite sufficient airspeed, the aircraft did not react to any of my control inputs and I just pancaked. By side-slipping I had exposed the control surfaces to the turbulent airflow caused by the gear, and the result I had expected did not materialise.

The events which followed happened so quickly that I had no time to think. I was still trying to regain control of the aircraft when the airfield appeared before me. I bent forward as far as possible, just before the aircraft impacted and somersaulted with a crash. The first thing I realised, when the aircraft had come to a halt, was that I was not hanging in my seat straps. The aircraft was sitting right side up and not lying on its back. Automatically, my right hand opened the canopy which, remarkably, was still intact. Carefully, I used my right hand to grope along my left arm, then cautiously along the length of my body, sides and legs. It was all still there, and I was able to move everything without too much discomfort. I was both astonished and thankful, a peculiar euphoria creeping into my mind. Then I realised that, although I felt little or no pain, a stream of blood was running down me. When I traced the line of the flow, it led to my face, which I touched with my fingers. There was a large open wound at the spot normally occupied by my nose. Air and bloody bubbles appeared at the bridge of my nose every time I breathed. Was I to go on through this world without a nose? I tried to turn my head sideways and suddenly all went black before my eyes and I nearly fainted. I held my head still, took pencil and paper from my pocket and noted the cause and the course of actions of the accident. This flight was not to be for nothing! Having made my notes, I took out my handkerchief and wrapped it around my face to cover the 'nose' in order to spare my rescuers the sight of my injured face.

Then I was wrapped in darkness. When I regained consciousness I saw my comrades, all as white as sheets, standing in front of me. I gathered all my strength and humour, so as to reassure them: I still felt no pain. I was then taken by car from the airfield to the hospital of the Sisters of Charity in Regensburg. The X – Ray showed a nasty picture: base of the skull fractured in four places; facial bones fractured in two;

upper jaw dislocated to the right; bruised brain and, on top of that, a split nose. All in all, I was very lucky to have Dr. Bodewig as my surgeon. I remember seeing the operating theatre and the staff when the veils of darkness descended upon me.

In March 1943 I had improved to the point of being able to leave the hospital, but I was not fully recovered as yet, and the question remained as to whether I ever would be...

CHAPTER TEN
Fritz Schäfer
Test Pilot and Master Engineer
at the Heinkel Trial Centre

This article by Fritz Schäfer is published almost in its entirety, because it is a typical example of German flight trials during the time before and during World War II. It also gives a vivid account of the training and education required for qualification as a master aircraft engineer, a career designed for those studying aircraft design and construction who were willing to put their knowledge to practical use by flying. Schäfer's report also contains the final answer as to why the Me 262 was preferred to the He 280.

Fritz Schäfer.

The day had come, but my dream of a career in flying was destroyed by the cancellation of our training course. War with Poland had begun on 1st September 1939 as I, and fifteen other academically trained engineers, attended a flying training course at Braunschweig-Völkenrode. This course was part of my training as a *Flugbaumeisterlaufbahn* (master aircraft engineer) and I was to graduate as a pilot, holding the C2 licence permitting me to fly civil aircraft of all weights. This was my third course as a *Flugbauführer* (Aviation Construction Engineer – as we called ourselves then) before taking the master's exam at the *RLM* (*Reichsluftfahrt-Ministerium*). During our three years training we were all employees of the *DVL* (*Deutsche Versuchsanstalt für Luftfahrt* (German Institute of Aviation and Trials). It was the *DVL* which had formally initiated the career of *Flugbaumeisterlaufbahn*. Along with our training as engineer pilots, we were seconded to other companies in the aviation industry from time to time, in order to gain a few months extra experience. It was up to the individual to choose the field of interest and training: we either went to aircraft manufacturers, companies making equipment for aircraft, or companies designing and building engines. During the whole time with the industry, we all remained employees of the *DVL*, and on their payroll. We received a so-called grant for trainees, which was an improved students' allowance.

Due to the advent of war, our flying training was interrupted. Military pilots were more important now, and pilot engineers were not so much in demand. 'What was going to happen?' was one of the questions on our mind. Whoever one listened to, the story was the same: 'The war will be over in a few weeks: it won't last.' We all wanted to complete our three years training successfully and on time, and the outbreak of war did not worry us in the least. Initially, we had hoped that the halt to our training had just been an impulsive reaction which would soon be corrected. Sadly, this was not the case, and the flight-training section of the *DVL* at Braunschweig went on 'hold'. Some of the *Flugbauführen* were sent to companies they had previously worked for, and the others were given orders to join the *RLM*.

I was part of the group sent to the Ministry. Since I was specialising in aircraft armament, I was to work on planning how best to equip *Lufthansa* transport aircraft, and aircraft of other companies, with suitable defence armament. This task was to be completed with the highest priority. I had specialised knowledge through working with Mauser Waffenfabrik at Oberndorf am Neckar, as well as working in the weapons trial and test section of the *Luftwaffe* at Tarnewitz. Mercifully they soon remembered that we wanted to fly. I was very close to having my C2 licence 'in the bag'; the only stage left to complete was a qualifying cross country flight using, perhaps, a Ju 52 which the *DVL* would provide for this purpose. For the time being, I had to do without the C2 licence. At least, with my B2 licence I was able to fly all land aircraft of medium weight, including aerobatics and instrument flight. We did not much enjoy our desk jobs at the *RLM*: they were not stimulating employment for young *Flugbauführen*.

One day, together with two other colleagues (Eugen Speter and Herbert Kaulbach), I was sent to *Erprobungsstelle der Luftwaffe* (Trial and Test Section) at Tarnewitz, where, in conjunction with weapons trials, we were to fly again. The military airfield of Tarnewitz, on which *Erprobungsstelle der Luftwaffe* had quartered itself, was located on the Baltic Sea between Wismar and Travemünde, right next to the seaside resort of Boltenhagen, Mecklenburg. It was difficult to reach without a car, and only a few of the privileged had one at that time; we underlings were not among them. Our journey was by *Reichsbahn* (National Railway), then by narrow-gauge railway and bus to the village of Boltenhagen, and then a walk took us the rest of the way. Initially, we stayed in Boltenhagen, where our thoughts were invaded by the continuous murmur of the surf on the beach, a new experience for us. In any event, this was to prove very soothing after the hectic weeks which lay before us.

At the Trial Section, the three of us were assigned to different groups. I was put into the group working on trials for fixed gun mountings. My two colleagues were allocated to the team working on mobile mountings and trials of visors. The asphalt runway of the Trial Section jutted out into the Baltic like a peninsula. Landings with a glassy smooth sea and absolutely no wind were rather difficult, due to reflections and the heat rising from the black asphalt. This created problems, especially for pilots not used to these conditions. We, 'the natives', soon became accustomed to these hazards. The Trial and Test Department also had firing ranges facing the open sea which had been declared restricted areas. Live ammunition was issued, and we were able to fire on targets floating in the sea. All the German companies developing weapons and arms, visors, mountings and ancillary equipment were permitted to use Tarnewitz for their testing and development, up to the 'ready for production' stage. They received support from the different sections, and each specialist Trial Section had suitable aircraft at its disposal which were made available to carry out the tests for the different companies and their equipment. Usually, these aircraft were flown by the pilots of the Trial Section, but the engineers, who wanted to do their own testing and firing, were also allowed to fly as long as they were suitably qualified.

When we arrived at Tarnewitz, many trials and tests by the industry, as well as the *Luftwaffe,* were in progress. Everybody who wanted to fly had his money's worth. We had ample opportunity to try out offensive and defensive weapons in the air, either as pilots of the different aircraft, or as the defence gunner. Flying was the most welcome interruption of our numerous duties, whilst writing-up reports about the tests and the results of the trials in the air and on the ground firing ranges was probably the least popular. For the times we flew, the Trials Section paid us additional flight pay, which noticeably boosted the allowance granted by the DVL. We gladly accepted the extra money, although we would have willingly have flown without it. Most important to us was that we were allowed to fly! We were very content with our work and, after the successful Polish Campaign, we looked forward to 1940 with relatively few worries. But, despite our confidence, we realised, from general conversation, that a very high demand was to be put on our trials programme before the war was brought to a satisfactory conclusion.

On 9th April 1940, at 08.00hrs, I took off from Tarnewitz in a commuter aircraft, an Ar 79, accompanied by a mechanic. We were under orders to make our way to Fassberg, an airfield in the Lüneburger-Heide (north east of Hanover). I was to visit the Rheinmetall – Borsig weapons factory in Unterlüß, where they were developing and testing aircraft armament. Within an hour, we were the airfield, and I saw below us a great bustle going on. Ju 52 transport aircraft were lined up in long rows, ready to be loaded, and large groups of soldiers were standing about. More soldiers were being off-loaded from coaches and lorries but, despite this military activity going on, I decided to land. Red flares were fired all around me, but I ignored them, feeling that my mission was also of great importance to the war! However, when I entered Operations, all Hell broke loose: 'What was I doing, landing right in the middle of a military manoeuvre!?' After a few more choice words, we were told that the occupation of Denmark and Norway had just begun. Nonetheless, after lunch, we were allowed to fly back to Tarnewitz.

The German long range reconnaissance air fleet had suffered greater losses over France than expected. A demand arose for better defensive armament than the commonly used MG 15. With this weapon, the operator had to change the drum magazines manually. In an effort to improve matters, the Trial Section had tested and improvised many different devices without achieving complete success. It was an example of the fact that Germany was in no way sufficiently prepared for a war in the West. However, we were tasked to do our best and, in my opinion, the best co-operative development by the Trial Section and the companies in the field of defensive weapons was the fixed rearward-firing machine gun. After the completion of the campaign in Norway and France, I was tasked with the trials of the improved MG 151/ 20 machine gun in a Me 109 F, and ordered to have it ready for production. For this exercise, I was almost exclusively on my own, including the air-to-air and ground-to-ground test-firing of the gun. As a result of this trial, I managed to have a very important safety feature incorporated into the gun mounting.

Schäfer's first task, the trials of the rim mounting for the machine gun.

On one of the last successful gun test flights, high spirits got the better of me and I flew over the heads of my ground crew at very low level. During one of the turns, the leading edge slats of the Me 109 operated, which was not unusual. However, what caught me by surprise was the fact that they did not deploy simultaneously! The outside wing extended the slat a fraction of a second earlier than the inside, causing the aircraft to roll nearly inverted. And this with only 30 metres (100ft) altitude! I frightened myself considerably, but the other wing slat decided to come out as well and stopped the roll – all was normal again, and so was my emotional balance. I reproached myself for being so careless, but once in a while a pilot needs a reminder of his own fallibility.

Right at the beginning of my stay at Tarnewitz I had had a similar experience. During the so called 'Open Day', the inhabitants of Boltenhagen and Tarnewitz were able to visit the site and see the aircraft of the Trial Section. Flight demonstrations were naturally included in the day's programme, and I was to fly a He 137. This aircraft was initially intended as a 'Stuka' type dive bomber, and this particular example was fitted with a Jumo 210 engine. It had an open cockpit and was normally used as a test and target aircraft by the Trial Section. I was accomplished in handling this very manoeuvrable aircraft but, sadly, a low cloud base imposed narrow limits on my flight demonstration. When the ceiling seemed to have lifted just a bit, I tried to perform a turn and pulled the aircraft up over the sea just beyond the airfield. I entered the clouds earlier than I had expected, and was forced to complete my stall turn on instruments. As I came clear of the clouds again, I was heading straight down for the water of the Baltic, which was closing on me rather rapidly. Instinctively, I pulled back on the stick, possibly a bit hard, without waiting for the speed to build up again. The aircraft merely reacted by shaking, and continued its nose dive. I realised that the airflow over the deflected tailplane was disturbed, rendering the elevator ineffective. Putting the stick back to neutral, I continued the dive and started an easy recovery with the increased speed. The airfoil was effective again, and I was able to recover the aircraft, just above the surface of the sea. From that point I continued in horizontal flight. Thank God, nobody on the ground had been able to see that I had frightened myself stiff. After landing, I parked the aeroplane without referring to the incident.

I had another narrow escape, also at Tarnewitz, when a Curtiss P 36, which had been captured during the Norwegian campaign, was allocated briefly to the Trial Section for flight tests. An impressive, robust, little bird with a dual radial engine, the Curtiss had ample room in the cockpit, and was altogether larger than our Me 109. It had a sturdy, retractable,

undercarriage and two separate rear fuel tanks. Checklists and
instructions were not available, but before a flight one gathered
all the information concerning the known flight parameters,
including what were thought to be normal engine
temperatures and pressures, as well as familiarising oneself
with the different flight controls. Basically, one simply set the
trim to neutral, opened the throttle and took off. Other pilots
also wanted to fly the machine and I had observed my
colleague, who had flown before me, performing a few rolls
and turns, and had been duly impressed. Having flown similar
manoeuvres, I then thought I would top them with a loop. I
pushed the stick forward, accelerated, pulled up for the loop,
but was not quite sure if I would make it over the top, and
therefore pulled a bit harder to tighten the loop. When I had
nearly reached the inverted position, and the airspeed had
reduced near to stalling, the aircraft entered a violent roll. I
thought I might enter a potentially fatal inverted spin, and
moved all controls to neutral. The aircraft responded by
dropping a wing and went into a vertical dive from which I
was, fortunately, able to recover. I landed without attempting
any other experiments. Again I had frightened myself, but I
had survived, albeit a little shakily. The next candidate to take
off with the Curtiss was Reck, one of the Trial test pilots. I told
him about my mishap with the unsuccessful loop and tried to
warn him, even though he had many more flying hours than I.
He listened to me patiently, and remarked in an almost
benevolent tone: 'Who knows what kind of manoeuvre you
attempted to fly?' He took off and started to cut his capers at
approximately 800 metres (2,627ft). He seemed a real expert,
but suddenly the aircraft started to spin. At first all the
bystanders, including myself, thought it was intentional, but
then the canopy was seen to become detached, a sure
indication that he was in trouble. Shortly after, the aircraft
impacted inland, and a few moments later we heard a bang
and waited for the black column of smoke to appear, but there
was no fire. For several seconds we were all paralysed as we
stood in the silence, staring in the same direction. Then we fell
into the well-rehearsed routine: sound the alarm, deploy the
fire crews, send the ambulance – full emergency procedure,
but all to no avail for poor Reck. A few days later there was a
full military funeral service in a hangar, and afterwards
everyone tried to forget as quickly as possible. Later, we were

He 177 with the tail developed by Fritz Schäfer.

to experience these occasions with increasing frequency.

In early November, 1940, I was appointed as works pilot with Heinkel at Rostock. Ernst Heinkel was a highly respected man in the Ministry. After all it was he who, before the outbreak of war in August 1939, had flown the World's first jet aircraft, the He 178, at Marienehe. Now a twin engine jet fighter, the He 280, had been developed under the leadership of *Direktor* Lusser. This aeroplane was to be flight tested with the utmost urgency, as it was intended that it should be employed in the front lines as soon as possible. The other lead project, the development and testing of the He 177 long range bomber, was also being forced through, and was to be made a success at all costs (which was to lead to the total loss of two aircraft and two crews). This type of aircraft was urgently needed in view of the war situation, and it was a difficult task for *Direktor* Lusser which he hoped to resolve with the help of the newly created department of *Ingenieur-Piloten* (engineer pilots). The test flight department at Heinkel had more or less refused to fly the He 177 because of the losses. When I arrived, two engineer pilots, Peter and Ahlborn, had already begun new trials with the He 177. 'You have been employed mainly for trials with the He 280', Lusser explained during my initial interview, 'but you are also to engage in the trials of the He 177 and other prototypes.'

My introduction to the Heinkel company was spectacular. On my very first day Lusser gave me a guided tour of the company. He explained the difficulties involved in developing the new prototypes, and outlined his intentions for the new *Ingenieur-Piloten* department. We also went out to the factory's airstrip, where Gotthold Peter had just landed after a trial with the He 177. Peter was an excellent pilot, a member of the *Akaflieg* (Flying Academy) and an academically trained engineer who had graduated from the *Technische Hochschule* (technical high school) in Berlin: he had been trained as a pilot by the *Luftwaffe*. He was fully occupied, trying to increase the speed step by step, and testing a new horizontal stabiliser by pushing the aircraft into a bunt with the engines at full power. Recording systems for the trial data were still in their infancy, and comprised basically only airspeed and altitude recorders, with no additional system for monitoring the dive. Suddenly, Lusser had the idea of me flying with Peter on the next trial, lying in the navigation dome and observing the stabiliser at different speeds. I was convinced that this would not deliver the required result but, on the other hand, I did not want to refuse. Lusser thought it excellent that an engineer pilot had come just at the right time to record the data.

Unenthusiastically, I put down my hat and coat and a parachute was strapped to my back, right over my best three-piece suit. I took a seat in the aircraft with the other three crew members, strapped in, and Peter took off again, climbing to 5,000m (16,405ft), before commencing further trials: increasing the speed in regular steps, ending at 3,000m (9,843ft). The speed was increased by 15km/h (9.32mph) indicated airspeed (IAS) and each trial was started again at 5,000m. Despite careful observation, I was unable to observe anything abnormal in the behaviour of the stabiliser. We had finally reached a speed of 550km/h (341.76mph) when I saw a brief shadow on the tailplane, and the aircraft broke into a violent pitching motion. There were four of us in the cockpit, while the fifth man was lying in the tail position. Someone shouted: 'Get out!' and I somehow struggled out of the high seat to reach the hatch in the floor of the aircraft in order to bale out. The engineer down below had already started to work on the opening mechanism of the hatch when Peter calmly said over the intercom, 'Don't bale out, I'll soon have this thing under control.' Despite the persistent pitching up and down, Peter smoothly pulled up and arrested our descent until we flew level again.

The engineer in the tail position reported that the left hand side of the stabiliser had broken off and was fluttering in the airstream. The right side was still intact, but the tail of the aeroplane continued pitching up and down. Peter stuck to his decision to land with the crew on board and, after we had observed the fire trucks and ambulances driving out on the airfield, we commenced our final approach, which ended with a relatively smooth landing. We were then able to inspect the stabiliser at close range, and marvel at Peter's success in regaining control and bringing both us and the aircraft back. This was my first day as a test pilot with Heinkel, and it was with a sense of relief that I retrieved my hat and coat from the person who had kindly held them for me. I left the airfield in the company of the Technical Director, reflecting upon what might lie ahead in my time with Heinkel.

The He 280 was to be fitted with jet engines, developed and manufactured by Heinkel and overseen by Dr. von Ohain, head of the engine development department. The fact that the airframe had been built prior to the final development of the engines required the He 280 V1 to be flown initially without engines, simply as a glider. For this purpose it was towed to an altitude of 4,000m (13,124ft) using a He111. After the release of the tow line, one was able to test the flight properties of the aircraft in the glide for about six minutes. The last 1,000m (3,281ft) of altitude were required for the approach, since a go-around or overshoot were not possible, and a point landing was obviously mandatory on every approach.

For these glide tests, two aerodynamically shaped bodies were installed instead of the engines. A large battery was carried in the forward weapons bay to power the electro-hydraulic retraction of the nose wheel, the operation of the air brakes and the flaps. Installing the heavy battery in a forward position had the same effect on the balance of the aircraft as if the engines had been fitted, and so the proper centre of gravity was preserved. My colleague and Master Engineer, Bader, had already begun the glide trials by the time I arrived at Rostock. Bader, as a staff engineer with the Trial and Test Centre at Rechlin, had officially taken over the trials by order of the Ministry of Aviation. I was to continue these tests as a works engineer.

Within Heinkel there was not a single person who was able, or even wanted, to take over this task. Bader personally gave me an introduction to the He 280 and, on my first approach, I

He 280 landing after its maiden (unpowered) flight.

came in a bit short and had to land in a neighbouring field with the nose gear extended. I was naturally very angry with myself, but struggled not to show it. Then the engineers responsible for the undercarriage, led by their boss *Herr* Schneider, came over with wry smiles on their faces and a cheery, 'Well done! Superb!' as they patted me on the shoulder: 'How good of you to add an undercarriage test on your very first trial flight programme!' The nose gear, by the way, had also been developed by Heinkel and was being used, instead of the usual tail wheel arrangement, for the first time in a German designed aircraft of the size and weight of the He 280. The advantages of the nose wheel (and the tricycle undercarriage in general) on jet aircraft are nowadays undisputed, but at the time we were developing and testing the He 280 we were very much in uncharted waters.

The glide trials which followed were mainly aimed at testing the stability of the design in the three main axes. This resulted in enlargement of the rudder and the control tabs on the ailerons. By changing the kinetics of the tabs on all the controls, the aerodynamic forces were reduced and balanced. The air brake was laid out as a dive brake without any influence on the aerodynamic loading of the aircraft. It was tested up to the speeds reached by diving from an altitude of 4,000m (13,124ft). These were extensive flight tests and trials, still without an engine, which reminded me very much of my time at the flying academy in Stuttgart where they were towing gliders.

I was soon introduced to the He 177 by Gotthold Peter, and was destined to play a great part in the continuing trials. In contrast to my first flight as an observer, of which I had nothing but bad memories, the subsequent flights with Peter left a very positive impression. The concept of the He 177 was a giant step forward and, as with all new creations, she naturally had 'teething problems'. It is a pity that the people responsible were not able to give us enough time to investigate and rectify many of the deficiencies we discovered. The demand for an aircraft with the performance of the He 177 was terrific, and the production in series started much too soon. As a result, the troops had to put up with faults which should have been cleared during the trials. But before I was able to really 'make friends' with the He177, the He 280 had to have its turn.

The Ohain jet engines were well ahead of BMW and Junkers developments. While these two large companies continued to study basic details on a wide basis, involving a vast number of personnel, Ohain, with limited resources, had built a very simple but operational engine. This simple jet had been running on the test stand for quite some time and, by March 1941, the engineers were at a stage where they thought they could guarantee a running time of one hour. A turbine speed regulator had not been developed, due to lack of time and, sadly, the maximum static thrust of the engine was less than predicted (only about 450kg, approximately 1,000lbs). This did not meet the requirements for propulsion of the He 280, as laid down by the designers, but it did mean that the thrust would be sufficient to get the aircraft off the ground.

Heinkel's secret of success was to be always the first and the quickest in whatever he did. For this reason he spared no effort on the He 280, and strove to be in the market long before the competition. The BMW and Junkers engines offered better prospects of success in the long run because they were already equipped with turbine speed regulators and axial compressors. If Messerschmitt's Me 262 had been powered by BMW or Junkers engines, Heinkel would have been left standing. Therefore, in March 1941, in an effort to stay ahead, two of Ohain's engines – designated He S 8 a – were fitted to the He 280 V2.

Dr. von Ohain had succeeded in building an operational jet engine within a relatively short time-frame, with limited personnel and a shoestring budget – a remarkable achievement! However, the project was still very much in the development stage: for instance, because the engines were leaking fuel, due to poor vaporisation, the cowlings had to be left off in order to avoid an engine fire during taxi-ing tests.

The plan was that the maiden flight of the aircraft fitted with jet engines should be made by my colleague, Paul Bader, from the Trial and Test Centre, Rechlin. In the meantime, I was to go ahead with the fast taxi-ing runs. I noticed that everyone expected me, as a Heinkel employee and the works Test Pilot, to include a 'short flight' in my taxi trials. However I was told that Bader was not to 'lose out' in respect of the maiden flight and the prestige that it would bring. After all, he had already performed the very first glide trial with the He 280. What was I to do? Professor Heinkel drove me up and down the 1,000m (3,281ft) runway in his Tatra, and remarked: 'One could easily taxi along this beautiful runway all the way to lift-off speed, and possibly even make a small hop into the air?' Then he gave me a mischievous look, and said: 'Naturally, you must not fly it yet, but you can do whatever else you please!'

I decided to execute a high speed taxi run and, if all was well, lift off and fly a short circuit pattern. Due to the short life of the engines, it was best not to waste any more time on taxi trials so, to ensure a safe lift-off, I had the fuel tanks only half-filled; the lighter the aircraft, the better the chances of lift-off. I was still not permitted to run the engines at full thrust and so, having had the engines started with compressed air, I began to increase the power whilst holding the aircraft on the brakes. Slowly, I increased the turbine speed to 13,000rpm, the 'red line' at the time, then released the brakes. The aircraft accelerated quicker than I had expected, a good start, and after using just over half the runway, I lifted off, leaving the gear and flaps down. My attention was focused on the engine instruments and, in particular, the turbine speed and jet pipe temperature. Both reduced with the increasing speed, but I had been told to expect this because the engines still did not have regulators. I had to push both throttles fully forward to maintain 12,000rpm and a jet pipe temperature of 600 degrees. These two readings were crucial if I was to generate sufficient thrust to take off and remain airborne. With an indicated airspeed of 250km/h (155.3mph), and an altitude of 200m (656ft), I continued with my extended 'hop' and completed the circuit. Passing over the Warnow, just prior to turning onto 'finals', the red 'low fuel' light flickered on. Having reduced the thrust to idle in the turn on to 'finals' and lowered the flaps, I pushed the aircraft down relatively quickly in order to touch down at the beginning of the runway at approximately 150km/h (93.27mph). The first flight of a twin engine jet aircraft in Germany had been performed: the date entered in my log book was 30th March 1941.

The first take-off of the He 280 without the engine cowlings.

Everyone at Heinkel was delighted. The event was to be properly exploited and used as publicity; Ernst Heinkel was very good at that. All the top people from the *Reichsluftfahrt-Ministerium* (Ministry of Aviation) who had an interest in the development of jet aircraft were invited for the following week. The delegates were led by *General* Ernst Udet, head of the technical department. They all came to watch the demonstration of the He 280 at Rostock, flown by Bader. I did not mind at all: I had already flown my three minute pattern, and was told that this would not disadvantage Bader's position in any way. The bonus for the maiden flight was paid to both of us!

From Left to right: Paul Bader, Ernst Heinkel and Fritz Schäfer. Both pilots are holding envelopes containing their bonus of 10,000 Reichmarks.

During Bader's demonstration, *General* Udet approached me and asked why I had already flown. I said that I had to take responsibility for that flight, and that I had thought it my duty as works pilot. He gave me an approving smile, and continued watching the demonstration with great interest. Bader was a member of the technical department at the *Reichsluftfahrt-Ministerium*, and Udet was his superior. I was happy with the outcome of the conversation, and soon got over the disappointment at not flying the demonstrations. During the week before Bader's flight, the engineers had managed to replace the fuel nozzles with others produced by the specialist company, L'Orange. This cured the fuel leakage, and Bader was able to fly faster with the engine cowlings properly fitted and with the gear retracted. It was an impressive flight but, when the aircraft landed, neither engine was turning. The rear bearings had seized: Bader had not gone as easy on the engines as I had on my flight. Luckily, none of the spectators noticed that the engines had stopped, and the aircraft was immediately towed to the hangar by tractor. It was clear that Dr. von Ohain and his engineers had quite a job on their hands if this obvious weakness in the rear rotor bearing was to be rectified.

Flight test of the Ohain engine, mounted under the belly of a Heinkel He 111.

To make better progress with the Ohain engines, a He 111 was modified to become an airborne testbed. A He S 8a engine was attached to the aircraft for testing the turbine shaft speed regulator, as well as a control for the variation of the exhaust cross-section. Both the Junkers 004 and the BMW 003 jet engines already had such regulators, thereby reducing the pilot's workload by enabling him to set constant engine parameters at varying altitudes and speeds. I performed many flights with the He 111, and we were, at last, able to find a temporary solution to replace these regulators. The He 280 V3 was cleared to fly again, following an improvement in the cooling of the turbine bearing. I conducted several high performance flights in order to attract the Ministry's attention to Heinkel again, since the competition by Messerschmitt with their Me 262 was ever threatening. During one of these flights, on 8th February 1943, bad luck struck once again. After a take-off across a railway embankment, with the undercarriage already retracted, there was a loud bang at a height of about 40m (132ft). I saw a long fiery tail coming from the right engine, and immediately pulled the right throttle back and closed the corresponding fuel cock. I succeeded in correcting the powerful yaw by using the rudder, and then there was nothing for it but to continue straight ahead and attempt an emergency landing outside the airfield: I knew the thrust of the left engine was insufficient to continue in level flight. Leaving the flaps in the take-off position, the warning horn for 'flaps extended' was sounding continuously as I searched for a suitable field for an emergency landing. With time running out, I finally saw one straight ahead, manoeuvred around several trees, pulled the throttle of the left engine to idle, opened the canopy completely, using the crank, and released my harness. If the aircraft were to somersault, which could easily happen, I wanted to be thown clear if possible. The tanks still contained about 1,200 litres (317US gal. / 264 imp. gal) of highly flammable benzene. If this caught fire, I would be sitting in Hell. (Benzene was used because we did not as yet have J2 Jet fuel which was not quite as flammable). As I approached the field, I pushed the plane towards the ground at a speed of approximately 220km/h (137mph) and touched down. Dirt flew up around me amid a terrible racket, and the aircraft bounced several times as if about to somersault, but then settled, skidding along as if on skis. We finally stopped, broadside on but right side up. I was out in record time, putting a safe

Emergency landing February 9, 1943.

distance between myself and the potential fire bomb, but nothing happened, no fire, no fuel leak. I had been extremely lucky once again.

After the nerve-wracking experience of the landing, I stood alone in the field, west of Marienehe, beside the aircraft. Then I saw people running towards me, coming from a hollow in the ground near the spot where I had initially touched down. Imagine my surprise when I saw they were wearing Russian uniforms! However, as they came closer, I saw their armbands, with *'Deutsche Wehrmacht'* on them. They were Russian prisoners of war, and were part of a barrage balloon unit. The Russians had seen my belly landing and shared my joy at its successful outcome. A German soldier, who was in charge of the POW's, came up behind them and also took an interest in my odd-looking aircraft. These barrage balloon sites had been installed all around the Heinkel factory for defence against air raids.

Approximately half an hour later, a convoy of vehicles worked its way to my improvised landing ground and a group of mechanics immediately started dismantling the aircraft. The damage was relatively minor, with only the engine cowlings and

Fritz Schäfer in the cockpit of the He 280.

the nose gear damaged. Needless to say, the right engine was a total loss: a heavy turbine blade had broken off and been ejected rearwards through the exhaust. Luckily no imbalance had developed while the engine was still running at 13,000rpm; had it done so, the engine could have been completely torn off.

I made a brief report to Professor Heinkel, and a meeting was set up for the following morning. It was to include all the leading personnel responsible for the development, production and operation of the He 280 and, incidentally, the manager of the canteen! Initially, I could not comprehend why the latter was required to attend the meeting, but it was to prove yet another shrewd move by the Professor. During the course of the meeting, Professor Heinkel demanded that the aircraft should fly again within four days. After taking stock of the damage and the work required, it was concluded that four days was a completely impossible target. At this point, Heinkel intervened and asked the head of each department what his requirements were in order to meet the four day limit. The broad consensus was: more staff, more overtime, institution of night shifts and, of course, additional meals for all involved. The extra meals were necessary because the workforce had to manage outside with their ration-cards, which provided only a minimum of food. Heinkel approved almost everything and, after having spoken to *Herr* Bernau – the canteen manager – he also sanctioned the additional rations for meals. Bernau always had things under control – and a few surprises 'up his sleeve' for special occasions like this. Once these matters had been taken care of, everyone present had to promise that he would report immediately if meeting the deadline became doubtful, or if he felt that further measures were required. Professor Heinkel called each department every morning and evening to ask about the state of the repairs. The result was that, after only three days, I was able to take-off again and fly the He 280 V3. Ernst Heinkel proudly announced, 'This is Heinkel speed!'

For the demonstration of the He 280 to *General* Milch at Rechlin, I was required to fly the first 'cross country' with a twin engine jet aircraft. Since our temporary nozzle regulator worked pretty well, I was able to adjust the engines to a fuel saving thrust setting. I took off from Rostock on 17th December 1942, soon after our master technician, Weber, had left with three mechanics in our *'Taifun'*. I flew at about 4,000m (13,124ft), above a broken layer of clouds, and landed on the long runway at Laerz near Rechlin. The whole flight took only 12 minutes, and I arrived well before the team in their *'Taifun'*. Before the demonstration of the newest types from the German aircraft industry, all the 'planes were lined up along the runway. Milch took the parade, together with his staff. He stopped in front of each aircraft and saluted each of the pilots, who were already sitting in their cockpits, by raising his Marshal's baton. My demonstration seemed to have pleased everyone, since a jet aircraft was something special at that time. On 18th December, I flew back to Rostock: the first 'out and return' in the He 280 had been completed safely.

He 280 V2 in flight.

The last attempt to introduce the He 280 to the *Luftwaffe* was initiated at Wien – Schwechat (Vienna, Austria). The design and development department had been moved there after several devastating air raids on Rostock. In the meantime, it was realised that it would be some time before the Heinkel jet engines would be ready for a production run.

The He 280 V2 had been taken to Schwechat by road, and for this demonstration we intended to fit the aircraft with Junkers 004-engines, which already had an admirable safety record. They were a little larger in diameter than the Heinkel engines, resulting in lower ground clearance, but with due care and caution the aircraft could be flown safely, and allow us enough test flights to ascertain whether their use on the Heinkel He 280 aircraft was practical. The message arrived at Rostock that the aircraft had been fitted with the Junkers engines, and was ready for flight at Schwechat. I was to go to Vienna immediately and demonstrate the aircraft to *Gauleiter* Baldur von Schirach. On 16th March 1943, I flew our *'Taifun'* to Wien-Schwechat, via Prague, non-stop: on landing, the fuel tanks were nearly empty. The He 280 V2 was waiting, ready to be flown, but surrounded by a Junkers engineering team wanting to make an engine run and take thrust measurements.

The demonstration was scheduled for the next day, and I wanted to have at least one short test flight with the new engines. Schwechat airfield looked like a construction site, because the runway was being extended by the Heinkel development section. One was just able to take off and land between the tracked equipment, building materials and tippers. The test run, thrust measurement, and adjustment took longer than I liked, and dusk was already falling when I was given the go-ahead to fly. I was soon airborne, and it was a pleasure flying with the new engines. They produced nearly double the thrust of the Heinkel engines (approximately 800kg (1,760lbs), and I had no worries about the adjustment of the turbine shaft rpm and exhaust gas temperature, thanks to the ingenious Junkers regulator. Highly satisfied, I began to set up the aircraft for landing, lowering the undercarriage and deploying full flaps. When I was well established on finals, approaching the runway, the landing speed seemed rather high, and the airport fence came towards me very quickly. I performed an overshoot, which worked out very well with the new engines. This time I noticed the flaps had not extended and so, during the set-up for the new approach, I used the emergency hydraulic hand pump, but to no avail – the flaps steadfastly refused to extend. The undercarriage was down and locked, or at least this was what the indications led me to believe and, since it was getting dark quickly, I would have to land without flaps. I approached the runway again, making a very flat approach, very low and as slow as I possibly could without getting too close to the stall point, and gingerly touched down. The speed after touch-down was still very high, and I was conscious that at the end of the runway was a fence and, behind it, a shallow slope which descended into a field where the DF equipment (Direction

Finder) hut was located. I was unable to deviate left or right of the runway because of all the equipment and building materials and, in addition, I did not want to slide down the embankment, for this would almost certainly result in the aircraft ending up on its back. In my opinion, the brakes were not going to stop the aircraft before the end of the runway, and so I opted to let her roll. As a result, I left the end of the runway, crashed through the fence at a relatively high speed, actually jumped the slope and touched down, on all three wheels, about 50m (164ft) into the field where the aircraft came to a halt.

After I had cranked back the canopy and climbed out of the cockpit, I found myself once again alone in a field beside my aircraft, enjoying the peace and quiet surrounding me. After a few minutes, the ground crew appeared on top of the embankment with obvious expressions of relief, having seen me disappear after going through the fence. I was pleased that the new engines remained unscathed, and the aircraft itself had suffered only minor damage. At first, the ground crew did not believe the flaps had not worked properly and so I left them to investigate further, confident that I would be vindicated. After a good night's sleep in the 'Grossherzogin Elisabeth' Hotel in Kärntner Strasse, which Heinkel had rented, I went straight to the hangar where the aircraft was being repaired. Shamefaced, the mechanics admitted that the hydraulic check valve had been installed the wrong way round. A ground check had proved that the flaps extended when on the ground, but not under aerodynamic pressure during flight. With the check valve installed the wrong way round, the flaps would have never come out while airborne!

After two days I was flying the Heinkel He 280 V2 again, and during the flight tests which followed, the flaps could not be faulted. With the new and more powerful engines, I wanted to test the top speed of the aircraft at an altitude of 3,000m (9,843ft), and decided on a route Pressburg – Wien. I was accelerating nicely, when the aircraft suddenly started an oscillating yaw. Increasing the speed only increased the violence of the motion. Looking rearward, I noticed that the two vertical fins were moving alternately up and down, causing the rear fuselage to produce torsion oscillations in the longitudinal axis. I decided not to increase speed any further under these circumstances, and aborted the flight test. My colleague, *Dipl. Ing.* Julius Schuck, who had moved from Rostock to Wien for the trials of the He 219 night fighter, later performed a flight on the He 280 V2, and made the same diagnosis. Ground evaluation showed that I had reached a True Air Speed (TAS) of about 800km/h (497mph). The aircraft was nowhere near safe in this state, and it was clear that the whole of the tail section required redesign and reconstruction. This would inevitably take more time and testing and, in the meantime, the Me 262 successfully continued its test series. Before long it was clear that Messerschmitt had won the race, and the development of the He 280 was accordingly cancelled in favour of the Me 262.

CHAPTER ELEVEN

Jochen Eisermann
To Bale Out Was Suicide

The following chapter was put together following several conversations with Kapitän Jochen Eisermann; hence it is written in the form of an interview. When I, as part of a selected group of German military personnel, took my course at the renowned Test Pilot School at Brétigny, Jochen was my instructor. Talking about flight trials and tests was our daily business and I am, therefore, very pleased that, through this article, I am able to keep these memories alive: in particular, the fact that Germany, up to 1945, not only took the fastest aeroplanes in the world into the air, but also developed the means to save pilots' lives by enabling them to eject safely from aircraft flying near the speed of sound.

*Jochen Eisermann at Brétigny (June 1956)
being briefed on an aircraft by his instructor.*

126

Wolfgang Späte (W.S.): On the Eastern Front alone, I twice had to abandon burning Fw 190s by parachute in order to save myself. On each bale-out I had injured myself by striking a part of the tail section; once the right thigh, then the left. When I reached the ground, I had to really bend my knees to absorb the force of the landing, and it was painful on each occasion. What was I doing wrong?

Jochen Eisermann (J.E.): When jumping by parachute, it was always important to clear the aeroplane in the correct way. With a slow flying aircraft, say at a speed of approximately 200 to 300km/h (124 to 186mph), it was possible to simply step over the side, rather like jumping from a vehicle on the ground; by stepping over the side you only had to fall between the wing and the tail. However, in a fighter or, later, a jet or rocket aircraft, it was not that easy. Either you were unable to get out of your seat, due to the aerodynamic or centrifugal forces, or you were sucked out violently by the slipstream. Once in the slipstream, you effectively began to decelerate rapidly, whilst the aircraft maintained its relative speed. For example, within 5 seconds you would slow down from 600km/h (372mph) to 200km/h (124mph). Thus, by the time you had reached the tail section of the aircraft you had just abandoned, there was a considerable speed differential. If you were then unlucky enough to hit the elevator or rudder with any part of your body, you could receive a severe blow.

W.S.: This is obviously what happened to me. The *Luftwaffe* had lost many pilots who had left their aircraft apparently cleanly, but whose parachutes did not deploy, the most probable cause being that they were rendered unconscious by striking their head on some part of the tail section. One of the best known cases involved one of our fighter aces, Joachim Marseille. He had to abandon his aircraft due to an engine fire, and rolled it inverted to allow a free fall out. But, in so doing, he must have hit his head, because he fell from a relatively great height without opening his 'chute. I observed a similar incident in Russia: one of my comrades had to abandon his burning Me 109 and announced his intention over the RT. We saw him jettison the canopy and pull the aircraft steeply upward to absorb the speed in a climb, and then saw him come out of his seat and slide along the fuselage towards the tail, passing over the elevator. He fell from an altitude of about 1,500m (4,922ft) without opening his parachute, and finally impacted the snow covered ground far below us.

There was much discussion on this subject among the pilots, as to what could be done to improve safety when baling-out and increase the chances of reaching the ground in one piece.

J.E.: As I have already pointed out, there were several methods which would assist the pilot in clearing the aircraft after baling out. When, for example, you wanted to leave your aircraft without the aid of an ejector seat, you were unable to do so while you were in a spin, a turn, or when recovering from a dive. During these and similar manoeuvres, your actions were heavily influenced by additional centrifugal forces, and your movements were severely hindered. I think you (W.S.) baled out of your Fw 190 at approximately 500km/h (311mph) on both occasions. This is a matter of great interest to me: how did you manage to get out of the aeroplane? I remember the Fighter General recommending us to push the stick all the way forward with our foot, which would result in negative 'g', the effect of which was to lift you up and clear of the aircraft.

W.S.: This was exactly the trick I was trying to use, and I still remember today, several decades later, that I had been pushed to the back of the seat and was unable to get out. When the nose of the aircraft was pointing vertically towards the ground, I took my foot off the stick and was lifted up and out of the 'plane as light as a feather. I did not feel the blow to my thigh, or its effects during the time I was in the air, but each landing brought with it excruciating pain, something I remember to this day.

J.E.: This description outlines a fairly dangerous trial with which I was tasked during 1943/45 at Rechlin. I was to test an ejector seat which had been developed by Heinkel engineers, using a dummy weighing 75kg. Eventually, Wilhelm Buss (see next chapter), our pilot in charge of parachute trials, performed three bale-outs for official approval and acceptance.

W.S.: Professor Ernst Heinkel was one of our foremost aircraft design and construction engineers, and was always a step ahead of the competition. After all, it was he who introduced the first rocket aircraft to the world, the He 176. In 1939, his He 178 was the first aircraft flying with a turbo-jet engine and the He 280 followed with two jet engines and flew several months before

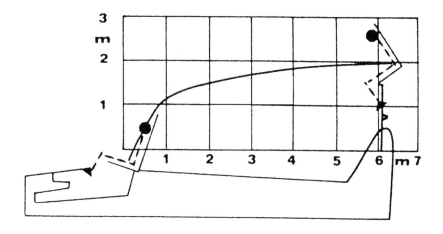

Erforderliche Bahnkurve eines Schleudersitzes.
Geschwindigkeit = 9oo km/h

Required trajectory of an ejector seat.

the Messerschmitt Me 262 even got airborne. Was it Heinkel, or one of his staff, who also invented the ejector seat?

J.E.: The ejector seat was invented by four academically trained engineers working with the Junkers company: Karl Arnold, Oscar Nissen, Reinhold Preuschen and Otto Schwarz. They were awarded the German *Reichspatent Nr.* 711045. Later, *Dr.-Ing.* Erich Dietz took out a supplementary patent for the addition of extra power cartridges to the seat. Junkers had not developed aircraft which flew in the higher speed ranges and so probably kept this invention under lock and key.

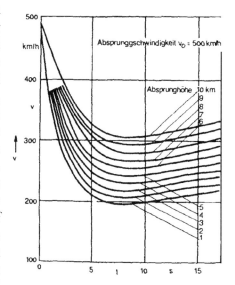

Speed of a man after having left the aircraft flying at a speed of 500km/h (310.7mph).

129

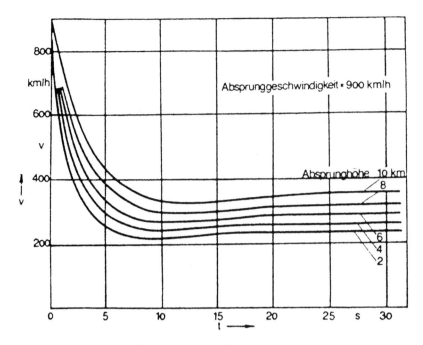

With an aircraft flying at 900km/h (559.2mph).

W.S.: However, Heinkel was the first to realise the necessity of equipping the flight crew with special equipment to aid abandonment of the aircraft in an emergency, especially at speeds of up to 900km/h (600mph). Heinkel predicted a top speed in excess of Mach 0.8 by the He 280.

J.E.: I imagine the process would have been something like this: the initial concept was born and the invention made patent. Heinkel then needed the patent, which he acquired. He was then responsible for the developing, testing and finally the production of ejector seats. I imagine Heinkel had to 'cough up' a very substantial licence fee.

W.S.: Which Heinkel aircraft was the first to be equipped with such a seat?

J.E.: Initially it was the He 176, the so-called '*Verrückte Raketenflugzeug*' (crazy rocket aircraft) in which Erich Warsitz had undertaken several daredevil take-offs. They had mathematically calculated that this '*Kiste*' (old crate) would be able to reach a speed of 850km/h (528.2mph). A successful conventional bale-out seemed very unlikely, even to the greatest of optimists within the Heinkel workforce. In addition, one had to accept that explosions in the type of engine being used were quite likely, necessitating immediate abandonment of the aircraft. This is why there were plans to make a part of the fuselage, measuring 1,500 mm (59.05 inches), easily separable from the aircraft. This forward section, containing the cockpit and occupant, would be released by pulling a lever.

W.S.: Was Warsitz, as a test pilot, ever forced to use this method?

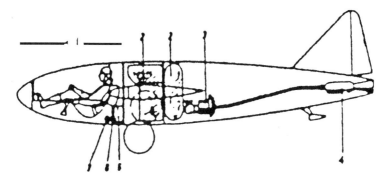

Cross-section of a Heinkel He 176.

J.E.: No, thank God! The He 176 was built in peacetime, so funding and time were available to put it to the test. Several wooden mock-up cockpits were built and released from a He 111. However, during the initial trials, the 'chute opened too quickly and became entangled with the cockpit. Because of this, the engineers invented an inflatable pillow which expelled the parachute by use of compressed air. A timer was installed in order to delay this action for five seconds, which was ample time for the section containing the pilot to clear the aircraft. Finally, a life-size wooden dummy was strapped into the seat and a full practical test conducted. Afterwards they discovered the dummy had suffered only a broken ankle upon landing... As I say, Warsitz fortunately never had to make use of this device, but its mere presence was a comfort to him, and possibly even more so for Heinkel and his staff.

W.S.: How was the ejector seat finally developed? The rescue equipment you describe on the He 176 was still very different in both concept and operation.

J.E.: Heinkel had completed the He 178, a single seat jet aircraft, before the outbreak of World War II. This aeroplane had a *'TL-Triebwerk'* *(Turbo-Lader- Triebwerk* – turbo-charged-drive – turbojet engine), which had been developed by the ingenious *Dipl. Ing.* Hans von Ohain, in conjunction with Heinkel. It was an engine with a radial compressor, and its performance was a touch inferior to the axial-flow turbines which were later developed by Junkers and BMW. However, with the jet engines von Ohain had developed, Ernst Heinkel was more than just a hair's breadth ahead of the competition. The test flights of the He 178 proved that the maximum speeds attainable by propeller driven aircraft could be exceeded by a substantial margin by jets. Indicated Air Speeds (IAS) were reached at which members of the crew could not 'step over the side' without risking terrible damage to life and limb. It seemed impossible to clear an aircraft travelling at, or in excess of, a speed of 800km/h (497.1mph). The He 178 was not ready for production, nor was it suitable for use by the *Luftwaffe*, but the subsequent development of an aircraft equipped with two jet engines, the Heinkel He 280, was to be built for service use. And, because of its predicted high speed capability, an ejector seat was planned for the He 280, right from the outset. At the same time, the He 219 night fighter was being developed: this aircraft had an unusually long fuselage, and, again, it was equipped with ejector seats, right from day one.

Heinkel He 219 in flight.

W.S.: It is stated in a report by the *DFVLR (Deutsche Forschungs- und Versuchsanstalt für Luftfahrt und Raumfahrt –* German Institute for Research of Aviation and Space Technology) that those tasked with research into the physiology of flight had begun extensive tests from 1938 onward. For instance, volunteers had been exposed to airspeeds of up to 485km/h (301.37mph) in a diving Ju 87 and, later, these tests had been continued in a wind-tunnel with ram air speeds of up to 720km/h (447.39mph). This level of aerodynamic pressure was considered to be the limit of tolerance, and then only when the subject kept his mouth and eyes tightly closed. The volunteers used during these trials were medical students, and pictures of the tests revealed horrible distortions of the face. Had Heinkel, at that time, also built test equipment to simulate a parachute jump at high speed?

J.E.: This is correct. The main problem associated with getting out was still how to ensure that the pilot avoided collision with the tail. The engineers had calculated that he needed to be ejected from the cockpit with very high initial acceleration in order to avoid the inevitable collision. At first the doctors shook their heads, because they felt there must be a maximum shock-loading to which the spine could be subjected. Therefore, Heinkel built a catapult track, operated by compressed air, for the scientific examination of the effects of vertical acceleration at different speeds. Before the catapult track was officially accepted and scientific trials begun, four of the staff tried out the machine in their spare time after work. Two engineers, a foreman and a fitter, shot themselves up the track

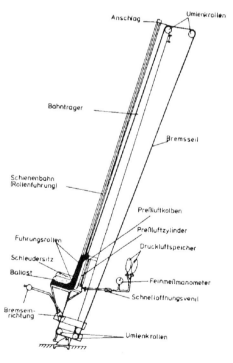

The Heinkel ejector seat test rig.

133

several times with increasing pressure. The next day, three of the four complained of back ache, and X-ray examination showed they had suffered small fractures to their vertebrae. Dr. Ruff and the *DVL (Deutsche Versuchsanstalt für Luftfahrt* – German Institute of Aviation Research and Development) later stated that the men had exposed themselves to a maximum of 26 g, and had reached the 'objectively bearable limit'. Given that they were just conducting ad hoc experiments of their own, they probably did not even take care to adopt the proper seating posture necessary to reduce injury in such tests.

W.S.: Well now, who was the first person to bale out of an aircraft with an ejector seat?

J.E.: On 13th January 1943, test pilot Schenk saved himself by ejecting from a He 280 on a ferry flight. Approximately six months later, on 20th July 1943, during a test flight over Rechlin, *Kapitän* Pancherz was involuntarily ejected from a Ju 290 by ejector seat, and landed safely by parachute. Shortly after this incident, the *Luftwaffe* Trial and Test Centre at Rechlin was tasked by the *Reichsluftfahrt Ministerium* (Ministry of Aviation) to methodically test the ejection sequence. The flying part of these trials landed in my lap, and Wilhelm Buss was to become the third man to use the seat, making a series of three safe ejections from our airborne test rig (See Chapter Twelve – Wilhelm Buss).

W.S.: What else was there to be tested after the ejector seat had worked properly during the first two ejections?

J.E.: The seat had worked 'properly' in as much as the trial pilot got out of the aircraft unscathed. However, the ejection sequence as a whole required substantial improvement. For instance, after ejection it was necessary for the pilot to pull a trigger to free himself from the metal ejector seat, and then pull his rip cord to open the parachute. One had to assume that the pilot who had just ejected from his aircraft would either remain dazed for a while by the acceleration, or even be injured, and therefore unable to make conscious decisions and deliberate movements. In a wind tunnel experiment, conducted by the DVL, one of the test subjects lost consciousness when he was suddenly exposed to an airstream at a speed of 720km/h (447.39mph). Pancherz reported that his ejector seat began to rotate violently when he ejected, making a reasoned assessment of his orientation impossible. In order to both slow and stabilise the flight characteristics of the seat, an additional parachute was installed. This was an automatic device which, five seconds after ejection, separated the seat from the pilot, at which point he was able to initiate his own 'chute at a safe distance from the aircraft. Later, triggers were to be replaced by fully automatic devices, but on top of all that, proof was required that the ejector seat would not only clear the aircraft at 200km/h (124.28mph) but also at a speed of 400 to 500km/h (248.28 to 310.7mph).

W.S.: The theories developed in the drawing offices had to be modified in the face of the practical evidence of the flight tests. How long did all this take?

J.E.: When I look at my logbook, I see that we performed fifty-eight trial flights between October 1943 and the summer of 1944, using two specially equipped He 219s. Final approval was given following three successful acceptance flights in May and June of 1944; thereafter, we declared the concept ready for production. Although I had never ejected, but only flown the trial aircraft, these flights arguably bore more risks for me than the subject who, after all, ejected at the last moment.

Following ground tests of the ejector seat at the Heinkel plant at Rostock-Marienehe, a He 219 was equipped with the seat as a flying test-bed. This aircraft was selected because its fuselage was very long, and this was one of the conditions which called for an

Jochen Eisermann climbing into the pilot's seat of a Heinkel 219 with the night fighter radar antennae and rear cockpit removed.

ejector seat. For the trials the rear gunner / observer's position, immediately behind the cockpit area, was modified to house the ejector seat and, for the purposes of this test, the rails on which the seat ran tilted forward into the direction of flight. The official requirements called for the seat to safely clear the tailplane at 500km/h (310.7mph). A He 219 (coded **DH+PV**), number six in the first ten prototype craft, was modified for the tests, with the otherwise enclosed cockpit stripped out except for a front windscreen. The *'Geweih'* (antlers), the front array of antennae for the night fighter interceptor, were removed and the automatic engine cooling gills changed for a manually operated system to reduce drag. All this was necessary to enable a brief acceleration to 500km/h (310.7mph). Cameras were mounted on each of the wings, and a large rear view mirror was installed to help me observe the firing of the seat. The pilot's seat, and that of the radio operator, were replaced with the ejecting type, as well as the test position at the rear.

Naturally, we did not put a man in the tail gunner's seat right away. We did, however, use a dummy made of cloth and the size of a man weighing 75kg (165lbs). I had to fly the aircraft and increase the speed up to the point at which the seat was to be ejected. I also had to operate the dummy's ejection seat from the cockpit. During these flights, all of the ejections, the technical mishaps and the accidents were filmed by a camera 'plane, a Do 217, flying alongside. In addition, there was a meteorology station on the ground, over which I was required to fly at a height of 1,250m (4,101ft) because cameras had been installed there as well. The final checks were made approaching this station, because it was located adjacent to the dropping area in Mirow, near Lärz, made available to us during these trials. Sometimes, in order to avoid air raids, I flew the trials at Udetfeld in Upper Silesia, one of our now widely dispersed facilities.

The dummy had to be ejected so that it reached the ground within sight of the met. station, and in this way was quickly retrieved and prepared for the next trial. Increasing the speed inevitably led to problems: during one attempt, the ejector seat, including the dummy, got stuck at the top of the rails. Since the rails for this seat had been installed tilted forward, it overhung my position and would have obstructed my exit had there been an emergency. On the seventh trial, the ejector seat did not clear the tail and damaged the right rudder, and I was only just able to land the aircraft. This also led to the reinforcement of the guide rails, because they had broken off at the top. We continued the trials but, only five flights later, and following a further increase in speed, we encountered the next problem. It was 14th January 1944, and the guide rails had been further reinforced, but I had my doubts as to whether they were at the root of the trouble. For safety, we decided to move to Udetfeld because it was a little more isolated, and there we met this new challenge. When I think back to it now, it still gives me the jitters, but at least this experience helped us find the cause of the malfunction.

We had reached a speed of 500km/h (310.7mph) during our trials. The previous tests, in which the seat had stuck on the rails, caused me to be very careful. I had been lucky to get the aircraft down in one piece during these incidents, and the strain inevitably began to show. I cannot say that I was in a funk before the next test, but I was certainly somewhat rattled: however, the requirements of the 'front line' demanded the speediest solution, and there was no place for 'ifs' or 'buts'! For some reason I decided to overfly the met. station at 1,500m (4,921ft) instead of the usual 1,250m (4,265ft), although I knew that the observers on the ground would probably not be best pleased with me because it would reduce the clarity of their observations and film record. Nevertheless, I started my run, and in order to reach 500km/h (310.7mph), I had to push the nose down a fair amount. The dropping zone came into view, and I triggered the rear ejector seat as we passed over the release point. Once more the seat stuck on the rails, protruding well out of the top of the fuselage, right behind my neck. Worse still, a few seconds later the automatic release mechanism deployed the dummy's parachute! In my rear view mirror I could clearly see a large white canopy hanging over the tail of the aircraft.

It was unfortunate that, in this case, the makers of the parachute had delivered exceptionally good German workmanship. The canopy did not tear and rapidly slowed the He 219 down to 200km/h (124.27mph) or less. We were on the edge of the stall, and so I had no alternative other than to push the nose down to try and gain some flying speed. To try to bale out in this situation would have been suicidal because the test seat was right above mine. I would inevitably be trapped and crash with the 'plane. Strangely enough, in situations like this calmness can descend and allow logical thought: I remembered that a parachute canopy will collapse when struck by an airflow hitting it from an angle. I throttled back the left engine and gave the right full power, at the same time applying full left rudder, yawing hard to the right. I looked in the rear view mirror and saw the billowing white silk wall disappear and hang like a big white sausage along the side of the fuselage. The aircraft accelerated and regained flying speed. I was able to recover, and finally landed with the 'chute all rolled up. Later, on the ground, I was able to look at the film taken by the camera 'plane and observe how my He 219 slowly went from a steep descent to within about 100m (328ft), of the ground, where I managed to make the transition to horizontal flight. The additional 250m (820ft) on the approach to the drop zone had saved my life.

This time we brought back the faulty seat still in the aircraft, and were able to look for the cause of failure in our own time. It was easily found, and my suspicion that the fault was not in the rails proved correct. Two days later, we flew to Wien-Schwechat to meet the Heinkel experts, *Dipl. Ing.* Schwärzler and *Dipl. Ing.* Franke, and they confirmed that it was the round piston in the propulsion unit which was jamming when it was subjected to lateral forces at the top of the barrel. A slightly oval piston was introduced into the launching mechanism and, after returning to our test site, I flew twenty-four trials without incident. All went so smoothly that, on 19th May 1944, our trial parachutist, Wilhelm Buss, was ejected from the aircraft for the first time. There were no further problems, and on 12th and 13th June 1944 Buss fulfilled the remaining requirements for acceptance with his last two test ejections: the seat was ready for production.

On his three trial ejections, I did not drop Buss over the land-based dropping zone, but over Lake Müritz, whence he was recovered by launch. Previously, whilst making other risky test jumps, he had broken twenty bones in his body. These injuries occurred mainly during the development of quick-release buckles for the parachute risers. These were required to allow a parachutist to release one or both of the main risers when landing in high winds, so as to avoid being dragged along the ground. Unfortunately, it took some time to get the quick releases working properly and, as a consequence, Buss had been dragged across the rugged terrain of the dropping area several times and badly injured. This was probably the reason why he made a rubber suit for himself, and subsequently preferred soft landings in water to hard touchdowns on land.

CHAPTER TWELVE

Wilhelm Buss

My First Bale-out with an Ejector Seat

The following report was written immediately after the end of World War II, and is an interesting addition to the previous interview with Jochen Eisermann

Aircraft:	He 219 (Night Fighter)
Speed:	250km/h ((155.35mph)
Ejection altitude:	1,000 metres (3,281ft)
Ejection pressure:	73 at (1,038psi)
Parachute:	Seat type

There was much excitement before my first launch in the ejector seat. The aircraft mechanic was in more of a hurry than I, and unintentionally catapulted himself out of the aircraft before it had left the hangar. Luckily for him, the air pressure had dropped and did not project him all the way to the roof of the hangar. Fortunately, he fell onto the wing of another aeroplane and not onto the concrete floor.

On the day the trial was to take place, the air bottle for the ejector seat was filled just prior to take-off, in order to prevent failure of the ejection due to lack of pressure. I climbed into the He 219 very carefully, because the aircraft was fitted with equipment for several different trials, and still carried all the gear for night fighter operations. There was very limited space, and only fractions of inches between the equipment and my body. I strapped myself tightly to the seat, and someone checked it over and wished me good luck, and a happy landing. The aircraft started to taxi, and I went over the sequence of events prior to take-off. I had taken several additional precautions in case anything should go wrong. There were time delay triggers on the seat belt and the 'chute pack, which would activate automatically if I were to be rendered unconscious after striking the aircraft. The timer on the seat strap was set to ten seconds, and the one on the 'chute to fifteen. My brief was to

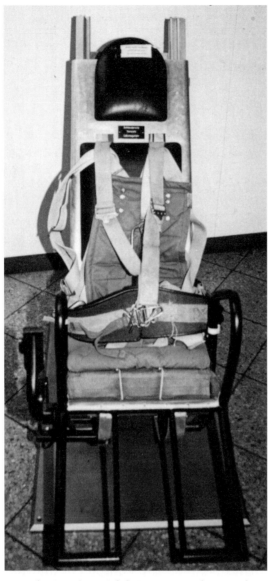

Reproduction of a Heinkel ejector seat in the Deutsches Museum.

release the seat belt and the parachute in only half the time set, to demonstrate to the ground crew that I was uninjured. We performed a test run on the approach path, to check if all the staff had taken their positions. The smoke signal from a boat confirmed all was well. On the second approach I fired a flare, and left the aircraft three seconds later. During the launch I sat in the seat facing rearward, my feet on foot rests, my hands holding onto grips on the side of the seat. On ejection, my wrists gave in and I hit my arm on an edge of the 'plane. The blow was not painful, however, and I was only aware of brushing along something with my right side. The ejector mechanism was set off with a loud bang, water and oil vapour swirled around, and there was a juddering thump in the seat which felt almost pleasant when compared to the previous ground trials. In an instant, I was outside the aircraft and somersaulting: entering the airstream felt surprisingly smooth; the same feeling as during free fall when the body gains speed and is supported by the resistance of the air. After leaving the aircraft, I saw the fuselage of the He 219 passing below. The somersaults were not unpleasant, although I was unable to determine the number of turns. When viewed later, the film showed four somersaults up to a point just behind the tail section.

With great satisfaction, I noted how tightly the seat had held my body: however, my feet had slipped off the foot-rests because I had unconsciously lifted them slightly. I had just put them back on the rests, when the drogue 'chute had opened. This could also be observed on the film taken by the camera aircraft. The shape of the foot rests, as well as my shoes (which had no heels) had partly caused my feet to slide off the rests. Immediately after the deployment of the drogue 'chute, I heard the sound of metal banging against the backrest of the seat. My trajectory was then smoothly stabilised, the noise having come from the activation of the spring which pushed the drogue 'chute out of the slipstream of the seat, as well as from the steel securing rings which held the drogue. I remained in the seat, descending for a few seconds, and was able to see very well, thoroughly enjoying the sudden silence around me. In the aircraft, I sat in line with the propellers of the two engines, with no canopy to deaden the noise which actually caused pain in my ears. I took a brief look at the drogue 'chute to confirm that it was properly deployed and that all was on track.

Measurements and calculations made later showed the seat descending on the 'chute at a rate of thirty-nine metres per second (127.95ft/sec). It was time to release the safety harness, and I separated from the seat immediately, letting myself free-fall for a further four seconds, then pulling the ripcord. Deployment was smooth and, having checked my canopy, I looked for the seat, and found it floating majestically below me. I continued watching until it splashed down, immediately turning the surrounding water bright green – small bags of dye were attached to the seat for easier location and recovery. Shortly before entering the water, I turned the release on the harness lock, then pressed it firmly just before I reached the surface. The parachute, still inflated by the wind, pulled the harness from my body and landed a few metres away. Since I had landed near a group of rocks, I tried to swim ashore, but after the first few strokes I felt a pain in my right wrist, saw I was bleeding and decided to wait for rescue by boat. Following the evaluations of this trial, the securing straps on the seat were moved forward so that the arms would not flay about during ejection.

My third ejection

The third ejection was an involuntary one. The camera aircraft accompanied us on the right hand side. As usual, I wanted to give the 'ready' signal by firing a flare, after which the ejection would take place. The cloud ceiling was at approximately 1,000m (3,281ft) and only partially broken; visibility was therefore impaired. I had bent forward to look over the side to check our position and was holding the flare gun up in my right hand with the safety catch off, but with my finger clear of the trigger. Unexpectedly, the pilot triggered the ejector seat and I found myself outside the aircraft. I had received a good 'kick' in the bottom, followed by the usual tumbling and turning of the seat. At the moment the seat was fired I had been looking out over my right arm and down the side of the aircraft. Therefore, as I was launched upward, my head involuntarily hit my right arm, causing it, together with the flare gun, to hit my right thigh. When I regained my composure, the drogue 'chute had automatically operated and I was still holding the flare gun. Since it was in my way, I finally let it go...

Remaining with the seat and floating down on the inflated drogue 'chute for a while, I eventually released the safety belts manually and the seat immediately slid away. Then I pulled the main parachute and landed within the airfield boundary. The film showed my arms extended during the ejection, and we were able to observe that the seat did not turn or tumble on any fixed axis. Due to the extension of my arms, and the consequent shifting body weight, the seat whirled and turned through the air in all directions. On this test it proved effective to have the catch for the shoulder straps on the back of the seat, at shoulder level, thus preventing the body from leaning or being thrown forward upon ejection.

CHAPTER THIRTEEN

Karl Schieferstein

From 'My Life as a Pilot'
– Glider Trials During the War

The DFS (Deutsche Forschungsanstalt für Segelflug – German Institute for Gliding Research) in Darmstadt employed more than a dozen pilots in 1935. They were assigned to each of the five Departments of the Institute: Heini Dittmar was test pilot for Alexander Lippisch, mainly involved with the testing of tail-less powered aircraft up to the DFS 194 and the Me 163; Hanna Reitsch was the glider pilot for Hans Jacobs' Aeronautical Department; and I was earmarked for the exclusive use of the Meteorological Department. The other pilots, Hermann Zitter, Schieferstein, Rudolf Opitz, Kurt Oppitz, von Jan, Klöckner, Stämmler, Reese, Scheuermann, Egner, Sahner, Münchhoff, Lettmayer, Schubert and others, were assigned to the Flight Trials Department, headed by Fritz Stamer. Maintenance and allocation of powered aircraft for trials and training, as well as of gliders, was the responsibility of that Department. Personnel and material were also available for other flight operations, on request.

It is a well known fact that the military had shown an early interest in glider flying. The crews for the DFS 230, the cargo glider developed by Hans Jacobs, were trained by instructors from the DFS at the Griesheimer Sand glider field. Those were the pilots who later landed near the bridges of the river Maas, on Fort Eben Emael (Belgium) and who accomplished heroic deeds on the Korinth Isthmus. Hermann Zitter led the training, performed in two-seat aircraft – which were tow-launched – requiring many instructors and tow pilots. Fritz Stamer was in charge of the pilots, who were also deployed for trial tasks. The Department for Flight Equipment, headed by Prof. Dr. Fischel, together with the Department of Aeronautics, under the leadership of Prof. Dr. Ruden, were both trying to find solutions for diverse problems.

In 1939, more than five hundred scientists, specialists and employees poured daily through the gates of the Institute. The German Reich not only attached importance to the research and development of gliding, but also contributed a large budget for this task. At the outbreak of war this changed immediately, and the money stopped coming in. Duties also changed drastically, and some of the pilots, namely Barabas, Carthaus, Egner, Rudolf Opitz and Heinz Schubert, became military

The Department for Flight Trials pilots grouped around a Röhn Sperber in 1937.
From the left: Zitter, three unknown, Von Jan, Münchhoff, Carthaus, Egner, Klöckner,
Rudolf Opitz, Stamer, Schieferstein and Stämmler.

pilots. *I was also conscripted into the Luftwaffe and, as a reserve officer
in the rank of Leutnant, flew reconnaissance missions over Poland and
France. Initially, there was a rumour that the whole of the Institute was
to be closed because the facilities provided were apparently no longer
required. Then the Heads of the Institute changed their minds (or
thought the war would soon be over) and planned ahead for peacetime,
when there would surely be glider flying again. Late in 1939, the DFS
was moved to Braunschweig, then to Ainring near Salzburg. During
this time the Departments managed to keep most of their technical and
scientific staff, as well as half a dozen test pilots.*

*When it became clear that there was going to be no quick end to the
war, the DFS began to test and evaluate equipment which was only, at
best, on the fringe of gliding. Examples included the development of
airborne towing systems, all the way up to the rigid connection of two
aircraft; the remote radio control of drones and guided weapons; rocket
assisted take-off and landing; gliding trials of aircraft for which engines
were not yet ready, and much more.*

*After the end of the war, the DFS was never the same again. For
decades, a large group of former staff got together annually for
contemplative conversations and talks. But, from all these meetings, not
one historically reliable record remains of the years of the DFS and its
achievements. The only record was a contribution by Professor Georgii,
who died far too early, which is only a rough overview of that time.
Eventually, two former test pilots put together an extensive overview by
describing their flying experiences, and the flight trials during their time
with the DFS: they were Erich Klöckner and Karl Schieferstein.*

The trials performed during wartime at Darmstadt, Braunschweig

144

and Ainring were not only of the highest interest in respect of the technology involved, but also demonstrated the flying skills and courage of those involved. Karl Schieferstein gave up his studies at the Technical College in Darmstadt on 5 June, 1934 to further develop his abilities as a pilot in both gliders and powered aircraft. He eventually joined the DFS as a test pilot and flying instructor. Later, he took over flight operations in the Glider Research Department, and held this post until 1945. He developed a lecture about his experiences, which he described, albeit modestly, for the benefit of his successors.

Karl Schieferstein in 1936.

Among many other things, Professor Walter Georgii introduced the investigation of high altitude glider flying into our programme. For this purpose, a special team was sent to the glider field at Prien, close to the Chiemsee, on the northern edge of the Alps. A Heinkel He 46 towed the gliders into the lee of the Alps and, with this high wing monoplane, we were able to reach heights of 5,500 to 6,000 metres (18,045 to 19,685ft). While I was climbing rapidly to these unusually high

145

The Wolken Kranich equipped for high altitude gliding.

altitudes in my glider, I would hear a spooky little voice repeating again and again, 'I want to go down, I want to go down.' (I can still hear it today.) I was flying a glider which was fitted with reinforced wings, and which had an oxygen system. However, I lacked not only the necessary clothing to protect myself against the cold, but also the appropriate experience, and eventually realised I was talking to myself! I quickly decided to turn north, fly out of the cold and down to levels where I could breathe unaided. This all happened well before World War II.

At the beginning of the war, in 1939, we moved to Ainring via Braunschweig. Ainring was a small airfield in Bavaria, not far from Salzburg. All our peacetime tasks, such as high performance gliding, training up-and-coming engineers, sports students, and complete units of airborne troops, were all cancelled. Fritz Stamer, Head of the Department for Flight Trails, found substitute tasks, such as the development of new towing methods. Our trial team consisted of six pilots, all well suited to work together: Zitter, Stämmler, von Jan, Oppitz, Klöckner and myself. There was also a Construction and Maintenance Department, situated in an aircraft hangar, which also housed Flight Operations, and was headed by *Ing*. Paul Kiefel. All these individual groups were staffed with able, qualified personnel.

Towing aircraft on a long line had been well proven, but was impossible to perform in poor weather, and under instrument flying conditions. This was why the tow line was shortened in increments, all the way to a length of 1.5 metres (5ft). Hermann Zitter and I flew these trials, using the He 72 and the *Minimoa* glider. We even managed to fly at night, as well as on cross country flights in cloud, using this short tow on the *DFS* 230, towed by a Ju 52. The idea of replacing the line with a rigid device occurred as a natural progression, not

A long tow being progressively shortened.

only for safety reasons, but also, for example, to prevent the rather frequent line breaks.

Stamer's Department, in co-operation with Dr. Trutz Fölsche – Head of the Department for Flight Equipment – developed a boom with a hydraulically dampened swivel arm. The aircraft had a robust universal joint which allowed it to swivel freely. This type of towing connection could be disconnected by the pilot either of the tug, or of the aircraft being towed. In a second version, the boom was fitted with a ball joint which allowed the swivel arm to be mobile in all directions. This design also had a damping system with which the degree of movement could be varied, and it was this model which was approved for production.

The rigid tow system was tried and tested with the *DFS* 230 in tow behind the Junkers 52, the Heinkel 111 and the Dornier 17. I vividly remember a very tough blind flying tow trial, myself flying the Do 17 and Zitter in the *DFS* 230. We were above the

Starrschlepp – Rigid tow. Ju 52 towing a DFS 230.

147

mountains in rather gusty weather with icing conditions prevailing. The air was as turbulent as our morale, particularly when, over the radio, Zitter said that he was unable to see the tail section of the Do 17, which he had to use as an attitude reference; however, we managed to land safely. By towing the cargo glider, a Go 242 loaded with thirty men, behind a He 177, we proved that the rigid tow system could also be used on larger gliders. To assist that take-off, both a Junkers 88 and a Heinkel 111, using long lines, were employed to get the tow underway.

Dr. Fölsche took part in the initial trials of the rigid tow system, which were flown by Kurt Oppitz, Hermann Zitter and myself. One day, at short notice, proof was required that it was possible to tow a second *DFS 230*, rigidly connected behind the first glider, also being towed. Oppitz was to tow this *3er-Zug* (aerial three plane train), using a Ju 52, with me in the middle

The Starrschlepp system with friction ball coupling.

and Fölsche as number three behind. During the very first test, vertical oscillations quickly set in, in fact immediately after lift-off, and Fölsche released the tow just in time. On the second take-off he tried to stay with us a bit longer, but his aircraft broke away violently, and was destroyed in the ensuing crash. It impacted the ground with such force during the oscillations that the tow-beam on the Ju 52 was bent and the damper torn out. The connection was now jammed, preventing my *DFS 230* releasing from the Ju 52. Together we swung up and down before deciding to land, still connected. During the turn to base the formation broke up, and both Oppitz and I landed at our airfield at Braunschweig – Waggum, looking somewhat the worse for wear but in one piece. Dr. Fölsche was quite badly injured, but soon recovered in the hospital, where we visited him from time to time. After that, the trial was taken off the programme because it clear that it was not feasible.

Towing several gliders, for instance, two side by side behind one tug, was quite common. In order to tow high gross weights, we were forced to reverse this procedure, and hitch several tow aircraft to the heavy cargo glider. During the pre-trials, we towed a *DFS 230* using five He 72 *Kadetten* (Cadets), and I was to fly on the extreme left hand side. I missed Stamer's signal for brake release, and so there I was, hammering away at full throttle to catch up with the others, eventually ending up dragging all the weight behind me. Quite deservedly, I ended up landing alone in the potato field, but at least we had demonstrated that towing with the use of five He 72's was feasible.

Towing trials using an unpowered Ju 52 followed. The Ju 52 which was to be towed had its middle propeller replaced by a release coupling. The engines on the wings remained shut down, and the tow was made up by three other Ju 52's. After this test had been satisfactorily completed, three Me 110s successfully towed a Me 321 *Gigant* (Giant), a heavy cargo glider. The *Gigant* had a wingspan of 55m (180.5ft) and a payload of 23,000kg (50,600lbs), adding up to a total inflight weight of 35,000kg (77,000lbs). Hermann Zitter was flying the centre Me 110, I

Troika-Schlepp (triple tow). Three JU 52s tow another with engines shut down and centre propeller removed.

149

flew on the right and Kurt Oppitz on the left hand side. Trying out this *Troika-Schlepp* (triple tow), Oppitz ended up in a bad position because he repeatedly drifted out to the left. The torque effect which caused this was counteracted by installing a release mechanism on the boom protruding from the right hand side of the tail on the He 111. After this modification, all worked well.

The task of getting an aircraft with a high wing loading airborne by towing it behind a slow transport was impossible. However, it appeared it might be achieved by trying the *Huckepack-Verfahren* (piggy back system). This idea led to the development of the *Mistel-Verfahren* (*Mistel-* system) at the *DFS*. Wooden rails for the wheels of a Klemm Kl 35 were mounted on top of the wings of a *DFS* 230, and a block for the tailwheel of the Kl 35 was attached to the rear section of the fuselage of the glider. A quick-release mounting held the Kl 35 nicely horizontal on top of the *DFS* 230, with the spring-loaded struts compressed. Oppitz flew the carrier aircraft, and I was put on top, possibly because I was a little smaller, and that is exactly where I remained for the rest of the trials. Paul Stämmler sometimes took Oppitz's place.

This combination was towed to altitude by a Ju 52 piloted by Zitter. The Kl 35, with its open cockpit, was a breezy but exciting place of work for me! At the very beginning of this trial, each pilot made his own control inputs without making his

Mistelschlepp DFS 230 glider with top mounted Kl. 35.

intentions known to the other aircraft. The burden of steering the couple lay with the pilot of the aircraft below, with my assistance from above when I could predict his intentions. This configuration was mainly designed to be separated in the air, and also to be able to land still coupled. The 105hp power plant of the Kl 35 proved insufficient to maintain horizontal flight, and was most definitely not powerful enough for take-off and climb. The airborne handling and performance of this launch pad was eagerly awaited by all and, when the time came to separate, it actually worked fairly well. The Kl 35 I was flying literally leapt up as the spring-loaded attachment struts launched me upward and away from the glider: I pushed the throttle forward and easily climbed away. As we progressed, the Kl 35 was replaced by the Fw 56 Stößer (Hawk) and, although this combination had a similar performance during the different evolutions of flight, the 240hp motor of the Stößer made even horizontal flight possible.

Naturally, from time to time, these trials were demonstrated to a selected audience. At the first of these impromptu airshows, we wanted to perform both a tow and a *Huckepack-Verfahren* (piggy-back) fly-past involving the *DFS* 230 / Kl 35 combination, which was to separate at the field boundary. The fly-past worked out perfectly, but when we attempted to release the Kl 35 nothing happened. An overshoot was impossible, and Stämmler exclaimed: *'Ach du lieber Gott!'* (Oh dear God!) Together, we tried to land smoothly, not knowing how my aircraft would behave because it had already been effectively disconnected. At the first contact with the ground, my Klemm jumped like a flea and I added full power, climbed away, and landed after performing an elegant turn, next to the *DFS* 230 which was rolling to a stop.

Professor Georgii came running over to congratulate us on this superb performance. The visiting committee, he said, was highly impressed. However it was only good fortune that our guardian angel had released the coupling just in time! Stamer, who had immediately noticed that things were not quite normal, came storming across the airfield. *'Karlchen* (little Karl), did you say anything?' he asked gruffly. 'Why,' I calmly replied, 'what's wrong?' Stamer just ground his teeth, but from the look on his face I could see that he wished I'd go to the Devil!

With the third version, we began to try a really high performance aircraft in this combination. The engineers

151

mounted a Me 109, with its undercarriage retracted, on a special carrier on top of a *DFS* 230, which had been fitted with modified and reinforced landing gear. This carrier only allowed release in the direction of flight, and the 109 was firmly strapped down, remaining under tension. Its tail was attached to a pylon, and the coupling of this support and tension system opened only at a certain angle of attack. The difference in wing loading of the two aircraft did seem rather high and, therefore, the whole concept was judged somewhat risky. For that reason Zitter opted to fly the *DFS* 230 from the second pilot's seat, leaving the forward seat, and something of a crumple zone, empty.

Mistelschlepp: Karl Schieferstein in the Me 109 and Hermann Zitter in the DFS 230.

This combination was able to take off without assistance, climb, separate in the air or land still attached. Putting Zitter in the rear seat as a precaution soon paid off because, upon release, the tail-wheel of the Me 109 went straight through the hood of the cabin, right in front of his nose. He did not like this at all, and neither did I; a more serious collision was only avoided by the quick deployment of the spoilers on the *DFS* 230, which caused rapid deceleration.

After completing the observations and finishing different tests on the airfield at Hörsching, near Linz, we wanted to go back to Ainring. It was Christmas Eve and, as a one-off, Zitter had taken our *Segelflug-Startmeister* (Senior Controller- Gliders), along as a passenger in his *DFS* 230. While flying cross country the left hand pylon, which held my Me 109 in place, either opened, or broke off. We were flying near Salzburg at the time and took the obvious option to release; however, the right hand coupling jammed, probably because the Me 109 was then flying tilted to the right by about fifteen degrees. In the absence of any other ideas, we continued our flight, although we had no idea if we would be able to land in this unusual and unstable configuration without crashing. I asked Zitter what his passenger thought of the situation, and he replied: 'Well, I haven't told him anything, and he can't see above and behind.' We performed a very smooth landing, which taxed our flying skills to the limit, and my Messerschmitt remained on top, still tilted at a jaunty angle. Again, someone must have been watching over us, and we wondered if it had anything to do with it being Christmas?

There were further *Huckepack-Verfahren* trials which nearly ended in disaster for me. I was to fly a special unmanned transport unit with a Focke Wulf Fw 190 mounted on top. The overall centre of gravity had become so high, that even taxi-ing created difficulties, and keeping the combination straight on take-off was nearly impossible. On the third take-off run it veered away atrociously, and the machine ended up on its head, standing on three points, but not the ones the designer had intended. I sat there, supported by the propeller hub of the Fw 190, and the nose and wing tip of the glider, its tail pointing straight up into the sky. The whole contraption swayed back and forth and, as I hung there in my seat harness, I hardly dared breathe. Later, after it was over, malicious tongues claimed that I had deliberately remained hanging on high, doing nothing more than rolling my eyes until the fire crew arrived and stabilised the situation.

In the course of time, new *Huckepack-Verfahren* were developed, either to aerodynamically test new jet aircraft, or in response to different military requirements. At the *DFS*, we tried and tested all kinds of various towing methods, systems and procedures. For example, the *Tragschlepp* (carrying tow) – here the aircraft to be towed hung below the tug aircraft. This method was, among other things, intended to help deliver aircraft as quickly as possible to their required area of operation, without using their engines. This method was applied during the trials of the 'Natter'. *(See next chapter for more details of the carry-tow and the 'Natter').*

The take-off for the *Tragschlepp* began as normal, with both aircraft connected by a line attached to their respective centres of gravity. The towing aircraft took off before the aircraft being towed, the latter being, at that low speed, unable to fly aerodynamically. The tug simply lifted its tow off the ground when the line reached an angle of 50°-70°, and carried it to an altitude where it was then brought to flying speed. At the beginning of the trial, a Ju 87 towed the *Habicht* (Goshawk), a glider used by the *DFS*: however, a tow using the He 111 and a Ju 87 without its propeller was much more impressive. A similar method was used to lift heavy aircraft off the ground with the aid of a glider. In this situation, the glider lifted off before the towing aircraft had gathered sufficient flying speed, and helped to lift the heavy aircraft off the runway. For these tests, a Do 17 and a *DFS 230* were used.

Trials for airborne link-up were undertaken to prepare the way for in-flight, or air-to-air, refuelling and, in order to extend the range of aircraft, external flying tanks were developed to be towed behind, flying independently – as opposed to being attached to the airframe – and linked with a supply hose.

The picking up of cargo, or parked aircraft at rest on the ground, had always been of great interest. A method was developed in which the energy during pickup was not dispersed by breaking the tow line, but by the predetermined destruction of different materials. During the first test, flying a Ju 87, I picked up a load of 100kg (220lbs). After that, I hitched up to a *Habicht* glider with Kiefel as its pilot. During this test, belt-type material, which had previously been sewn up and tightly packed into a cylinder, had to be pulled by the tow line, allowing the shock of pick-up to be absorbed whilst accelerating the tow. During a second trial, the line was layered into a *Schleppkasten* (tow case or tow box), and had to shear through a series of plywood slats as it was pulled out. The thickness and, therefore, the strength of each plywood slat could be calculated and altered to suit the load to be picked up. We were eventually able to hitch and pick up a *DFS 230* weighing 2,000kg (4,400lbs), flying a He 111 at a speed of 200km/h (124.3mph). The ground run was only 200m (656ft) with acceleration at an acceptable level. The pickup itself was performed with a hook, which was lowered during approach, engaging a loop on the coupling pack of the glider. *(The various types of tow and carry are described in much more detail by Karl Schieferstein's colleague, Erich Klöckner, in the following chapter. Ed.)*

I had towed many an unmanned flying machine for Dr.

Karl Schieferstein in the Ju 87, performing the Tragschlepp with Paul Kiefel in the Habicht below.

Lippisch, some of which were on lines up to 300m (984ft) long. When there was a requirement for the trials to be performed in northern Germany, I towed these aircraft cross country. An unscheduled intermediate landing, due to bad weather or for refuelling, was sometimes unavoidable, and I always had some fun when the police demanded to meet the pilot of the tow.

Performing the so-called *Wolga – Startverfahren* (Volga Launch), land vehicles such as caterpillar tractors, and both electric and steam powered vehicles, were used to tow-launch cargo gliders, as well as overloaded powered aircraft. The tow line was run through pulleys to increase the tow speed by as much as four times. The two towing vehicles (for example, two electric locomotives) drove off in opposite directions but in line with the tow. The tow line would pass around a pulley on the first loco, which would be moving in the direction of the tow, whilst the other pulled the line away in the opposite direction, doubling the speed, and considerably increasing the power of the tow. One steam loco (still in common use in those days) was also sufficient for a launch. With a 1,000m (3,281ft) line, and the *DFS* 230 with an all-up weight of 2,000kg (4,400lbs), I reached release altitudes of between 200 to 300m (656ft to 984ft) using these methods.

At the end of 1944 we tested the first launch of a *DFS* 230 from the waters of the Chiemsee. Both the tug and the glider were equipped with floats, and the tow line was kept afloat by attaching cork to it at regular intervals. One morning we decided our tests were over, because British aircrew had used our aircraft for target practice during the moonlit night!

With the steady advance of the front from the West in 1945, continuation of the trials was not only senseless but also, largely, impossible. The collapse in May finally brought an end to our research and our trials.

Troikaschlepp: Three Me 110's towing a Me 321 Gigant.

CHAPTER FOURTEEN
Erich Klöckner
Trial Reports from the DFS

From 1935 to 1945, Erich Klöckner was assigned as chief test pilot to a large number of trials carried out by the DFS (Deutschen Forschungsanstalt für Segelflug – German Institute for Gliding Research). In 1939, he distinguished himself by becoming the first glider pilot to reach 9,280 metres (30,447ft), thereby establishing an absolute altitude record, flying in the lee waves of the Central Alps. One year later, he even reached the edge of the stratosphere in a glider, climbing to an altitude of 11,460 metres (37,599ft). Few remember today that it was he who made the first test flights in the 'Natter', having first performed several tow trials. The reason can probably be found in the fact that, for years, the project was concealed with some embarrassment because it appeared to be of 'Kamikaze' status of which many were more ashamed than proud. Only the imminent disaster of losing World War II offered the opportunity to find means of turning this seemingly crazy venture into reality.

The 'Natter':
An Act of Desperation

Erich Klöckner.

Beginning in October 1944, trials for the 'Natter' were undertaken by the DFS (German Institute for Gliding Research). These trials, using a launching vehicle, were performed on the airfields at Ainring and Neuburg. The 'Natter', when completely developed, would by manned by a pilot, launched vertically from a gantry, and was to be powered by rockets.

The original concept was that it would take a powerful weapon system into the air to combat enemy aircraft. After completion of this task, the pilot would bale out and both he and the'Natter' would descend by parachutes.

Stamer, the head of the department for flight trials within the *DFS*, told me at a meeting, 'You will take over the trials for this equipment.' He went on to say, 'You have acquired the appropriate experience during the trials of the Me 328...' and continued by trying to explain the project to me. From the pensive expression on my face, he obviously noticed that I was not very keen to take over this task. He therefore tried to reassure me by remarking, 'You have sound knowledge in towing, you have experience with the 'Argusrohr' (pulse-jet type engine by Argus-Schmidt) and the ram-jet engine by Sänger. You are the man best prepared for the job.'

What was this *'Natter'*, and what was it to do? When, in 1943/1944, it became clear that the existing German air defence system, using *Flak* and fighters, was not able to prevent enemy air forces flattening one German city after the other, the hectic search for new methods was on. Even the Me 163 rocket fighter did not fulfil the high hopes placed upon it. Despite low production cost and excellent in-flight performance, it had two major disadvantages: the rocket engine had only four minutes running time at full thrust, and the landing was a most hazardous operation. In addition, the fact that the weapons fired along the longitudinal axis of the aircraft, combined with the high intercept speed, did not give even the most experienced pilots a fair chance of making a 'kill'. Only when the Me 163 was flown at reduced speed was the pilot able to achieve a hit, but he himself was then exposed to the massively superior enemy defence fire. The Walter engine was produced in series and required relatively little material or time to make, but the fuselage, though partially made of wood, was still too expensive. This is how the idea was born to build an aircraft which:

1. – was able to take-off vertically (dispensing with runways) and engage in combat with the enemy visually;

2. – was inexpensive and, even after a single flight, would have fulfilled its purpose as a 'throw away' aircraft;

3. – would be able to break through the enemy

defences by penetrating from below at a very steep angle and, because of its superior speed, would be relatively immune to attack;

4. – could be flown by enthusiastic young men after only a short period of training; and

5. – after having reached firing range, would be able to deliver a devastating salvo against one or more enemy aircraft. Then the pilot would separate from the aircraft and descend to the ground by parachute, while the aircraft would also be recovered by 'chute.

From the experience gathered on the Me 163, we knew that requirements 1 to 3 could easily have been realised. Numbers 4 and 5 were impossible right from the start, and the whole project was doomed to failure. Wolfgang Späte had to re-train a number of pilots in his *Erprobungs-Kommando 16* (Trial Detachment Number 16), at Zwischenahn. One of them was, as a very remarkable exception, an official from the *Reichsluftfahrt-Ministerium* (*RLM* – Ministry of Aviation), a high ranking staff engineer by the name of Walter Reyle. He was a professional engineer, aircraft designer and constructor, holding the appropriate position in the *RLM*. As a bearer of the golden Party badge, he enjoyed *Gnadensonne von oben* ('protection from above'). During re-training for the rocket fighter, he finally managed to get the Me 163 B airborne and flew it after several daring take-offs. During one of these training flights he made contact with several USAAF fighters without being able to engage in combat, since his training aircraft was unarmed. Reyle was one of the driving forces who were able to convince the *RLM* to invite tenders for the project from the different aircraft manufacturers.

One suggestion resulting from this was originated by *Dipl.-Ing.* Erich von Bachem, and was designated Ba 349 – the *'Natter'*. It was handled with top priority and classified *'Geheime Reichssache'* (Top Secret) and, despite all its faults, the *'Natter'* was later to prove of great interest to the

The core of the trial team for the 'Natter'. From left: Dipl.-Ing Fielder and colleague from the Bachem Company), Hermann Zitter and Erich Klöckner.

Allies. (After the end of World War II, several different Allied organisations, tasked with the evaluation of captured German technology, applied for further information. However, only a few documents, and just three or four reasonably complete 'Natters' were, by then, available.)

For the initial development, it was decided that the tactics would require vertical take-off as soon as visual contact was made with the approaching enemy. In order to achieve this, an extraordinarily high climb rate was required. The fire-power of the 'Natter' was to be so great that the enemy would be destroyed after only a short burst. Due to the high differential speed of the 'Natter', compared to the enemy aircraft, there was only a very short time – approximately one to two seconds – in which the pilot was at an acceptable range (very short, even for the best fighter pilots!).

Operation: Lift-off from a vertical launch gantry 10 metres (32.8ft) high. Automatic steering by rudders partially penetrating the hot exhaust, detachable booster rockets, and a main rocket engine with variable speed. The whole machine sequentially disassembling to a pre-programmed sequence, whilst airborne, with the fuselage finally separating for the high speed engagement.

Rescue of the pilot by parachute and recovery of the fuselage, including the steering mechanism and booster rockets, on cargo type parachutes.

Armament: thirty-four 7.3 cm (2.87 inch) rockets to be fired in one salvo, lasting 0.4 seconds.

Employment: Defence against attacking enemy bomber aircraft.

Technical specification of the 'Natter': Wingspan 3.6m (11.8ft), overall length 6.0m (19.7ft), height of fuselage 1.3m (4.27ft), width of fuselage 0.9m (3ft), chord of wing 1.0m (3.28ft), chord of the empennage 1.0m (3.28ft). Lift-off weight (fully fuelled including booster rockets) 2,270kg (5,004lbs). Wing loading at full lift-off weight 568kg/cm (approximately 8 p.s.i): while flying empty without use of booster rockets 233kg/cm (approx. 4psi)

Propelled by a variable, liquid fuel, Walter HWK 109 509 A2

rocket engine, producing a maximum thrust of 1,700kp (3,748lbs). Additionally, four solid fuel booster rockets were attached, adding thrust of 1,200kp (2,646lbs) each. These booster rockets were automatically jettisoned after they had burned out. During launch there was a total thrust of 6,500kp (14,330lbs) available for ten seconds, and the average acceleration during lift-off was calculated at 2.2g. The highest projected altitude was 16,000m (52,494ft) at an average climb speed of 675km/h (419.4mph). The fuel was to be sufficient for 7 minutes at full thrust, and the calculated horizontal speed at 5,000m (16,405ft) was 1,000km/h (621.4mph). By using different profiles for wings and tailplane, a speed of 1,160km/h (720.8mph) at an altitude of 10,000m (32,809ft) and 1,420km/h (882.36mph) at 16,000m (52,494ft) were theoretically possible. As Rüdiger Kosin mentioned in his book 'The Development of German Fighter Planes', the *'Natter'* project was cancelled by the *Rüstungsstab* (Office for Arms Acquisition) as early as 5 January 1945. He remarks: 'Why the trials went on until the enemy troops arrived can only be understood in conjunction with the psychosis of the war coming to an end.' He also states: 'Besides the many primitive hand-made wooden parts, the Bachem 349 contained sophisticated equipment such as rocket engines, weapons, regulators, instruments, autopilot, oxygen equipment etc; requiring a substantially undamaged supply industry. It was the lack of essentials of this nature which held back delivery of fighter aircraft to the *Luftwaffe* by the aircraft manufacturers...'

Bachem, with his technical designer, Willi Fiedler (who later joined Lockheed), and *Prof. Dr.-Ing.* Kurt Petrikat, were the intellectual fathers of the *'Natter'*. In agreement with the *RLM*, a framework was set up, and fifty trial craft scheduled to be built. The initial ten were to test the flight characteristics, determining whether the design was right, whether the machine was manoeuvrable and sufficiently stable in flight, whether the extreme forces acting on the pilot were tolerable, and whether the operational range was sufficient. The next ten trial craft were to be used mainly to test the vertical take-off characteristics. During these tests, the initial guidance system, weight, centre of gravity, thrust – as well as the size of the tailplane – were to be varied. A further ten were to be used to investigate the feasibility of recovering the pilot and aircraft, as well as the initial launch equipment, by parachute. The trials showed that the solution of these problems required much additional painstaking

The Bachem M 2 'Natter' with fixed undercarriage.

development work and tests as prerequisites.

Understandably, I was mainly interested in the trials testing the flight properties of the first ten test craft, since I was to be the test pilot. Bachem was well known as a glider pilot in the Rhön competitions, and later became technical director of the Fieseler Aircraft Company in Kassel. Later, he started a company in Waldsee, Württemberg, delivering parts to the aviation industry, and, whilst there, he designed and built the first trial aircraft, designating them Bachem BP 20 M1, M2, M3 – and so on. During my two visits to Waldsee, and at several meetings at Ainring, I got a detailed idea of the job I was to do. Two departments within the *DFS*, Flight Mechanics, headed by Dr. Ruden, and Flight Trials, headed by Fritz Stamer, were to manage the whole project. Initially, a flight trial programme was set up which contained the following:

> The trial *'Natter'*, BP 20 M1, was to be literally dragged aloft by a He 111. After reaching the prescribed altitude, a transition would be made by the Heinkel entering a shallow dive and increasing airspeed to the point where the *'Natter'* would, hopefully, begin to behave like a normal glider under tow. The intention was that this should allow instrument readings to be taken, and thus determine exact values of rudder pressures, rudder effectiveness and inertia. Similarly, evaluations such as stall characteristics, slow speed control performance, and

the behaviour of the aircraft in the turn were to be tested in tandem with the input of trim during acceleration. On completion of the test schedule, the He 111 was to bring the aircraft over the airfield, where the test pilot was to bale out. The aircraft had neither undercarriage nor skis on which to land, and so, shortly after the pilot had abandoned the '*Natter*', and was observed descending safely towards the ground, the pilot of the tow aircraft was to reduce airspeed and release the '*Natter*' in a shallow dive, just prior to its reaching the ground. Release of the tow line was the duty of the observer, lying in the belly of the He 111. Clearly, a very competent pilot had to be found to fly the tow aircraft!

In fact, wind tunnel tests using a scale model 1:2.5 were to be performed at the *DVL* at Braunschweig before practical flight trials were to commence. However, it was not possible to perform these trials before 30 January 1945. Time was pressing, and this was why, regardless of the measurements and their results which were to be taken from the model, the first practical trial was prepared at the *DFS*. It at least comforted me to know that the towing aircraft, a He 111 H-6 (coded DG+RN), was to be flown by our most experienced test pilot, *Flugkapitän* Hermann Zitter (known as 'Zappel'). He knew all the tricks and was the best there was for this task. It was clear to me that I was about to make the most adventurous test flight of my career.

The M1 '*Natter*' was set up on a three-wheeled cradle, which had been specially designed and built for the launch. The aircraft sat loosely supported on blocks which matched the shape of the fuselage. The front wheel of the trolley was free to pivot, but had no steering control. However, it was raked backward in its swivel and, therefore, simply followed the direction of pull by the tow aircraft. The tow line was forked, with each end hooked to a wing tip, right on the line of the centre of gravity. The He 111 itself also had a coupling underneath the fuselage, securing the line precisely on the junction of the longitudinal centre line and the centre of gravity. The line was made of hemp, ten to twelve millimetres in diameter, because it provided elastic qualities which tended to dampen jerks during the launch and tow. An insulated cable was attached to the tow line to provide radio communication between Zitter and myself.

We were ready to launch at the beginning of November

1944, and a group of mechanics, led by the engineers Wrede, Kiefel, Pap and several others, hurried to Neuburg to help to complete final preparations. I had gone over all the details of this flight with Zitter, and we were absolutely positive that we could rely on each other. We flew from Ainring to Neuburg in our He 111 on 3rd November, with a VIP aboard – Stamer, the Head of the Institute, came with us, illustrating the importance of this mission. From noon, the runway was closed to all other traffic, and we agreed to take off after the light cross-wind had moderated, since it would have caused serious problems for our three-wheeler.

The complete tow set-up was ready to launch in the early afternoon, and Zitter and I calmly went through the most important details one last time. Finally, we assured each other with the words: 'It will all go well!' Zitter, joined by his mechanic and observer, walked to the He 111, and I climbed into the M1, observing that there was only a little residual cross-wind. As calm and collected as I could be, I rechecked all the controls, giving special attention to the canopy release mechanism and to my parachute. A knee board was strapped tightly to my right thigh, a pencil was ready in a clip, and the stopwatch on my left wrist was set to zero. Just as I lowered the canopy, Stamer came over to the aircraft, held the canopy up, and squeezed my hand, just like a priest administering the last rites to an innocent man sentenced to death. He looked me in the eyes and, like a truly stoic German, said: 'I wish you a good flight!' He meant well, of course, but at that moment I wished he'd go to Hell! – although I didn't say so. Luckily, I had a hide like a rhinoceros, and immediately resumed my pre-flight checks.

I closed and locked the canopy, rechecked communications with Zitter, and asked him to wait one minute with the engines running. I always needed this minute before critical missions to prepare myself psychologically for what lay in store. When the canopy closed above me, there was no contact with the world outside. Then, in those few moments, I could concentrate my mind completely on the task in hand. As ready as I could be, I shouted, 'Let's go!', and Zitter pushed the throttles smartly forward. I felt the acceleration and was pushed back into my moulded seat as we increased speed rather rapidly. This modified He 111 had an immense surplus of power and, in addition to that, she was carrying only minimum fuel. We raced along the runway behind the He 111, with me sitting in the

'*Natter*' , which was still laying in its cradle of blocks on the launch trolley. Shortly before the end of the runway, Zitter pulled the He 111 up into a steep climb: it was eager to fly, but not so my '*Natter*'. Within seconds, the He 111 had climbed about 80 – 100m, and the tow line turned into a drag line – with me hanging below the Heinkel! The launch trolley overtook me the moment the '*Natter*' was lifted out of it, crashing into the fields after performing a few somersaults. I shouted: 'Well done Zappel!', realising, with some satisfaction, that we were climbing away rapidly. Moments later I added: 'You're buying the drinks!' After all, he was at the safer end of this tow-line. There was no immediate response, so I added: 'Everything okay with you?' This only elicited a mumbled, *'Ja, ja'*. It was evident he was having problems of his own trying to stabilise the tow. There was only one course of action open – continue the climb!

We finally reached an altitude of 3,000m (9,843ft), and it was time to try to make the transition from hanging vertically to horizontal flight: this could be tricky because the '*Natter*' was such a small aircraft, designed for high speed, and equipped with very small control surfaces. However, we had developed a successful manoeuvre whilst testing the Me 328, and hoped it would work as well in this situation. After communicating briefly with Zitter, he went into a shallow dive to increase the airspeed and, predictably, the more he accelerated the more effective my control surfaces became. I eventually achieved a climb by pulling the 'stick' all the way back and giving her full up elevator. The '*Natter*' responded quickly, and I soon found myself above the longitudinal axis of the Heinkel, clear of the uncomfortable buffeting of the prop wash and wake turbulence. We were in an acceptable towing configuration, with my aircraft flying and responding to control inputs quite normally. I was able to execute every point of the test-programme, and my knee board began to fill with notes and data. As the test progressed, we had to take short breaks in order to enable me to write down my observations. During the years I had been trial flying, I had developed a kind of flight-trial 'shorthand', which saved me from writing long statements during the test flights. Later, on the ground, sitting at my desk, I had more time and was able to write up a more meaningful trial report.

After forty-five minutes, we had completed the programme, and the Heinkel was flying straight and level and reducing speed. At the right moment, Zitter pulled the He 111 up into a

The 'Natter' in Tragschlepp below a He. 111 piloted by Hermann Zitter.
Erich Klöchner was about to make a parachute descent prior to the 'Natter'
being brought in by the Heinkel.

climb, as I reversed my earlier actions and dropped back
through the prop-wash, ending up hanging nearly vertically
beneath the Heinkel again. 'Zappel' flew a wide turn to
approach the airfield from east to west, reaching the western

boundary of the field at an altitude of 800 – 1,000m (2,624 – 3,281ft). Everything was working 'as advertised' and, as we continued our approach, I passed a message of caution to 'Zappel': 'I 'm unlocking the canopy. Watch out! Now!' It was drawn up to the right and cleanly away backward. I unstrapped myself, making one last call to Zitter: 'See you in the canteen!' Then I disconnected the communication cable, stepped into the moulded parachute recess in the seat, and performed a headlong dive overboard. My body somersaulted several times in the air, and I waited until I was head-down before I pulled my manual parachute release. Shortly afterwards, I heard the comforting muffled rippling noise above my head as the 'chute deployed. Once more the illusion of being born again came over me, an almost euphoric experience which was especially apparent whilst free-falling. All I wished for was a soft landing! Parachutes in those days had a rate of descent of about 9 – 10m / sec (29.5 – 32.8ft / sec). There was little wind, and I descended towards the ground without drift. 'Oh my God!', I thought, 'The ground is closing on me rapidly!' Actually, in this case, it was the concrete runway, and it was rushing up toward me at alarming speed. With this thought in mind, I hit the ground with my legs slightly bent, my head dropping between my knees as I rolled over like a hedgehog. I have to admit I was slightly dazed, but soon rolled out of the parachute cords and stood on my two feet, intact. At that moment I was very grateful to 'Fips', our man responsible for the rescue equipment!

Moments later, 'Zappel' released M1 smoothly onto the turf, causing only very little damage, which was soon repaired. Stamer was the first to greet me, and he was obviously relieved. Patting me on the back, he laconically remarked: 'The earth has you back,' and, after a brief discussion, we agreed to fly back immediately to Ainring in the He 111. Happy as I was with this, I never did get to see Zitter in the canteen!

The next morning I delivered my detailed flight report to Stamer, Dr. Ruden and Prof. Georgii. I kept a carbon copy, and since it was a National secret, I stuck it under the drawer of my desk. However, despite my best attempt at secrecy, one day it disappeared. It contained a few very positive statements about the controllability of the *'Natter'*. I had especially praised the effectiveness of the controls in the range of 150km/h (93.2mph). It also contained some negative remarks, particularly regarding the opening and release of the canopy. It had to be opened from left to right, and tended to jam, even at the relatively low speed at which it was normally opened and jettisoned. Although untested, it was reasonable to expect that it would be impossible to open the canopy at higher speeds. My suggestion was to open the canopy by raising it at the front, and let it be drawn away by the slipstream. This suggestion was only adopted by the time M3 flew, but the repaired M1 and M2 kept their unmodified canopies.

In the meantime, on the Heuberg near Sigmaringen, a launch gantry had been designed and built and several unmanned 'Natters' had been launched, more or less successfully, by using solid fuel rockets. At the beginning of February, my second trial flight followed with the M1. There were no problems worth mentioning and, this time, I touched down on the turf and landed on my feet without falling over. The M2 arrived at Neuburg an der Donau, and was fitted with a tricycle undercarriage taken from a K.135. After fitting the gear, the pilot sat a little closer to the ground, compared to when the machine had been blocked-up on the original launch-trolley. One no longer sat on the 'second floor' – so to speak – and the nose-wheel had been made steerable via the rudder pedals. 'Zappel' and I felt relatively confident dealing with this unusual tow, even though the take-off, the flight, and my landing by parachute placed enormous psychological stress on both of us. Behind my back they called me, 'Mann mit den starken Nerven und dem schwarzen Hut' (man with the strong nerves and the black hat). In my view only the latter was correct; I certainly had 'nerves' but, fortunately, I was able to control them when the occasion required a cool head.

The M2 was already equipped with a large parachute, fitted in the rear fuselage, intended for recovery of the machine after it had been abandoned by the pilot. It was only fitted for future data collection flights, and as a 'tranquilliser' for me, but not for actual use at that stage of the trials. For my part, I had always had faith in the parachute packed by Fips. The first take-off on the tricycle undercarriage was more precise than those on the un-steerable launch trolley. After lift-off, the 'Natter' proved rather nose-heavy, but this was easily corrected by moving back the trim weight in the nose section. Having completed collecting the data, I made my preparations for landing in what had become an established routine. After consulting the 'man above', I actuated the cockpit cover release, but had to use all my strength to push the hood open, as it had jammed again. I had already said good-bye to 'Zappel' and, having eventually got the canopy to yield, I executed my accustomed full length dive over the side. This time my body did not make any turns or somersaults whatsoever, and I was so fascinated by the free fall that I continued a few hundred metres extra, as if I were sliding downhill on my belly. My right hand found the 'D'-ring on the rip-cord, and I gave it a firm tug. There was the familiar 'whoosh' above me, accompanied by a firm jerk on my harness and, once more, I was sailing down to earth just like an experienced parachutist. Having touched down safely, I was able to observe the landing of the 'Natter' on its new undercarriage. 'Zappel' approached the field in a very smooth dive, with the M2 hanging 80 – 100m below the Heinkel. Achieving a smooth landing would, however, require a flying masterpiece. He made a careful approach and, when the tricycle undercarriage was about one metre above the ground, the observer released the tow line and it touched down; a perfectly normal landing until one of the struts broke off and the fuselage was damaged.

During this trial phase, nearly the whole team was staying in the Hotel *'Zur Krone'* in Neuburg. We regularly took our supper in a restaurant associated with a butcher's shop, and there was food and drink as if it were peacetime. There was a rumour that the reason for this was not that we were working on a defence weapon, but that the owner had two daughters he wanted to marry off. We never told him that nearly all of us were married!

There were endless air-raid warnings one night, with bomber formations from Italy flying over our heads on north-easterly courses until the early hours of the morning. Later, we were to learn it was the night when Dresden was bombed, and when thousands of people died in its flaming ruins. Yet the radio continuously broadcast new special announcements, reiterating the motto:*'Nur durchhalten – bald kommt die Geheimwaffe!'* (Just hold out – soon comes the secret weapon!) Each of us knew that victory could not be ours. After that terrible night, all the subsequent flights I performed with the *DFS* were just a hopeless fulfilment of my duties.

The third *'Natter'*, the M3, was ready for launch. She had reinforced struts, and a canopy which opened front to back! Launch, flight, and the recording of my observations went as planned. A large number of instruments had been installed and, in addition to this, a camera had been fitted on the right hand side of the cockpit behind my head, saving me a lot of writing. After returning to the field, we came in for a previously well practised 'two piece' landing. I unlocked the canopy, which immediately flew backwards, delivering a hard blow to the back of my neck as it went. For a moment I was more shocked than dazed, and it took me a few seconds to put my feet on the seat and slide out over the side. I pulled the rip-cord immediately and heard the comforting sound of the 'chute deploying above me. Looking up, I saw the familiar and reassuring sight of my parachute, and the tension of the bale-out subsided. It was then that I felt a rather severe pain in my neck which took my attention for a few moments. I was probably concentrating too much on this and, as a consequence, my landing was not very elegant. 'Zappel' brought the 'Natter' smoothly to the runway, where it rolled to a halt after touching down. When I complained about the blow to the neck, it was initially suggested that I might consider remaining in-situ, letting 'Zappel' bring me in for a landing. With due respect to Zitter's flying abilities, no discussions were required about anything of that sort. I considered that a drag-in landing would be a far greater risk for me than taking to my parachute.

My safety was not the main consideration during the tow trials, but it would come into sharp focus when the 'Natter' was equipped with its rocket engines and flying at high speed. The canopy had a new, but ineffective, connecting brace made of a steel pipe with a diameter of approximately 10-12 mm (.39 to .47 in). When it was opened and flipped back, the locking latch delivered the blow I had experienced to my neck. In my opinion, depending of course on the speed, there was a real danger of the pilot being decapitated while attempting to abandon the machine.

As already mentioned, the 'Natter' was to be used as a manned, rocket propelled, anti aircraft weapon. The approach to the enemy was to be carried out at an angle of approximately 15° from behind and below. At a distance of 50 to 100m (164 to 328ft) the rockets were to be fired using the appropriate lead angle. After a successful 'kill', or if a shot had failed to hit the target, an attempt was to be made to attack a second or third aircraft by turning towards the bombers flying ahead. It was thought possible for very proficient pilots, after firing all their rockets, to fly a 360° turn or a loop, in order to set themselves up again behind the enemy, and bring them down by ramming. This vision of tactical employment presumably came from the bureaucratic ivory tower of the *SS*, since the *RLM* could never have thought of anything so bizarre. Experienced fighter pilots to whom I spoke about this only laughed. The inventors of these tactics thought the bale-out and landing by parachute after shooting down the enemy was the easiest form of recovery. First, the pilot was to dive away from the enemy, then reduce his speed by pulling up. All he then had to do, in theory, was to unstrap himself. By moving a lever, the forward part of the fuselage was

The launch of an unmanned 'Natter' using rockets.

171

to be jettisoned, and the recovery 'chute deployed. After this, the main fuselage section, containing the cockpit, decelerated quickly and the pilot could easily make his escape from the machine. This would then descend with a calculated sink rate of 12 m/sec (39.4ft/sec). Having fallen a safe distance from the machine, the pilot would open his own parachute. By using this type of recovery, the pilot, as well as all major parts of the aircraft – especially the engine – were to be saved and used again.

So-called *Halb-Piloten* (half-pilots) were to operate the *'Natter'*. They were only to be trained in the machine's approach to the enemy, which they were to practice in a type of simulator. The students were not required to learn the most difficult techniques, namely take-off and landing, because the aircraft was automatically guided on take-off until the booster-rockets burnt out; landing, other than by parachute, had never been intended. Conventional twin-engine aircraft were reconfigured to function as trainers for this exceedingly short course. These had a *'Natter'* cockpit in the nose, and the student lay in it, learning to guide the craft towards a predetermined point. I returned to Ainring and reported verbally to Stamer and Prof. Georgii about the progress of the trials. It was at this time that I found out that the *RLM* had handed the responsibility for this project to the *SS*. That same afternoon I was sitting at my desk, putting the report of my first M3 trial to paper, when there was a knock on the door. Before I was able to say: *'Herein'* (come in), Dr. Ruden stood in my room with two high-ranking *SS* Officers. Dr. Ruden introduced me, I asked them to take a seat and, without further ado, discussion commenced about the *'Natter'*. I was asked how many flights I had made, and what my impressions were. Finally, it was disclosed that the original programme could not be carried out because of time constraints and, thenceforth, manned flights using rocket propulsion were to be made.

I read my hand-written flight report to the gentlemen, expressing my conviction that without modifying the canopy it should not be flown, since I believed there was a very real danger of the pilot having his neck broken by the release of the canopy. Further, that I would want to see at least five or six satisfactory launches, using dummies, as a prerequisite before I would be available for the first live launch.

With zealous enthusiasm, which at times took the form of emotional blackmail, they tried to convince me that there was no time, that the *'Führer'* needed the weapon, and that nobody

---

FORSCHUNGSFÜHRUNG
des Reichsministers der Luftfahrt u.
Oberbefehlshabers der Luftwaffe

Professor Dr. W. Georgii .

(Bitte in der Antwort vorstehendes Geschäftszeichen,
das Datum, und kurzen Inhalt anzugeben)

BERLIN SW 68, den 11. Nov. .1944
Jerusalemer Str. 65
Telegramm-Adresse: Reichsluft Berlin
Fernsprecher: Ortsverkehr: 52 00 24, 21 82 41, 12 00 47
Fernverkehr: 21 80 11
Hausapparat: 6096

Herrn

Flugzeugführer E. Klöckner
DFS Ernst Udet, Inst. F.

Flughafen Ainring /Obb.

Mein lieber Klöckner !

Nach Durchsicht des Flugberichtes über Versuche am 3. 11. 44 in
N. an der Donau ist es mir ein herzliches Bedürfnis, Ihrer mit einem
besonderen Gruss zu gedenken und Ihnen in Gedanken die Hand zu drücken.

Ich danke Ihnen sehr für Ihre Einsatzbereitschaft.

Meine herzlichsten Wünsche begleiten Sie auch weiterhin

Ihr

Georgii

A letter of appreciation to Erich Klöchner from Prof. Georgii.

should shrink from his National duty to defend the Fatherland in its hour of greatest need. The word *'Ritterkreuz'* (Knight's Cross) was mentioned, and, a while later, something about a pistol, as they paced the floor, vacillating from rewards and encouragement to crude threats. I told my visitors several times that I was willing to continue the trials, but only under the conditions I had already detailed. Finally, they left without a word of farewell. The next afternoon, a soldier in flying uniform came to me with orders to be trained in the theory of flying the *'Natter'*: I was to give the briefing. I think his name was Zuebert. He gave me the impression of being a daredevil, although he seemed pleasant enough. I explained everything to him in detail, including the deficiencies of the system. After leaving me, he went to Neuburg where he underwent technical instruction. I never knew whether or not he flew the '*Natter*'. A few days later news arrived from Heuberg that, on 1 March 1945, Lothar Siebert had undertaken the first manned launch of a '*Natter*'. It had, unfortunately, resulted in his death.

Wilhelm Buss: Witness of the Manned Launch

Wilhelm Buss was a parachute specialist with the Luftwaffe Trial and Test Centre at Rechlin. He had also taken part in the ejector seat trials (see Chapter Eleven – Kapitän Jochen Eisermann and Chapter Twelve – Wilhelm Buss). After World War II, Buss went to the USA where he published several reports about his experiences in Germany on tests and trials. He had also been enlisted to help with the parachutes for the 'Natter', about which he had grave misgivings. He was an eyewitness of the fatal launch of Lothar Siebert on the Heuberg. Among other things he writes:

'When I talked to Siebert, he was firmly convinced that nothing could happen to him. Not because of the fact that everything was in order with the construction, but because he was convinced he was born under a lucky star... On the manned launch there was a drogue 'chute for deployment after the '*Natter*' had reached its ceiling altitude. During this flight, Siebert would certainly need the support of a 'lucky star'.

The launch took place, with Siebert as pilot. The '*Natter*', weighing two tons, reached a speed of 600km/h (372.8mph) in a vertical climb. Shortly after lift-off, the plexiglass canopy blew off, and this could have caused Siebert to lose consciousness, or worse. The engine of the '*Natter*' continued to run all the way to the ceiling altitude. Then the craft went into a steep dive and disappeared, crashing into the Danube valley'.

Hans Zübert: Flight Report of the '*Natter*'

In 1985, Hans Zübert was featured in the mass media in such sensational headlines as 'The First Rocket Man', because, it was reported, he was the first man to have been shot into the skies in the 'Natter'. A modest and retiring man, Zübert protested that his former achievement did not warrant such extravagant acclaim. The Press, however, eager as always for a lucrative 'scoop', ignored his objections and elaborated on the story to such an extent that Zübert was eventually made a member of the American Test Pilots' Society.

Despite all this, it would be wrong to say Hans Zübert did not deserve considerable credit. He did actually fly the 'Natter', and in all probability is the one and only pilot to have flown this 'projectile' in free flight and survived. However, he was not propelled into the air by rockets, but was carried to an altitude of 5,500m (18,045ft) by a Heinkel He 111, and there released. He bravely mastered the prescribed test programme on the BP 20 M8, and baled out safely at the end. Only one human being ever flew the 'Natter' in free, vertical, flight using the full rocket thrust on take-off. This, as we have read, ended with both Lothar Siebert and his machine in a thousand pieces. Maybe it was the similarity in name that made the Press attribute more to Hans Zübert than the actual truth?

In any case, his flying achievement was outstanding – if only because he proved the supporters of the project right in saying that expensively trained fighter pilots were not required to fly this weapon. It only needed brave young men who did not even have to be trained in take-off and landing, but only in steering and aiming a machine which was already airborne. The flying ability of Hans Zübert was well above these minimum requirements, although he was not equipped with the qualifications and knowledge of a test pilot holding an academic grade. He had been testing parachutes before the war, and trained as a pilot in 1943, under the command of Kapitän Walter Horten. One day Horten asked him,'Wouldn't the testing of the 'Natter' be an attractive task for you?' Hans Zübert agreed without hesitation. He was, as his comrades of those days and even now believe, something of a daredevil who, without hesitation, took on the most dangerous and questionable tasks. Nevertheless, he carried out the required test flight with the coolness and sensitivity of an experienced trial pilot. In retrospect, one has to say he was fortunate that there was only one trial flight. That way it ended like a happy fairy tale, and he is still alive today.

To the Stratosphere in a Glider

It seemed, on 11th October 1940, that the Föhn wind (a wind peculiar to the mountain regions which creates so-called 'mountain waves' – also called the Chinook in the American Rockies) for which I had been waiting so long, had finally arrived. I hastened to Ainring airfield, long before the start of my working day, and sorted out the things I needed to take along: fur gloves, battery-belt, heating pads for my shoes, a special face cream to protect against cosmic radiation, sunglasses to protect my eyes from strong ultraviolet, fur over-boots, oxygen mask and a thick fur-lined flying suit.

The meteorologists had also arrived, and we agreed that a high altitude glider tow was worth trying. Before sunrise, the whole of the eastern sky became a beautiful blood-red, and we observed several high altitude cloud formations over the eastern Alps. Their structure indicated the possibility of a wave formation at even higher altitude, the dramatic lighting of the sky enhancing the impression that the clouds were, indeed, very high. Over the central Alps, we were able to make out a contoured wave cloud at cirrus level, sharply cut off at the southern edge and slowly dissipating on the northern edge of the mountains. At the intermediate altitude, several smaller banks of clouds could be seen which did not necessarily indicate Föhn wind conditions, but we decided they really just obscured the view of the large wave cloud above.

A sudden, and unexpected, formation of ground fog in the *Salachtal* (Salach valley) stopped all flying activity on Ainring airfield, including our glider tow, at least for a while. The big wave was still to be seen, its front edge seeming to move south. The question was, would there be northerly winds up aloft? As it turned out, the fog was a false alarm and soon dissipated and, at about 08:30 hours, we finally took off.

The glider had been specially prepared for high altitude flights, and I had already been sitting in it for quite some time. It was a *Kranich* (Crane), made by Jacobs, and equipped with reinforced wings and speed brakes. The *DFS* used it for 'risky flights' in cloud and this is why it was usually known as the Wolkenkranich (cloud Crane), registered D 11-169. The rear seat of this double-seater did not have a stick and, therefore, usually had enough room for a meteorological observer, as well as additional equipment. That day, however, I flew it alone and was pleased that we were getting started, such was my thirst for action. In the tow aircraft, a He 46 – coded D-IBKA, were the pilot, Paul Stämmler, together with the meteorologist, *Frau Dr-Ing* Ursel Pielsticker. Near ground level, we had a westerly wind and the atmospheric pressure was dropping.

After an uneventful take-off, I followed the tug as it towed me along the northern edge of the foothills of the Alps, climbing in order to avoid the turbulence which was evident up to 3,000m (9,843ft). Near Traunstein we turned south-westerly, heading toward Innsbruck and, in the meantime, the large Föhn-wave had developed enormously and had spread, with a few gaps at extreme altitude, all the way west to the Wetterstein mountain-range. On line with the Kaiser mountains, we turned southward as strong Föhn cloud was just developing over the central Alps, which seemed to promise fabulous gliding conditions. We reached an altitude of 5,000m (18,045ft), just abeam Zell am See, and overhead the Salzachtal (Salzach valley). In this area I felt a slight descent, and then a climb a few seconds later: this was repeated three times, but the upward current was too weak. I kept my hand on the release handle and, full of excitement, waited for the first wave and the predicted higher rate of climb. Still heading southward, we were able to tell from the structure of the cloud above that we would shortly reach the area of the main updraught. At a position north-west of the peak of the Glockner, I finally released at an altitude of 5,700m (18,701ft). This obviously occurred at the right moment as, within a few moments, I was in an updraught, rising at 1.5 to 2 m/sec (5 to 6.6ft/sec) and nicely placed at the front edge of this typical Föhn wave cloud, rising high above my position.

The wind velocity seemed fairly high at this altitude, resulting in very low ground-speed on my southerly heading. In this calm updraught I climbed higher and higher, not making a single turn. This gave me ample time to re-check my high altitude equipment: the oxygen mask was in good working order, the ultraviolet lenses were protecting my eyes, and a brief look at the oxygen pressure gauge indicated that everything was perfect. I had no trouble breathing oxygen, having put the mask on before take-off to adjust the flow and the fit on my face. This preparation had proven best during previous high altitude flights.

As before, when using the Föhn phenomenon for gliding, there was a distinct Föhn wall, a bank of clouds approaching from the south, and tending to dissipate north of the Glockner-Venediger-Massif, but the mountain tops were not visible. Normally the Föhn wall ran from east to west during the almost freak conditions, but this time its northern edge was stretching from the Venediger to the Glockner, then southbound to the Fernblick-Ankogel and on to the Hochalmspitze. The wave-cloud itself was extending north and began almost vertically above the northern edge of the Föhn wall, and from my lofty perch I could see there were occasional patches of ground fog on the northern Alps.

On my steady course south, still climbing at a rate of 1.5 to 2 m/sec, I reached the front edge of the leeward cloud in the sunshine. The base of this cloud was at 8,000m (26,247ft). Between 7,000 and 8,000m (22,966 and 26,247ft), the climb rate reduced a fraction. When I noticed the forward top edge of the cloud slowly disintegrating, I turned south-east, heading along the sharply contoured cloud. By doing so, I regained the previous climb rate of 2 m/sec. The cloud, viewed in cross-section from north to south, was wedge shaped, with the tip of the wedge in the south. The top front edge seemed to reach the windward side of the central ridge of the Alps at an estimated 13,000 to 14,000m (42,652 to 45,933ft).

The low temperature began to make itself painfully felt in my feet, despite the occasional use of the heating pads. Furthermore, I was only able to move the stick using both hands, the ailerons crunched and complained at the smallest of deflections, and the fuselage made awful cracking noises due to the wood and metal shrinking in the extremely low temperatures at that altitude. (In the silence which usually prevails in a glider, this is particularly noticeable). The cloud had now fully developed, and showed a very pronounced shape. There was no doubt in my mind that I would be able to reach, and even surpass, the 10,000 metre (32,809ft) mark that day. However, since the altimeter, which had been installed in the front panel, was only calibrated up to 10,000m (32,809ft), I made the decision to stop the climb when it showed 500m above, no matter what rate of climb I was experiencing at the time. According to the aviation doctors, an uncontrolled climb could pose a potentially fatal risk. They had speculated that 12,000m (39,371ft), in an un-pressurised cabin, would be the absolute altitude attainable. Above this, they had suggested, the oxygen in the blood would boil out, even whilst breathing pure O_2. Their theory was that high altitude death would occur within seconds and, probably, without warning. I had known about these physiological phenomena for quite some time and, therefore, went through a self-checking routine during my climb. By looking into a mirror, which I had fitted solely for this purpose, I observed that my face was occasionally strangely contorted. Sometimes, feelings of anxiety were followed by sudden euphoria – during which I would have loved to open the canopy and step out! Taking my gloves off, I found, to my consternation, my fingernails turning blue. Previous high altitude flights, and decompression chamber tests, had taught me that this was a sign of anoxia.

The updraught varied in strength, at times up to 4m/sec (13.1ft/sec), and I was now approaching the 10,000m (32,809ft) limit. Unusual turbulence at this level induced in the aircraft abrupt pitching and yawing movements, and I had the feeling that it might stall – even though the air speed indicator read 70-80km/h (43.5 to 49.7mph). This 'wobbly' layer was to prove only 100m (328ft) thick, and I was soon continuing my flight along the front edge of the cloud. The altimeter then indicated more than 10,500 metres (34,499ft), and the time of climb through 10,000 to 10,500m seemed rather long. However, it has to be said that I was estimating my altitude on the un-calibrated section of the face of my altimeter; my instinct was that I was actually much higher. Physically, I felt fairly good except for the dreadful cold and a perception of increasing pressure in my head.

Despite this uneasy feeling, I continued looking south, where I was able see an incredible distance. I was able, for instance, to see all the way to, and beyond, the northern Adriatic sea, including the Po River Delta with its dirty, brown water pouring into the blue of the Adria. When the humid air masses of the Mediterranean are pushed northward, and are stopped by the Alps, they rise and cool, the water molecules condensing during the ascent and forming clouds. These clouds partially rid themselves of the water by precipitating devastating downpours, which quickly swell numerous small rivers and streams, taking along dirt and mud in suspension into the river Po. This dirt and mud colours the river a dirty-brown, and this spectacle of nature was revealed before my eyes.

The cloudless sky in the south no longer looked blue from this altitude; it seemed darker, nearly black – I had never been given more convincing proof of the earth being round. The sight-line from the cockpit to the horizon was noticeably steeper than at 500 to 1,000m (1,641 to 3,281ft). I had never reached this altitude before, and it had a sort of magic effect on me. In my state of euphoria, I felt I could have flown into space. But, at the same time, I was all alone in my '*Sperrholzkiste*' (ply-wood box) and felt the urge to go back home, back to Mother Earth.

The gigantic wave-cloud was still in the north, with yet another above it, the edge located even further south. The possibilities that day seemed endless: if only I'd had a pressurised cabin. The top cloud was surely at the '*Perlmutter-Bericht*' (mother-of-pearl level – 23,000-25,000m, 75,460 to 82,023ft). My flying instinct told me, 'You have to break off, break off immediately!' My respiration rate and my pulse increased, but I was still climbing at 2 m/sec (6.6ft/sec). Suddenly, a strange feeling came over me, and I spoke to myself aloud. I wanted to deploy the air brakes, but really did not have the energy to do so. I could not fly back to the north, because of the enormous Föhn cloud, and I did not want to penetrate it with my super-cooled aircraft. Experience showed that these clouds normally contained a fair amount of water, even at these altitudes, and this would have resulted in immediate and dangerous icing conditions. I therefore pushed the nose down and proceeded southbound to find an area of down-draught. Instead, I entered another up-current, rising at 3-4 m/sec (9.8 to 13.1ft/sec). Pushing the 'Wolkenkranich' down, and accelerating to 150km/h (93,2mph), only reduced the climb rate to 0 or 1m/sec (0 to 3.3ft/sec). This was equal to a rate of climb of over 5 m/sec (984ft/min) and, at this point, a feeling of great fear came over me. I had to descend, I wanted to descend, but I could not! The thought struck me for the first time: 'For heaven's sake! How will I ever get down?!' With a few words of self-encouragement, I calmed myself and found that by flying an easterly course for a time, I came to an area with a strong down-draught, and no turbulence. Then, by descending in a spiral, I managed to lose altitude quickly, and at 8,000m, (26,247ft) I arrived below the base, and in front of the edge of the cloud. However, even at 8,000m it was still damn cold, and in order to reach warmer air masses as quickly as possible, I gathered the last of my strength and deployed the air brakes, not retracting them until reaching an altitude of 4,000m (13,124ft).

With the wind now behind me, and in a steady descent, I flew towards Ainring at a cracking pace. The pride I felt at the successful outcome of my task gave me the strength for the last, but rather difficult, phase. Still super-cold, the whole of the canopy had become instantly covered with several millimetres of frost as I entered the humid lower air so that visibility was zero! I smashed the sliding window with my left elbow, providing sufficient visibility to make a safe landing. Shortly before 12 o'clock, I touched down at Ainring, the point whence I had set out to achieve my dream. Unable as I was to get out of the seat unaided, I was lifted out by my colleagues and eased onto my feet, but suddenly felt weak. This soon passed, and Dr. Ewald Hucke, the medical advisor tasked with looking after us, did his utmost to help. Three fingers of my right hand were frozen white, the lobes of my ears under the fur cap were frozen stiff, and we feared they would break off. Although they didn't, I had trouble with them for years afterwards.

The barothermograph, which had been installed in the nose section, was evaluated by the meteorological section, and found to indicate an absolute altitude of 11,460metres (37,599ft), and an outside air temperature of minus 56°C (minus 68.8°F). The rest of the day was spent at the medical station, and that evening I rode home on my bicycle. Professor Georgii caught up with me in his car and invited me for dinner at the *'Neuwirt'*. Gii (our nick-name for the Professor) had brought a bottle of red wine along, and I am not sure which of us was happier that night, the Professor or myself.

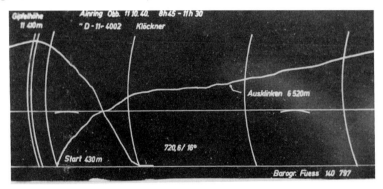

The barograph readout for the flight of 11th October 1940.

The findings of my high altitude research flights formed both the initiative and the basis for the research programme begun by an American cloud research team in California ten years later, headed by Professor Klemperer and Dr. Joachim Küttner. The altitude of 15,000m (49,214ft), predicted by Professor Georgii in 1939, was nearly achieved on flights performed by this group. An altitude of 11,460m (37,599ft) has never again been reached by a glider in Europe. The absolute altitude of 11,460 metres achieved with a glider was, at that time, a world record. However, the FAI in Paris had not, at that time, decided parameters or criteria to recognise this achievement and, in any event, we were right in the middle of a war and so no records could be registered.

Initial Trials of Solid Fuel Rockets

After we had moved to Ainring, in the summer of 1940, one of my first flights involved testing solid fuel rockets, manufactured by Rheinmetall-Borsig (better known for their machine guns). These rockets were to serve as take-off boosters

181

on cargo gliders, and we were to investigate whether steerable rockets would improve take-off. The Kracht Institute, which had been tasked by the *RLM* to complete the trials, had a test-stand erected at the western edge of the airfield to ascertain which jet exhaust casings were most suitable. They soon found that only materials with high melting points were of any use, because the jet pipes soon melted away and the thrust was lost. Also, during these early tests, they developed an electric igniter for the rockets.

Test rockets were fitted to the heavy cargo glider, the *DFS* 230, one rocket under each wing. A button was installed in the instrument panel which, when depressed, was to ignite the rockets simultaneously – at least, this was the theory. The trials manager, *Herr* Mayer, and I agreed that enormous acceleration was to be expected if the calculated total thrust was correct. However, how this would affect the flight no one, including myself, knew. It had simply never been done before. The first take-off was planned for a Saturday afternoon because of the high security classification of the trial. Nobody, except Mayer and his helpers and the Doctor, was at the take-off point. The *DFS* 230 was set up at the far south-west corner of the airfield to offer the maximum take-off distance. I took my seat in the cockpit while, outside, the rockets and the ignition system were checked just one more time. Finally, I was given the signal: all clear for take-off. I pressed my back into the seat and raised my right hand to indicate that I was ready. I counted: 5 – 4 – 3 – 2 – 1 – 0 – Ignition, and the rockets were ignited. The take-off felt like a blow in the back, my head was thrown way back and something similar happened to my arm. The right hand, holding the stick, moved back and pulled the aircraft into a steep climb. With the rockets blasting away, I was shooting up into the sky at an angle of about 35°. Despite my preparation, I was slightly dazed by the unexpected acceleration, but I reacted immediately and controlled the climb. A few seconds later, the rockets had burned out, ending the forward thrust. The altitude gained was approximately 80-100m (262 to 328ft), which gave me ample room for manoeuvre, and to bring the empty cargo glider safely back to the airfield.

Thus ended the first take-off of a cargo glider, assisted by solid fuel rockets mounted under the wings. My first demand was for a headrest and an armrest for take-off. After this request had been met, I performed several similar take-offs with great success.

Landing and Subsequent Take-off in High Mountain Regions

In the middle of February, 1941, I was called to Stamer's office to be introduced to a new plan: a cargo glider, loaded with a small amount of ballast, was to be towed up to an altitude of 3,000m (9,843ft) using a Ju 52. The cargo glider pilot was then to release, and fly a steep approach to land on a small site on the Zirbitzkogel, stopping with the aid of a brake-'chute. The landing area was to be blackened with soot to make it easily identifiable. After unloading, he was to take off with the assistance of solid fuel rockets, and glide down to land at Zeltweg airfield. 'Do you have any reservations about undertaking such a flight?' Stamer asked me. I told him I was convinced that the operation was feasible from the flying point of view. On this recommendation, it was decided to go through with the experiment: *Herr* Mayer, of the Kracht Institute, was to be responsible. As an introduction, we flew to Zeltweg in an He 46 and, from there, on to the Zirbitzkogel Massif to have a look at the approach, and to familiarise myself with the details of the area.

On 24th February, all the preparations were complete, and I flew the *DFS* 230 cargo glider (Coded **NC+SA**) from Ainring to Zeltweg, towed by a Ju 52, piloted by Karl Schieferstein. The additional personnel required flew in the Ju 52. After landing, Mayer and I drove to Judenburg, and that afternoon climbed to the mountaineers' lodge, located just below the Zirbitzkogel on the Schmelz. Due to the fresh snow, and the steep slopes, we worked up a good sweat. We arrived just as it got dark and Dr Kampe, the meteorologist, as well as Herrn Hennemann, the rocket specialist, were expecting us. The two of them had already familiarised themselves with the local wind and weather conditions.

In the early hours of the morning, we set off to inspect the intended landing site. The boundaries of the area had already been marked and measured 20 by 40 metres (65.6 by 131.2ft), dropping off sharply about 100m (328ft) beyond the landing field. I thoroughly inspected each centimetre of ground, from the intended touchdown zone, marked by a red landing T, all the way to the precipice. Satisfied with my inspection, I climbed down to Judenburg, and drove back to Zeltweg. The following day, at around noon, Karl Schieferstein towed me from Zeltweg to the Zirbitzkogel with a Ju 52. There was high pressure and a nearly clear sky, requiring us to fly several turns in order to reach 1,000m (3, 281ft) overhead our intended landing point.

Releasing the tow without hesitation, I steered the cargo glider towards the landing field, and pressed the button to deploy the large brake 'chute. There was the familiar shudder, and the *DFS* 230 rapidly lost speed. By pushing the nose down, I was quickly able to stabilise my approach, and with an angle of about 50°, and a final speed of 140-150km/h (87 to 93.2mph), I tracked straight towards the landing spot. From previous experience I knew that I had to aim about 20-70m (65.6 to 229.6ft) short of the touch-down point,

The last stage of the approach to Zirbitzkogel.

depending on the angle of the approach. I had on an excellent pair of snow glasses and was, therefore, able to see the surface of the snow very well. There was no blinding glare or distortion during approach and, while plunging towards the landing T, I recognised a few people standing in the deep snow nearby, creating an additional landing reference. As practised numerous times before, I recovered the aircraft just prior to landing by fully deflecting the elevator up and touching down with the skid precisely on the touchdown markings. I had released the brake 'chute beforehand, to avoid landing short. Opening the canopy I was met with loud applause. My audience comprised Professor Georgii, Dr Kampe, Mayer, Hennemann, two staff officers from the *RLM* and a few curious guests from the lodge: I have to admit my landing pleased me just as much!

After a brief welcome and a hot cup of tea, served personally by Dr. Kampe, the cargo glider was turned around on the spot, and prepared for the rocket take-off on the reciprocal course to the landing. The intended line had an average incline of 15-20°, and a total length of about 50-60m (165 to 197ft), beyond which there were some bushes and small trees before the drop into the valley, some 1,200 metres (3,937ft) below. It was clear to me that a false start on this mountain top would prove fatal. Similarly, failure of a rocket on either side would have meant the end.

I had already taken the pilot's seat while Mayer, in his usual painstaking way, carried out an inspection of the aircraft and rockets. As I strapped myself in tightly, he gave me the 'all clear,' and the spectators were asked to step aside. One brief look to the side, and I raised my hand to signal my readiness for take-off. Once again, I counted 5 – 4 – 3 – 2 – 1 – 0 – Ignition and, with the rockets roaring, I slid down the slope. Coming free nicely, I picked up speed and, at an indicated air speed of 170km/h (105.6mph), pulled back on the stick, whereupon the aircraft climbed steeply into the sky at an angle of 45-50°.

The rocket assisted launch on the Zirbitzkogel.

During the final stage of the rocket burn, the thrust was uneven but it had no effect on the aircraft flying at an IAS of 170km/hr. Immediately after ignition, the aircraft had a tendency to rear up but, by controlling the elevator, this was effectively overcome. The rockets, having burned out, abruptly quit after thirty seconds, and I flew in the direction of Zeltweg in a smooth glide, arriving overhead the field at 400m (1,312ft), and landing near the parked Ju 52. The glide ratio was 1:18, and a second landing, with subsequent take-off, was performed the next day. For all involved, especially the Kracht Institute, this trial was a great success. However, I have never discovered if this method of landing and taking off in the mountains was ever put to practical use by the forces.

Short Field Landings with Brake-'chute and Retro-rockets

It was obvious that rockets could be used not only to launch cargo gliders but also, by reversing their thrust, to shorten a landing run. Hermann Zitter, from the Stamer Institute, was the first to perform a research flight using this method. It was fascinating to see how the cargo glider, after release from the tow aircraft at an altitude of 1,000m (3, 281ft), and with a fully deployed brake-'chute, descended in a steep dive towards the landing site (sometimes at an angle of up to 80° nose down). Recovery was performed immediately above ground level and, following a short burst of the retro-rocket, the aircraft would come to an almost immediate standstill. A fully laden cargo glider could be stopped after only 9 metres (29.5ft) of ground run! This combined brake-landing-system was to prove extremely precise.

The braking retro-rockets fitted in the nose of a DFS 230.

A further tactical requirement was to put up a smoke screen around the aircraft after landing, in order to obscure visibility. For this purpose, a large number of so-called 'anchor-rockets' were attached to the nose of the cargo glider, and ignited electrically. They added to the retro-rockets' deceleration, and also emitted a large cloud of white smoke which, for a short time, completely enveloped the aircraft. This period when the glider was obscured was to be used by the troops, who were being transported in the cargo glider, to evacuate the aircraft and deploy. At Peenemünde, I was able to successfully demonstrate this procedure to a committee of military experts during an exercise which simulated an operational mission.

Because of the success with gliders, this technique was soon extended to powered aircraft. Once, whilst at Rechlin, I demonstrated how, by using a brake-chute, a Ju 52 could be landed from relatively high altitude on the shortest runway at the smallest of airfields. After the war, the use of brake 'chutes was extensively introduced to international aviation, especially in the military sector.

Using the braking rockets engulfed the glider in smoke as required.

Unsuccessful Rocket-jump across the Danube

On 15th April,1941, I was tasked with a demonstration to the General Staff. I was to make a rocket assisted 'jump' across the Danube, near Straubing, with a *DFS* 230 cargo glider, fully laden with ballast. This was to demonstrate that it was possible to launch a fully loaded cargo glider from cover, right across the river, land on the other side and establish a bridgehead. On the morning prior to the demonstration, I flew the *DFS* 230 (**KG+BT**) to the take-off point. I was towed from Ainring by a He 46, and landed on the south-west bank of the Danube. Rocket-Mayer sat in the cargo glider with me, his support crew having gone ahead by road. All the interested military parties, as well as Professor Georgii, Stamer, Kracht and Doctor Hucke from the *DFS*, stood on the north side of the river. Communication was only possible by the use of megaphones, since the Danube was very wide at this point.

The support team manoeuvred the cargo glider into the take-off position and, after a brief consultation with Mayer, I had the aircraft aligned parallel with the Danube, so that I would not fall into the cold waters of the river if the rockets failed. The spectators on the north side were already getting impatient, and calling across: 'Are you ready?' Sure, I was ready, concentrating on the task before me, one last inspection of the ignition system, and was given the go-ahead. Pulling the harness even tighter and pressing my arms and head backwards into the rests, I raised my left arm to signal that I was ready – 5 – 4 – 3 – 2 – 1 – 0 – Ignition. There was a deafening cracking and banging, and dust, mixed with dry particles from the meadow, whirled up all around. Then parts of the aircraft started flying through the air, and I was first hanging head-down in my seat straps then, shortly after, the other way up. I was totally disorientated and the cargo glider, or rather, what was left of it, cavorted about in a crazy dance from Hell which seemed to last an eternity (it was actually only 30 seconds!). Eventually all was quiet; not a sound was to be heard. I was hanging in my harness, laying on the left side, and the aircraft was a complete write-off. The left wing was missing completely, the right one had lost its outer third, and the tail had been partially broken away.

Sounds of screaming and loud questions came from the other bank of the river: 'What's going on? Did anything happen to Klöckner? What's happened?'. I was able to free myself from the wreckage, and stood next to the sad remains of my glider, dusting off my flight suit. I had suffered no injuries, not even a graze but, despite that, I was quite shocked. Once again my Guardian Angel had spread his wings over me.

After a short period of speechlessness, I was myself again. From the bottom of my heart, I roundly and loudly cursed the damnable electrical ignition system. Ever since I had witnessed its failures on the test stand, I had taken the ignition system with a 'pinch of salt'. And wasn't it typical that it should choose a demonstration to the General Staff to show how badly it could work? They seemed even more disappointed than the Heads of the Institute, and solemnly filed away as the support crew reluctantly gathered the debris.

What had actually happened? The rockets on the right side had ignited correctly, but not those on the left. The demonstration was over, the bridgehead had not been established, and the *DFS* had lost a battle. There was a Fieseler *Storch* standing in the meadow: I still don't know who left it there, but I went straight over, got in, and flew straight back to Ainring.

The Parachute – our Life Saver

On 19th May, 1942, I once again sat in a cargo glider

(**NC+SE**). My task was the evaluation of a newly developed multi-stage ignition system for solid fuel rockets. This system was to be developed to enable the pilot to ignite additional pairs of rockets, following the burn-out of the previous set, providing four 'burns' in succession. The theorists who had masterminded this idea expected a gain in altitude of 400 – 500 metres (1,312 to 1,641ft) using rockets alone. For my reassurance, and as proof of his confidence, the head of the trial, *Herr* Mayer, came and sat behind me. A He 46 towed us up to an altitude of nearly 4,000m (13,123ft), and we were set to burn off four pairs of rockets in succession, expecting to gain additional altitude with each stage. At the initial briefing I had demanded a release altitude of 4,000m to give us the best chance of survival in case of failure, given that my already shaky faith in the electronic ignition system had been more than slightly dented by previous experience. Before take-off, the ignition specialist swore blind that everything was in order and nothing could go wrong. On top of that, he pointed to the fact that Mayer was also in the aircraft, although I didn't find this overly comforting.

After reaching the designated altitude, I released the tow and counted 5 – 4 – 3 – 2 – 1 – 0 – Ignition, and then calamity took its course. I had hardly touched the button, igniting the first set of rockets, when I hit my head violently on the right hand side of the canopy. The usual deafening banging and hissing began again, and the cargo glider was forced brutally into a left hand turn which I was unable to counter or control. Seconds later, a piece of the right wing broke off, and the aircraft went into a flat spin with everything silent. All the rockets had fired on the right hand side and had now burned out, but not a single one had fired on the left, and all attempts to stop the spin were in vain. I shouted to Mayer: 'Get ready. We have to get out!', and opened the canopy, which immediately blew away, making a terrible racket. Since Mayer was sitting behind me, I had to bale out first for him to follow. I attempted to get overboard as quickly as possible but failed, due to the high centrifugal force of the spinning glider pinning me against the side. My intention was to get out of the aircraft on the left hand side as usual but, each time I tried, I was pushed back with tremendous force. Eventually, I realised that I should try the right-hand side, in order to take advantage of the forces of the spin and get clear of the aircraft. Still crouched down, with my feet in the recessed seat, I turned around, stood up, and pushed away, using the left

189

side-wall as a step. In an instant, I was out head first and on my back, but clear of the aircraft.

As I tumbled downwards, I saw heaven and earth appear before my eyes in rapid succession. It was only when I spread my arms and legs that the tumbling subsided, and I stabilised in a head-down dive. Grabbing the release handle, I pulled it hard and then had another fright because I found myself holding the handle, including the release wire. I thought I had torn the manual release right out of the parachute, but this was normal, and the next moment there was a bang above my head, and I felt each and every tightly fitted harness strap bite into my body as the parachute deployed.

'Saved!', was my first thought, and then, very close to me, the cargo glider spun past and I realised Mayer had not yet baled out. Watching the tumbling craft, a horrible vision of him being unable to escape, for whatever reason, came to me. I only had a few split seconds to observe the stricken aircraft, because I was swinging back and forth on my 'chute in the wildest of pendulum movements. Each time I swung sharply to one side or the other, I thought the parachute would tip over. Again I was able to snatch a glance downward and the thought struck me: 'It's too late for Mayer now!' But, at that very instant, I saw him clear the aircraft, dragging his 'chute behind like a flag. The parachute deployed and, for a few seconds, he hung in his harness whilst the aircraft crashed to the ground and was completely destroyed. The next moment, Mayer followed, and disappeared up to his waist in the soft boggy ground. I was able to observe this spectacle clearly from an altitude of 200m (656ft), but had to give my attention to ways in which I might soften my own landing, as the earth was rushing up to meet me. I was still swinging like a pendulum when my knees struck the bank of a dry ditch on the moor, and I felt a sharp pain in my back as I fell into the ditch. I lay there while the parachute collapsed over me, thinking to myself again: 'God bless you, my Guardian Angel!'

In the hospital at Bad Reichenhall, the doctor's diagnosis showed I had chipped the fourth lumbar vertebra, and I was discharged from hospital into the caring hands of my wife. Eight days later I was sitting in a Ju 52 again. Mayer had escaped the aircraft at practically the last second. He had also initiated his escape by attempting to get out on the 'inside' until he, too, realised it was impossible. It had taken me from 4,000m (13,123ft) down to 800m (2,625ft) to escape, whilst

Mayer had got out at about 150m (492ft) above ground level – and lived to tell the tale!

After that, I performed another fifty or more trial flights using rockets, but never lost my suspicion of the electronic ignition system.

Crash During Drag 'Chute Trials

A new drag 'chute, of the strap or band type, was to be flight tested on a heavily loaded *DFS* 230 at Nellingen airfield, near Stuttgart. The trial team were: Paul Stämmler, as the tow pilot with his He 46 and, as a specialist engineer, *Dipl.-Ing.* Knacke. I was the cargo glider pilot because of my experience, not only on the *DFS* 230, but on all types of different aircraft. We had already found that, after deploying these airborne drag 'chutes, approach angles of up to 85°, nose down, could be achieved. The trial flights at Nellingen were to test the new band type brake 'chute, up to the maximum take-off weight of the *DFS* 230. This project enjoyed the highest priority, and was classified *Strenget Geheim* (Top Secret). We were told that much depended on a positive outcome, but it was not until much later that we found out what its practical use was to be.

A few flights without cargo revealed that the band type 'chute, with its comparative lack of resistance to the air flow, had a positive stabilising effect on the flight path. Step by step, the load was increased, with the addition in weight in units of 100kg (220lbs), composed of sand bags, and each flight path and every dive angle was measured and noted. A prerequisite was that the 'chute was always to be triggered at the same point along our track, at the same altitude, and at the maximum safe speed. The values and data thus collected enabled us to plot a chart which would enable the pilot to determine the distance from touch-down at a given altitude, where to open the drag 'chute, and how much to allow for the wind factor.

The glider had a two-wheeled, detachable, undercarriage, weighing more than 75kg (165lbs), which was re-attached following landing. The drag 'chute was mounted, like a lace package, a good way down the rear fuselage of the glider. The pilot was able to deploy the 'chute by pulling a handle in the cockpit, after release from the tow aircraft. The glider then slowed substantially, and went into a dive. Naturally, there was also a means of jettisoning the drag 'chute from the glider. Casting-off from the tow aircraft, and release of the tow line, was performed by pulling a tow-coupling release handle. As we prepared for the next flight in the sequence, the last 100kg (220lbs) of ballast were added to the load, and the glider prepared for flight. Obviously, the ground-run increased with the addition of every 100kg, and this was why I made some last minute arrangements with Paul Stämmler. The *DFS* 230 then had a take-off weight of 1,900kg (4,180lbs).

The take-off went as usual, the roll was fairly long, but this was expected, and most of the runway had been used up by the time I cleared the ground and was able to pull the gear release handle. Then, unexpectedly, the gear dropped away to the ground but bounced up again, much higher than usual, striking the underside of the glider. Although it did not damage the drag 'chute pack, it became entangled in the rigging lines. To my horror, the glider became acutely unstable, although I had no idea why. It reared up, then immediately dropped its nose into a steep dive, while the tow aircraft performed similarly violent pitching movements. I mistakenly tried to release the tow by pulling on the release handle for the drag 'chute, using brute force, but nothing happened. The glider was now beginning to yaw around the vertical axis and Paul started a gentle left turn, towing me in the direction of the airfield. The glider did not react at all to my control inputs and then there was a short, sharp jerk as the tow line parted. Again to my horror, I saw that the altimeter showed a fraction less than 100m (328ft), and I was barely able to keep the aircraft level. The elevator was totally unresponsive, and then the aircraft suddenly reared up as if it were trying to stand on its hind legs, then dropped its nose in a stall and plunged towards the ground.

Only seconds to the end of this world! In those few seconds, my whole life seemed to pass before my eyes as I pushed and pulled all the way to the stops, but with no response from my rogue aircraft. Nearly vertical, we dived towards an enormous tree, and the last conscious experience I had was hearing terrible noises as we crashed into it. After lying unconscious in the medical station on the airfield for more than three hours, I was reported as asking what the firemen were doing there, although only a doctor and the nurse were present. I had, apparently, noticed the fire brigade three hours earlier, as they cut me out of the wreckage, and was hallucinating. Three days later, my thinking returned to some semblance of normal, following severe concussion, and I was nursing a 20 cm (8.9 in) split in my scalp and a nose broken at the bridge. My companion had struck the measuring apparatus in the front of the glider with his face and was seriously hurt, but we had survived against all odds. Considering the circumstances, it wasn't so bad!

Despite the accident on the last flight, the trial was rated a success, and we later found out what had made these landing trials so secret: Benito Mussolini was rescued, using this very technique. Several fully manned cargo gliders, led by Otto Skorzeny, landed on the Gran Sasso Massif, using the tiny area in front of the building where the dictator was being held.

Parachute Trials

I already had personal experience which convinced me that we could not do without the parachute as a life saver. However, its safe use was only guaranteed up to the oxygen border line, above which special precautions had to be taken. In order to enable the pilot to free-fall through the higher altitudes, which offered little oxygen, to the comparatively safe levels around 4,000m (13,123ft), an automatic parachute release system had been invented and required testing. With this type of barometrically actuated parachute, a crew member would be able to bale out of an aircraft at very high altitude, and free-fall down, even unconscious, with the parachute being opened automatically. The first parachutes using this equipment were tested by strapping them to dummies, the size and weight of a man, then dropping them from great heights.

A somewhat macabre incident occurred during one of these trials when a dummy was dropped from a Do 17 at an altitude of 7,000m (22,966ft). The 'chute was to be released between 1,000 and 800m (3,281 and 2,625ft) above ground, but it failed and the dummy impacted the ground on a moor, close to where some people were working. The aircraft had not even landed before a 'phone call was received at Flight Operations, informing them that a man, with a parachute still strapped to his back, had apparently just fallen to his death on the Ainringer Moor. 'And,' said the caller, a woman, 'his arse, wearing *Lederhosen*, is still sticking out of the ground!' The rescue team arrived at the scene, where a large crowd had gathered in awkward silence. They all felt deeply for the 'deceased' and, indeed, the rear, covered with leather, was just to be seen above the surface. The 'chute pack itself had burst open upon impact and deployed, billowing about in the wind.

One of the men in the rescue team got a pick-axe, and swung it right through the aforesaid *Lederhosen* in order to be able to pull the dummy out of the moor. At that moment, an elderly woman cried: 'You desecraters!', and began beseeching someone to fetch the priest. It took some persuading to calm her down, and convince her that it was only a dummy. (These test dummies did have thick leather padding on their backsides in order to absorb the shock of the opening parachute.)

Numerous dummy releases and laboratory tests resulted in a different solution, in that a parachute with an integral oxygen system was invented. It consisted of a high quality steel pipe by which the parachutist was provided with oxygen during descent.

A Parachute Jump

During a company sports day at the *DFS*, I was asked to drop our highly respected parachute service man, 'Fips' Hönig, by parachute. We trusted him implicitly as our officially licensed parachute packer and, quite in keeping with this, he felt he had to demonstrate that the flying personnel could rely on the 'chutes which he had packed. So, during this sports day, he took the opportunity to do one of his self-imposed demonstration jumps. We climbed into a Klemm 35, with him sitting in the front, and myself in the rear seat. We had arranged that I would over-fly the field from east to west at 1,000 metres (3,281ft), maintaining a reduced speed for the drop. Fips had climbed out of his seat, and was sitting near the trailing edge of the wing, hanging onto the side of my cockpit. From time to time he looked down, and his face turned paler each time. At the point he was to jump, he signalled for me to go around and make a new approach. I couldn't see why, but thought he must know best.

The same thing happened again on the second approach, and it became clear that, for whatever reason, he was scared stiff. I thought about what I might do to help bolster his morale as we made the third approach. He, in the meantime, had crouched down on the wing, unable to move, clinging to the edge of my cockpit. As we approached the jump-point for the third time, he still showed no sign of leaving unaided, and we had already reached the field boundary. I made my decision, and banged my fist down on his fingers as they gripped the cockpit edge. Taken completely by surprise, he let go and fell off the trailing edge of the wing into the abyss. The 'chute opened, and Fips descended smoothly, managing to guide himself right onto the chalked-out drop zone on the sports field. After I had landed, he rushed over to say how pleased he was that I had, in a rough and ready way, helped him to conquer his fear.

By-Products of Flight Trials – Snow Ski Trials

During the first winter of the war, a trial of high priority arose from the requirement to land, and launch, aircraft on skis. The first trial aircraft were the Go 145, Hs 126 and the Fi 156 *Storch*. Taking off, flying, and landing with the skis created no problems: however, the fluctuations in the weather, and the inconsistency of the snow did. One of the greatest problems was that the skis froze to the surface of the snow, or to the frozen ground after the aircraft had been parked. The greater the aircraft weight, the more firmly the skis stuck. The engineers drew a beautiful diagram which showed the correlation between pressure on the skis, air and snow temperature, and the corresponding coefficient of friction. With this we knew a lot about the adhesive properties of snow under the aircraft skis, but when we attempted to taxi out of the parking position the machine would stand as if bolted to the ground; nothing would move it, even the application of full power. The trouble started at temperatures above 0°C (32°F), when the thin layer of water formed by the skis sliding across the snow froze when the aircraft came to rest. The aircraft was then, to all intents and purposes, glued to the ground.

Many ideas had been tried in order to tackle this problem, including the invention of a ski heater, which did nothing to help. Another attempt involved the installation of a number of small explosive charges under the skis. When the pilot wanted to taxi out, he selected full power and detonated the charges, the resulting low level tremor freeing the aircraft. Although this method proved successful, it was far too complicated. The simplest solution was a vibrating plate invented by Dr. Ratzke. It was simply screwed to the top of the skid, and gave a burst of vibration when electrical current was passed through it. This cleared the skis every time: I actually had the opportunity to try this system on a He 111 at Posen in March 1942 and, indeed, it worked perfectly.

Large Radio-Controlled Model Aircraft

Trials which did not require a test pilot to fly, but often to observe only, were the tests of large, unmanned, model aircraft.

These models had wing spans of several metres, were radio controlled, and driven by large model engines. They were intended for use by the military for low level reconnaissance, using on-board cameras. These types of 'planes were also used as airborne targets (drones) during practice firing by anti-aircraft units. Later, the further development of these large model aircraft by German engineers in the USA was based on the knowledge acquired at the *DFS*.

Das Personen-Abwurfgeräte (PAG) (Personnel Dropping Device)

The so-called *PAG* was also part of the trials programme of the *DFS*. This craft came in different sizes, with a maximum capacity of three persons. By using it, agents were to be dropped behind enemy lines, on land or in water. It was made of plywood, and was of hollow construction. Designed to be carried in the bomb bay of an aircraft, it was attached to the bomb callipers. The intention was that these *PAGs* were to be released over the target area, and descend on four parachutes with a calculated sink rate of 5 – 6 m/sec (16.4 to 19.7ft/sec – 984ft/min to 1,182ft/min). The one designed to land in water had special equipment, including an easily released hatch, and an electrically driven propeller to enable passengers to reach the shore.

During flight, the passengers lay face down in the direction of flight, looking down through an acrylic window. After release, the cylinder descended in the vertical, with its

The motorised PAG, underway with Paul Stamer and Paul Kiefel aboard.

passengers standing upright during landing. The cylindrically shaped body of the *PAG* had a crumple zone which substantially absorbed the impact energy. The occupants were strapped tightly into harnesses to help mitigate any residual effect. It was not within the scope of the *DFS* to perform test drops with the *PAG* using *DFS* personnel: its task was only to devise an operational transport and release system. The dropping of personnel was to be performed by experts, drawn from a special unit, but I had the opportunity to observe one of these releases as pilot of an observation and camera aircraft. Admittedly, I thought I was a tough guy at that time, but I probably would not have had the courage to be dropped in one of those contraptions! From the very first drawing to the completion of trials of the first thirty craft took the *DFS* just three weeks. Production was increased to 200 *PAG*s a month, with the *DFS* in charge. Some parts of the production line were dispersed to a factory in Freilassing.

The packed parachute in the tail of the PAG.

Test of Dr. Sänger's Ram Jet Engine

The airfields at Hörsching and Neuburg / Donau were working fields for the *DFS*. They had hard paved runways, and so trials requiring long runways and open countryside were performed there. Hörsching was only 110km (68.4 miles) away from Ainring, and could be reached in only half an hour by air, making it the preferred test area when Ainring airfield proved too small. In September, 1942, Dr. Sänger and his team were transfered to Hörsching. The *RLM* was not really interested in Dr. Sänger's ram jet engine project, because its development was taking up too much time, and the fuel consumption of the engine was very high. The first practical trials had been undertaken by *Kapitän* Paul Spremberg at Fassberg airfield, examining the different sizes and diameters of jet pipes, using a high temperature jet engine. Dr. Sänger fell back on a French patented design, dated 1908, which was the brainchild of René Lorin. He had developed a pipe which he called a 'ram jet engine', which operated as air entered freely at the front, and was compressed in an area at the centre. Fuel was then injected and ignited, and exited the rear end of the pipe at high temperature (near 2,000°C, approximately 3,632°F) and velocity. *Prof.* Georgii had managed to convince the heads of the trials section to reactivate the test programme at Hörsching. Flight implementation was to be my responsibility.

The test engine was mounted on the back of the fuselage of a Do 217 E2, with the fuel supplied from a tank inside the aircraft. It had been calculated that the motor would develop an equivalent of 20,000hp at maximum speed and full thrust. The tube itself had an overall length of 10.63m (34.88ft), a diameter of 1.5m (4.92ft) at the combustion chamber, and a total weight of 2.5 metric tonnes. On 16th September, 1943, together with Peter Kaffenberger, an experienced flight mechanic, I flew the Do 217 E2, under its own conventional power, from Ainring to Hörsching. As expected, the take-off run had increased due to the installation of the ram jet. The speed for lift-off had also increased from 140km/h to 170km/h (86.99 to105.63mph), and the cruise speed had decreased from 440km/h to 320km/h (273.4 to 198.84). Turns, using a maximum bank of only 40-45°, were possible if a little sluggish. Take-off for the first 'hot' flight was performed on 21st September, and we climbed to an altitude of 3,000m (9,843ft) for safety. Dr. Sänger took up position on the lower flight deck, and all crew members were connected by intercom. At the scheduled altitude of 3,000m we levelled-out at a speed of 320km/h (273.4mph). Since we had no idea what the pitching moment at the time of ignition would be, we thought this would be a safe range.

With the ignition of the engine, there was a muffled, growling bang and at the same instant I felt a firm push on my back. The jet was obviously providing a fair measure of propulsion , and I was surprised to note how small the pitching moment was; I was, in fact, able to compensate by using elevator trim only. Another, less positive effect I noticed during this first 'hot test run', was an uncomfortable vibration which was easily discernible, even in the control column. These vibrations could, I felt, endanger the stability of the aircraft and its controls.

The ram jet was flown with regular fuels of different mixture ratios. A new ignition system was tested and proved suitable during the trials. Using full thrust, the speed was increased to 400km/h (248.55mph) in level flight, and a second flight that afternoon ended similarly to the first. With every flight, we increased the speed by adopting a steeper flight path. This showed a direct link between an increase in thrust and an increase in speed. However, again, as the speed increased, so did the vibrations caused by the ram jet. We soon knew exactly where they came from: the rear exhaust section of the jet pipe. The frequency of these vibrations, caused by the hot gas jet, could have been changed by installing variable nozzles on the intake and exhaust end of the diffuser, thus eliminating the fault, but the lack of time forced us to do without any modification.

After a break of nearly two weeks, the next take-off was planned, and this time the data collecting phase was to start at an altitude of 7,000m (22,966ft), and at a cruising speed of 720km/h

The Sänger ram jet engine mounted on top of a Do 217 E2, in a dive at 720km/h (447.4mph) on 7th October 1943.

(447.4mph) – the V max (maximum permissible speed) of the Do 217 E2. I rang up Egon Fath and Paul Spremberg at Dornier to gather information on how the Do 217 behaved at a speed of 720km/h. Basically, all I learned was that exceeding this speed, even without external stores, would be very dangerous. There was only one thing left for me to do; find out for myself.

The 4th October was to see my take-off into the unknown. Despite being heavily loaded, the aircraft climbed nicely all the way to 7,000m (22,966ft) and, after confirming contact with all the stations involved, I gave the order for ignition. With the engine burning, and having taken all the measurements prescribed in the programme, I transmitted: 'Attention, beginning to increase the angle of descent, commencing a shallow dive.' I pushed the nose down easily and she rapidly increased speed, the pitch of the propellers continually increasing. The higher the speed of the aircraft, the more thrust came from the ram jet. Kaffenberger had continually to trim nose up, as all my attention was focused on the intended top speed of 720km/h and the increasing nose down moment. The tendency to pitch down increased in such a way that it was soon no longer possible to rectify it with trim. At an IAS of 720km/h, the aircraft started to shake and rattle badly – time to reduce speed and recover!

Recovery from this attitude, nearly 50° nose low, created a problem, since the ram jet could not be completely shut down. The two engines of the Dornier had been throttled back at the initiation of the dive, and with Kaffenberger's help (I had had the foresight to have a special harness made for him) we were able to pull the aeroplane out of the dive and level off, using both elevator and maximum trim inputs. The recovery radius was enormous, and I was very glad that the first high speed data collection run was over.

Having reached the field, I entered the downwind leg approximately 100m north of the runway and continued onto base and finals as usual. Approximately 200m (656ft) from the threshold of the runway, and at a height of 50m (164ft), I noticed we were coming in short, due to the heavy jet engine on top of the Do 217. I quickly pushed the throttles forward in order to stretch the glide, and then it happened. The right engine picked up immediately, but the left one did not even twitch. This induced a severe yaw to the left and, within seconds, the heading had changed by 50° away from the runway. Only a steep turn could have brought us back, but at that height, and with minimum speed, it would have surely been the end of us all. There was only one thing for it, a belly landing outside the field boundary. 'Gear up!' I shouted to Kaffenberger, then 'Flaps full down!' At that moment the aircraft gained a bit of lift, but then we touched the ground. Because the Do 217 E2 had a full-vision cockpit, the lower acrylic windows were smashed, and piles of dirt were ploughed into the aircraft. Dr. Sänger was in it up to his knees, and was unable to free himself, and I too had trouble freeing my feet from the soil. We came to a halt just 20m (65.6ft) away from a barn in the field.

The airfield fire crew arrived very quickly at the scene of the crash and, after a short while, we were all standing quietly next to the aircraft, completely unhurt. Finally, Dr. Sänger broke the silence: shaking my hand vigorously, he said: 'Thanks to you, we are alive!' A few days later I was told that the throttle linkage had broken off, due to the effect of the exhaust gas vibrations, something I had pointed out right after the very first 'hot flight'. I had made similar observations – without the dramatic crash landing – during the trials with the Argus Schmidt jet engine. The pulsating vibrations caused by this engine went through the aircraft at a frequency of 50 Hz, painfully affecting the wrists.

In March,1944, the trials were resumed, and between then and the end of August, I performed thirty-three test flights at speeds ranging from 320 to 720km/h (198 to 447mph). From September onward, further trials were prohibited due to the lack of fuel. From then on, Dr. Sänger performed his tests and trials using models with blowers in wind tunnels, utilising smoke or water channels.

Dr. Sänger and Irene Bredt came to visit from time to time, and stayed with my wife and me as our guests. With us they could indulge themselves, because we had good connections with a farmer, and always had a plentiful supply of food. As a scientist, Dr. Sänger was not entitled to any additional rations. Once, during a walk, he told me that the time would come when people would fly into space and would land on the moon, and that all this would be achieved using rockets. I have to admit that I looked at him in astonishment, thinking he had lost his mind. He also mentioned an engine which would one day enable mankind to travel at the speed of light: he called it the 'ion engine'. He was a fascinating man to listen to and, considering how technology has developed, years ahead of his time.

First Tests of the 'Argus-Tube'

As is clear from the title: *Deutschen Forschungsanstalt für Segelflug* (German Institute for Gliding Research – *'DFS'*), its main interest was scientific research in the field of gliding. During the war, some unusual duties replaced gliding, or were added to the everyday tasks. One of these additional jobs was to conduct the glide trials of aircraft for which the engines had not been fully developed. As mentioned earlier, for me this meant performing some dangerous tows in the *'Natter'*, together with two dozen test gliding flights on the Me 328, being towed up to altitude by a He 111 and then released. These improvised trials, with only the airframe of the Me 328, had obviously impressed someone, because I was tasked with the flight tests of the intended engines, twin Argus-tubes. This was an engine with 150kg (330lbs) of thrust designed to propel unmanned craft and glide-bombs (V1 for instance). It was a Pulse Jet Engine, not much more than a tube on the outside with a butterfly shutter valve on the front end. Thus it was also called the *'Argus – Rohr'* (Argus stovepipe). Ram air entered the combustion chamber through the butterfly valves, where fuel was injected as the shutter at the front closed. Sealed at one end, the mixture was then ignited and the hot exhaust gases left the rear of the tube at high velocity, generating thrust. The flaps opened and closed, or pulsed, at a rate of approximately 50 Hz. The flight trials of these Argus-tubes were to be my duty, with the first engines attached to a *DFS* 230. These engines had to be started

The Argus-Schmidt pulse jet, mounted under the wing of a DFS 230.

on the ground, by blowing compressed air into the front end, to replace the missing ram air. (This was why the V1 had to be catapult launched from the ground or dropped from an aircraft in flight). In the early stages of the trials, the engines frequently flamed-out when the speed dropped too low or, sometimes, when they were throttled back.

The test configuration was a *DFS* 230 which had two Argus-tubes installed under its wings and was towed up to an altitude of 1,000m. With the throttle in the start position, fuel was injected into the combustion chamber and, simultaneously, the ignition was switched on. This was followed by a muffled bang, and a noticeable push forward. The thrust was controlled by a throttle: however, the thrust available reduced markedly when the speed decreased during the climb. With increased speed the thrust increased proportionally (because of the increased ram-effect).

After completion of the first flights using jet engine thrust, I noticed that my right wrist was painful. The reason for this was soon discovered: the vibration frequency of the hot gas section was, as mentioned before, 50 Hz, and the steel framework of the aircraft developed sympathetic vibrations which were transmitted to the wrist, via the stick. Perhaps it seems a trivial condition, but for a while I had to stop flying because my wrist was so painful that I could not control the aircraft properly. During my enforced lay-off, other pilots of the *DFS* flew trials with the Argus-tube, and I remember one case where the rear door of the aircraft was suddenly torn from its hinges due to the vibrations. An improved version of this type of engine was later installed in the V 1.

About 170 to 180 V1s were equipped with pilots' seats, the conversion being intended for manned operations, and had the code name '*Reichenberg*'. These manned missiles were to be carried close to the target area, then released by the pilot and flown to the target. It was up to the pilot whether he stayed with the V1 and steered it all the way to the target, or baled out and saved himself by parachute. In January, 1945, I was present at Rechlin-Lärz when trial and training flights were being performed for this operation. To my knowledge, none of these manned V1's were ever used in action: however, during landings following training flights, several accidents occurred and the pilots suffered severe burns. The fuel tanks were very basic, only intended for short flights, and every landing with this craft on its skids was a hard one, causing the tanks to leak fuel which would immediately ignite.

First Flight Trial with the Me 328

In the middle of 1942, I was requested to help in the development of a new pilot seat in the trial workshops of the *DFS* at Ainring. A new flying machine was being built under the strictest secrecy, and was introduced to me as P 1079. I was to make recommendations for changes, and at that time I did not know that this machine would become the Me 328. It was in the final stages of development, and I was to take over the flight trials. No one seemed to know, or perhaps wanted to tell me, the envisaged role for this aeroplane. Only after I insisted did Felix Kracht, the Head of the Institute of Aircraft Construction, tell me about the future use of these *Sperrholzbombers* (plywood bombers). The Me 328 was being designed as a throw-away aircraft, inexpensive and generating minimal production cost and time. The design specified a cylindrical fuselage, 6.8 metres (22.3ft) long, with a wing span of 6.4metres (21ft), and a wing area of $7.5m^2$ (80.7 sq.ft). The ailerons were only 10cm (3.93 in) deep, requiring the machine to travel relatively fast in order to be effective. I was told it was to be a multi-role aircraft. For instance, it could be a bomber or, by use of the *Mistel* (after mistletoe – the tree parasite) system, as a parasite-fighter, flying into enemy bomber formations and being used as an airborne bomb. The pilot again had the option to bale out before hitting the target.

The Argus-Schmidt pulse engines were to be used as the propulsion system, and the Me 328 was launched on a two wheel carriage, jettisoned after lift-off. Landing was made on an unsprung skid. At the end of July, the first prototype was ready to fly, and Kurt Oppitz and I flew a He 111 to Hörsching to complete preparations for the first launch. The Heinkel we flew was to tow the airframe of the Me 328 aloft, because the engines were not yet ready. The first flight test was to be performed by being towed up to altitude, released and gliding the Me 328 back to the field. I was so familiar with the seat, it felt I had already flown it for ages. It was very hot at the end of July, and three days had already gone by, hanging around and waiting. One day there was too much turbulence (thermal currents), on the next there were thunderstorms, and then the wind was too variable. To reduce the risk to myself, I had insisted on optimum conditions, and this included a comfortable temperature. I wanted peak performance from the engines of the He 111 before I would take responsibility for the launch. 'Just in case,' the administration of the *DFS*, in co-operation with Messerschmitt, had taken out a substantial flight accident insurance for me, the premium for which, I learned later, was nearly 5,000 *Reichsmark*.

On 1st August, 1942, we waited for the heat of summer to cool in the evening. I had already been sitting in the aircraft for nearly one and a half hours, with the canopy wide open when, suddenly, I felt an ominous stirring in my gut. Releasing the harness straps, I removed my parachute, climbed out of the kite, jumped off the wing, and ran. Relief! I just made it to the 'throne' in time. When I returned, everybody was laughing – *Prof*. Georgii, Caroli, the trial manager from Messerschmitt, and all the experts who always attended maiden flights.

There were about twenty people standing around as I walked over to Oppitz, who was sitting in the tow aircraft, and we made our final arrangements. He was to stay on the ground as long as possible, up to the point where he could just make it over the fence at the eastern edge of the airfield. I had grave reservations about the speed being insufficient to pull the aircraft up, and through the prop-wash of the tow.

As I climbed into the aircraft again, Prof. Georgii came over and shook my hand, wishing me a good flight. Having respect for my superior, I tried not to let him notice that his gesture did little to calm my nerves. We were ready to go, the evening had cooled off a fraction, and the He 111 was already in take-off position with its engines running. The tow line was connected, and I closed and locked the canopy. Now I was all on my own again, well almost, since I hoped my Guardian Angel was fairly close at hand. Five seconds of 'eyes closed' and I was focused on the task ahead. I raised my arm, and the signal was passed on to Oppitz via a flag. At ten minutes to eight the tow aircraft started to roll, and I was right behind. During the first part of the ground roll, I could hardly see the He 111 because of the high nose section of the Me 328 reducing forward visibility. The He 111 lifted off quite quickly and, although my speed was increasing, I was still rolling, rolling, rolling. Eventually, I noticed some response in the controls, and not a moment too soon, as Oppitz was already coming close to the edge of the field where he was required to pull up. That was when I pulled on the stick, and the Me 328 literally jumped into the air. I was not only comfortably airborne, but had gone right through the prop-wash and the wake turbulence to rise high behind my tow.

As an experienced glider pilot, I had released the gear at lift-off, and now flew along on the long tow as if it were for the umpteenth time. With a wing loading of 150kg/m² (30.66lbs/sq in), the Me 328 was easily held in a steady tow, flying at a speed of 250 to 260km/h (155.3 to 161.6mph). The controls were, surprisingly, fully effective at that speed.

From take-off, the flight went as planned, and I released at 3,000m (9,843ft). Kracht had already warned me that the aircraft might be a bit unstable in the longitudinal axis, due to the small wing span, and that was exactly how it was. At a speed of 380 to 400km/h (236.1 to 248.6mph), the smallest aileron input induced a roll. Our flight profile for the glide phase only allowed an altitude band of 2,000m (6,652ft) for data collection, and with a sink rate of 7 m/sec (1,378ft/min), I only had about four minutes to take brief notes on my knee board. A slight push forward with the stick was sufficient to increase the air speed to an IAS of 500km/h (310.7mph). I traded the excess speed for altitude, just as I did in a glider, but at a far higher speed and sink rate.

The large recovery radius surprised me. The set-up for the approach and landing had to be prepared from an altitude of 1,000m (3,281ft). I was required to reach predetermined points over the ground at certain altitudes, in order to turn onto finals with an IAS of 200km/h (124.3mph), and to aim for the grass part of the field. I passed over the hedge on the airfield boundary at a height of 1 metre (3.3ft) and set the Messerschmitt on the ground. If I ever wanted to wish something terrible on someone, I would condemn them to eternal landings at 170km/h (105.6mph) on a skid with no suspension, on a dried out, bone hard, bumpy grass runway – I cried out in pain as I felt the jarring through my whole spine.

Me 328 in Mistelschlepp. Alternating as pilot of both aircraft was Gretchen Ziegler from the Test Centre at Rechlin.

The clock showed eight-fifteen and the earth had me back. One minute later, Oppitz landed with the tow aircraft. Then I did not mind the handshakes at all.

In all I made twenty-four flights on this, and the next prototype, again without engines, some using the *Mistel* System. Gretchen Ziegler made several more trial flights with the Argus-Schmidt-Tubes mounted on a *DFS* 230. Eventually, due to insufficient thrust being produced by the proposed engines, the Me 328 project was finally cancelled.

Luftkoppelung und Luftbetankung – Inflight Coupling and Inflight Refuelling

The department of aircraft equipment of the *DFS* had developed a system to link and release aircraft in the air. This was a completely new and innovative idea which was to demand ingenious solutions to difficult problems before it could become a practical reality, requiring the likes of Felix Kracht to be consulted from time to time during the trial programme. The tow line, which was always wobbling along in the slipstream of the tow aircraft, created the main problem with its own instability.

After lengthy trials, also involving the department for flight tests, they succeeded in developing a triangular-shaped device which was attached to the end of the line. After the attachment of this device, the line stabilised nicely in the turbulent air behind the tow aircraft. I took part in this airborne linkup operation, performing numerous trial flights. A Ju 52 flew ahead, unreeling a line from a rig in the tail section, to a length of 60 to 80m (196.9 to 262.5ft). The stabilising device on the end of the line looked like a funnel, and I flew behind, in a twin engine Fw 58 *Weihe* (Harrier), closing in on it. The Fw 58 was equipped with a telescopic rod, installed in the nose, and on the tip of this rod there was a barb type arrangement. The relatively short rod had to be flown in as close as possible to the funnel and, at the optimum moment, a button was pressed and a small, spring-loaded, device shot out of the tip of the rod, triggering itself as it entered the funnel, and the coupling was complete. To release, you had to pull on a Bowden cable control, and the attachment mechanism withdrew its locking barb, slipped the tow, and left the two aircraft to fly their own ways. This required precise flying in order to link up at the first attempt; more than one propeller had been irreparably damaged during this trial series, especially when they came in contact with the funnel while flying in turbulence.

This method of inflight linkup also helped bring about inflight refuelling. After the War, the technique was developed into air-to-air refuelling, now used routinely by military forces worldwide. All this owes its foundation to work such as that described above in those few years at institutions like the *DFS*. However, once the airborne link-up and release had proven feasible, there were those who sought to develop its potential too far. Some imaginative heads filled with fantasies, coming up with such ideas, for instance, as sending bombers to the US towing their own fighter escort! After having defended the bombers against the enemy, the fighters would hook up again and be taken back to home base by the bombers...

During the trials, new tasks, techniques and procedures were added as we progressed, and new ideas were born. One of these tasks was to launch by using either a normal or short tow, and then, after lift-off, to pull the aircraft in close by means of a winch until a rigid tow could be attached.

Vom Kurz – zum Starrschlepp – From Short to Rigid Tow

For a glider to fulfil its task, it has to be taken up to a given altitude. At first, a hill or the side of a mountain sufficed; later, a tow aircraft was employed. The *DFS* researched this type of tow in all its variations. The most important aim was to reduce the distance between the towing and the towed aircraft, so that the glider pilot did not lose sight of the tug while flying in cloud. To determine the length of the shortest practical line, it was shortened in increments, down to 1.5 metres (4.92ft). With line lengths of less than 10m (32.8ft), the slightest of displacements of the towed glider in the horizontal or the vertical caused high line angles. Only an experienced pilot was able to counteract the pitching or yawing moment without overcompensating. If this was not done, the oscillation quickly increased, inducing a porpoise-like effect in the tow aircraft which could become uncontrollable. Towing with the very short line obviously increased the danger of collision.

What could be more obvious than the idea of replacing the thin tow line by a rigid rod or bar? This thought originated from Dr. Trutz Fölsche, head of the Department for Flight Equipment at the Institute. A rigid tow, 3m (9.84ft) in length, was installed in the rear of the tow plane and connected to the towed aircraft by a universal coupling. Dr. Spilger performed a power monitoring exercise which proved that the loss of performance, compared with the long tow, was insignificant. In January, 1940, one of these short tows was demonstrated at Braunschweig to the representatives of the *Generalluftzeugmeisters* (General of the Air Staff), by Karl Schieferstein and Dr. Fölsche. Even though this method improved safety when blind flying, the rigid tow was not accepted, the main reason being that the tow rig was still too heavy. However, a conversion by Weserflug, of Lemwerder, reduced it to 150kg (330lbs). Then, when Dr. Kiefel, of the Department of Flight Equipment, developed a new universal joint for the tow plane, the weight was further reduced to 66kg (145lbs). The swivel arm, which had a length of 1m (3.28ft), was fitted with an ingeniously constructed metal ball brake system. Working with Zitter and Oppitz, I performed the trials for this equipment, using first a He 111, then a Ju 52 and, finally, a Do 17, all towing *DFS* 230 gliders. These tests showed satisfactory results for the rigid tow system, which was then approved for use by the forces. Whole wings were equipped with these systems, and were able to tow in poor weather and even at night. The tailplane of the towing aircraft remained visible at all times by the pilot of the cargo glider, and he was able to adjust his horizontal attitude throughout the flight, even in strong turbulence.

A Go 242 in Starrschlepp behind a Heinkel 177.

The most crucial piece of information gathered during our trials was that if oscillations, especially pitching in the vertical, were to be avoided, the weight ratio of the towing and the towed aircraft should not be higher than 3:1. This rule of thumb was sufficient, even though the differences in wing loading of the two aircraft played a large part in the stability of the whole tow train. A further problem was created by the trim adjustment of the two aircraft. I remember that during one of these rigid tow trials, the two aircraft were trimmed in such a way that the *DFS* 230 started a loop immediately after release, and broke up. The pilot, Oppitz, was able to save himself by parachute.

At Braunschweig, they also tried to tow-launch two cargo gliders in tandem (one behind the other) using the rigid tow behind a Ju 52. They called it *Kettenschlepp* (chain tow) and during two launch trials Oppitz flew the Ju 52 tug, with Schieferstein behind him in a *DFS* 230, and Dr. Fölsche in a second '230 towed behind that. This three ship arrangement built up enormous oscillations very quickly, and the second launch ended with the crash of the 'tail end Charlie' flown by Dr. Fölsche, who had to be taken to hospital with a fractured spine.

Der Deichselschlepp – The Draw Bar Tow

The range of an aircraft is, of course, limited by the fuel it can carry. Additional external tanks can increase it, but also create more drag and consequent overall loss of performance. An aerodynamically shaped flying container, filled with fuel and towed behind the aircraft, had to be an advantage. The *DFS* was, therefore, involved in the development of the *Deichselschleppgerät* (draw-bar tow system) SG 4004. Theoretical tests, as well as practical experience, showed that less power is required to tow an airborne cargo container than to carry the load in the aircraft itself. Orders had been given to develop an unmanned, self-contained, flying cargo carrier which could be towed behind aircraft, even at relatively high speeds. Initially, the SG 4004 was used, consisting of a rectangular wooden wing with a span of 2.9m (9.51ft), and an area of 7 m^2 (75.35 sq.ft) Under this wing, a fixed undercarriage from a Kl 35 was installed, which was neither retractable nor detachable. The SG 4004 had a height of 1.2 metres (3.94ft) and a ground clearance of 1m (3.28ft). The unladen weight, complete with the 12m (39.4ft) draw bar, and including the shafts to connect it to the aircraft, was 330kg (726lbs). The special shafts were added to avoid obstruction of the field of fire from the tail gun position of the He 177. The draw bar itself was connected to the He 177 in a such a way as to enable it to swivel easily in the vertical,

Heinkel 177 towing a SG 4004A.

through approximately three metres (9.84ft). The rear section of the bar, where it was attached to the tow, was connected by a vertical bolt, allowing it to move in the horizontal plane. Roll movements were dictated by the tow aircraft.

I was assigned to the flight trials, with Peter Kaffenberg as flight mechanic, and *Ing*. Güttler as trial engineer. The flight trials were performed at Neuburg, because of its long, hard surface runway. While Kaffenberg and I were sitting in the cockpit of the He 177, Güttler was in the tail gunner's seat to both observe and film the performance of the *Deichselschleppgerät* whilst under tow. The intention was, at a later stage, to take the fuel tank mounted on the SG 4004, and open fire upon it from the tail gunner's position on the He 177, observing and filming its behaviour during the subsequent explosion.

Initially, we flew without the fuel tank, and found a lift / drag ratio of 1 : 7.4. With the installation of the fuel tank, this was reduced by 17%, to 1 : 6.1. Lift-off was achieved with an angle of incidence between the tow bar and wing chord of 9° and, via the intercom, Güttler informed us about the behaviour of the 'trailer'. From the beginning, the whole system showed very good flight characteristics. Even manoeuvres such as steep turns and rolling movements were no problem, and rudder inputs by the tow aircraft during take-off caused only minor yawing of the trailer. During the climb, cruise and descent, no negative effect of the trailer on the tow aircraft was noticed. As long as the maximum take-off weight of the trailer had not been reached, it lifted off before the tow aircraft, and only at full take-off weight did both aircraft lift off simultaneously. I was able to reach air speeds of up to 620km/h (323.1mph) during level flight, with the trailer at maximum take-off weight, without noticing any uncomfortable effects.

As mentioned, the trial programme included the task of creating conditions which could arise if the fuel container was hit by gunfire; also of jettisoning the trailer at speeds of 400km/h (248.55mph) while still three-quarters full. A simulated engine failure on one side produced no alarming results, and landing with the *Deichselschleppgerät* still connected did not create any problems on either hard or soft surface runways. Following the satisfactory completion of this trial, it was decided to develop further devices for the transport of bombs and fuel, using this principle.

The SG 5041 (VI without pulse motor and fitted with an undercarriage) fitted for rigid tow behind a Heinkel 177.

Das Sleppgerät – The Tow Device SG 5041

The boldest and largest draw bar tow system project the *DFS* was to develop was the SG 5041. This was a reconstructed V1 (without the engine), fitted with fixed landing gear, on which spats were incorporated to streamline the wheels. Total launch weight, depending on additional bomb load, was 3-5,000kg (6,600 to 11,000lbs), and flight trials were performed using the twin jet engine Arado Ar 234. January,1945, saw me picking up the Ar 234 V1 from Sagan / Lausitz. This field had already been evacuated because of the approaching front, but two brave men had waited to hand the aircraft over to me despite the approaching Russian tanks and audible rumble of artillery in the near distance. Although I had only had one introductory flight on this type at Rechlin, I managed to take off after having blown the snow off the runway by taxi-ing up and down.

All the effort was, however, to no avail because the trial ended with an accident. During the very first take-off in the Ar 234, with the SG 5041 in tow, at Neuburg airfield, a tipper

The first and the last launch for the SG 5041 using the rigid tow behind the Arado 234 jet, moments before the trial came to an end in dramatic style.

wagon filled with dirt was pushed across the end of the runway, a sign of the disorder common towards the end of the War. The Arado 234 just cleared the tipper, but it was too late for the SG 5041. It crashed into the obstacle and was completely destroyed. However, even though this was the end of the trial, it had at least meant entry into the jet age for me.

Tragschlepp – The Carry-Tow

Within the *DFS*, all imaginable methods of towing an aircraft into the air were scientifically researched, as were the different towing systems. These methods are well publicised in specialist literature, and are usually described as very polished procedures. As one who took part, I would like to pen a few words concerning the sometimes adventurous flight trials which became necessary in order to complete these various towing operations.

The idea of the tug *carrying* the tow developed when aircraft with high wing loading were to be taken to altitude in order to test them in the non-propelled glide. Up to that point, the pilot of the tow aircraft, such as the He 111 we used initially, retracted his gear immediately after lift-off to reduce drag, and accelerated until he had reached a speed which enabled him to pull up with the tow airborne behind. However, the time came when the propeller driven aircraft used for towing were not able to achieve the speeds required to launch the towed plane, not even when using the longest runways available. The next development was to climb to an altitude where the aircraft which was to be towed was lifted off the ground. This required the line to be connected at the centre of gravity of both aircraft and, when sufficient altitude had been gained, speed was increased, usually in a dive, so that the pilot of the towed aircraft was able to pull up into the normal long tow position. This method was first employed, as you will have read, with the '*Natter*'.

Tragschlepp – Ju 87, with propeller removed, being carried aloft on an 80mm line, under a He. 111. For this trial Erick Klöckner and Hermann Zitter alternated their positions as pilots of the two aircraft.

During the initial flight trials of the *Tragslepp*, a Ju 87 acted as the tow and the *DFS Habicht* (Goshawk) was carried; Hermann Zitter in the *Habicht* and *Ing*. Kiefel in the Ju 87 *Stuka*. Trials generated loads on the attachment cable of up to 1,500kg (3,300lbs), produced by pushing down the nose of the *Habicht*, which only weighed 300kg (660lbs), and deploying the air brakes. During the course of these trials, we came up with a new pairing of a He 111 (to be flown by Zitter), and a Ju 87 (to be flown by Klöckner). The propeller of the Ju 87 had been removed, and the tow couplings attached to the centres of gravity of both aircraft. The *Stuka* was connected to the Heinkel by a forked cable and shackle and, as far as we could tell from the He 111, the forces on the linkage were increased in flight to about 5,000kg (11,000lbs). Line angles of 70° or more were achieved, just as with the *Habicht*, by pushing the stick hard forward and deploying air brakes. I took part in the continuing trials, and while being towed at low altitude, with me hanging in the Ju 87 below and behind, the stress was understandably high. The thought of the line parting with no height or time to escape, and me, in the truest meaning of the word *Runterfallen*

214

(fallen from the skies), crossed my mind more than once! The trials proved that the *Tragschlepp* could also be used on other projects; for instance, wire guided bombs, mines, etc.

Fangslepp – Aerial Pick Up

Ever since reading in the paper that Udet had picked up a handkerchief from the ground with his wing tip, and the day I had witnessed this during an airshow in Cologne, I was fascinated by this feat. In my whole flying career, I had never had the chance to try it myself. Udet had imported this flying gimmick from America, where the art of picking up not only handkerchiefs, but all kinds of objects in flight, had been extensively developed by the US mail service, and by the military. It was, therefore, inevitable that the idea of loads being collected from the ground by flying aircraft was to be resurrected in World War II. The *DFS* began looking into this problem although, I must admit, at a very late stage.

In order to pick up heavy loads in a fly-past, it is necessary to increase the speed of the load to that of the passing 'plane within seconds. As already mentioned, the techniques involved can be extensively reviewed in the appropriate literature. I had the opportunity to observe the procedure during flight trials successfully conducted by *Ing.* Paul Kiefer, who had developed the so-called *Fangschleppkasten* (aerial pick up box).

It was clear that picking up a glider which was waiting for dispatch, or which had landed and, perhaps, discharged its contents, could be an extension of this success. The procedure involved a line which had to be captured by the low-flying tug, and then pulled out of a container. Inside the container, the line had been looped through layers of wood, which were cut through by the line as it was pulled out, thereby progressively absorbing the shock, and accelerating the tow. Using this method, we picked up a *DFS* 230 in daylight with loads up to 2,000kg (4,400lbs). I was also involved in night trials, during which we successfully picked up several cargo gliders from the Donauried, later casting them off to land at Neuburg. Soon, however, the advent of the helicopter was to make the *Fangslep* (aerial pick-up) obsolete.

Mehrfachschlepp – Multiple Tow

The towing of several gliders at the same time (not in tandem), using only one powered aircraft, had been tried successfully during the early days of glider flying. Up to three gliders, or cargo gliders, were towed by a Ju 52 or He 111. Measurements and calculations made by the *DFS* showed that the power requirement for a triple long tow (three aircraft in tow), was equal to that required for a single rigid tow. This multiple tow was further developed in the operational wings, and even cleared for use at night.

The so-called *Umgekehrten Mehrachschlepp* (reversed multiple tow) was used to launch heavy transport, or giant cargo aircraft, by hitching-up several powered aircraft as the tow. These trials began in 1938, at Darmstadt, where five Heinkel *Kadetts* towed a cargo glider aloft. Later, this principle was used to tow the Me 321 *Gigant* (Giant). These so-called *Troika Schlepps* (triple tows) were tested with many types of aircraft, and aircraft combinations, including the Me 110 and the He 111.

Five Heinkel He. 72 Kadets, towing a DFS 230, piloted by Erich Klöckner. This variation of the Troikaschlepp was developed by the DFS.

Tragschrauber-Schlepp – Rotational Airfoil Tow

A small aircraft with a rotary airfoil (basically an autogyro) had been developed by Focke-Achgelis, to be launched from the deck of a U-Boat running on the surface, and towed astern when required. A speed of 30km/h (18.64mph) was sufficient for a kite type launch of this very basic helicopter, enabling the pilot to carry out observation at some altitude.

In co-operation with the *DFS*, *Professor* Focke developed, and built, a rotor system on top of a *DFS* 230, calling it the Fa 225. This was then flown by Paul Stämmler, towed behind a Ju 52 at Ainring. After release, this craft flew back to the field in an auto-rotational glide.

The experimental Fa. 225, a DFS 230 glider fitted with a rotor instead of wings.

Mistel-Starrschlepp – **Rigid Tow.**

During the course of time, the *DFS* had made a science of the air-to-air coupling of aircraft. It had proved that, by putting two aircraft together, a higher performance could be attained than that which could be achieved by one (as in any good marriage!). They towed one, two, or three aeroplanes behind each other, and side by side; then a giant cargo plane with three aircraft in the *Troika Schlepps*; they experimented with both extremely long and short lines; then with a rigid pipe or tow bar; finally, they mounted one aircraft on top of another, and separated them in the air.

One day, Paul Stamer wanted to know if it was possible to fly a *Mistel-Kombination* (configuration) in cloud. He had a *DFS 230* with a Fw 56 *Stößer* (Hawk) mounted on top as *Mistel-Kombination* , rigidly connected to a He 111 as the tug. This rigid tow formation was manned as follows: He 111 – Klöckner , *DFS* 230 – Stämmler, and Fw 56 – Oppitz. All involved knew that this kind of launch was inherently very risky, the instability of this configuration being well known from previous trials, and the high centre of gravity of the *Mistel-Kombination* did not make the task any easier. On 19th October, 1942, the combination was launched from Ainring airfield, with only 800 metres (2,625ft) of runway available. After having lifted off, very light vertical oscillations began, as experienced during solo tow: however, these oscillations increased rapidly to an intensity not previously experienced by the *Mistel* pilots, or by me in the He111. They quickly became so violent, even during the take-off, that the *DFS* 230 hit the ground hard several times. Quick thinking as ever, Stämmler, thank God, released the tow.

The next impact was so strong that the Fw 56, mounted on top of the cargo glider, was torn from its mounting, damaging the empennage: and half the elevator was broken off, but Kurt Oppitz managed to land the Stößer without too much difficulty. The cargo glider, as a result of the hard impact, bounced uncontrolled into the air, hitting the ground in a field outside the airfield boundary, right wing first. There was no take-off abort for me; I had to continue my flight, otherwise I would have landed on the hut containing the NDB (Non Directional Beacon) which stood on the extended runway centreline. At the very last moment, I managed to lift off, the wheels and elevator of the He 111 passing through the boundary hedge, but I was airborne.

Apart from the less than happy result detailed above, the launch nearly ended in catastrophe for another reason. In the right seat, next to me, sat Schorsch Keller, the flight mechanic. During the take-off, with the *Mistel-Kombination* still connected, he suffered some kind of panic attack and, jumping from his seat, tore open the top cabin window and began shouting, apparently in fear of his imminent death: 'It's not going to work! It's not going to work!' He then tried to squeeze himself through the window. There was nothing else for me to do, but to grab him roughly by the seat of his pants and pull him back down into his seat where he sat, motionless, until we landed. I felt sorry for him, as Schorsch was one of our oldest and most respected flight mechanics, but he just did not have the nerve any longer for this type of dangerous situation.

This rigidly connected *Mistel-Kombination* trial was the first using a He 111, and also the last.

Das Mistel-Gespann (Mistel-Team) *Ju 88 – Me 109*

The *Mistel-Kombination*, Ju 88 – Me 109, was based on an idea by *Kapitän* Holzbauer, which was to combine a Ju 88, loaded as a huge unmanned flying bomb, with a Me 109 mounted on top, its pilot acting as the guidance system. Close to the target area, the whole thing was to be put into a shallow dive, aiming at the target, and when the track and dive angle

The Großbomber, a Ju 88 loaded with explosive in flight with an Me 109 in the Mistelschlepp configuration.

were correct, the Ju 88 was to be put into autopilot. The pilot would then disconnect his Me 109 from the giant bomb, and fly back home with his tanks still full, the fuel for the outbound flight being drawn from the tanks of the Ju 88.

The Kracht department within the *DFS* was tasked with the flight trials of this project. Their task was to gather knowledge for future application, and the first flight trials were, again, put into my hands. The Me 109, which I was to fly, was mounted on top of the Ju 88 by two triangular trestles at the front, and a single vertical support strut in the rear. Each of the two front connecting points was secured by a special bolt, fitted with an explosive locking pin, which would be released when I pressed a button in my cockpit. The Me 109 would then be able to seperate. Kurt Oppitz was to pilot the Ju 88 during our trials, to give us the best chance of not losing the aircraft on the first attempt.

As we had hoped, the take-off was normal, and I quickly became accustomed to my position, relatively high above the ground. We climbed to 3,000m (9,843ft), and began checking the flight characteristics during turns, and in the landing configuration, as well as throttling the lower engines back. These tests also included shallow dives with a brief application of full power. After completion of the programme, the plan was to separate the team. We went into a very shallow dive and I pressed the firing button for the pins: the Me 109 reared up to the left, turning hard right by 10-15°. Then there was a terrible metallic rending and the aircraft jerked free. The violence of the Me 109's initial turn was so abrupt that my head was thrown against the left side of the canopy. A large lump appeared on my left temple, forcing me to go to the medical centre after landing, and get an ice bag for my head. In the meantime, a heated discussion developed over the fact that only the left pin had fired. Fortunately, the one on the right had simply broken off at its predetermined breaking point. It took quite some time for me to recover from the shock but Oppitz, flying the Junkers 88, had noticed nothing untoward!

The days that followed were dedicated to the further development of the giant bomb: the *Mistel-Kombination* soon found its way to the troops, and was used operationally during the last days of war. It is well described in a book by Arno Rose – *'Mistel, die Geschichte der Huckepack-Fleugzeug'* (Mistel, the Story of the Piggy-Back Aircraft).

Mistel-Gespann – Ju 88 & Me 109
moments after separation.

Der Fliegende Steg – The Flying Footbridge

The fact that it was possible to tow all kinds of manned, and unmanned, flying objects through the air was well known and well proven within the *DFS*. The idea that one could transport a complete bridge to a predetermined spot was really something unusual fifty years ago. Today, with the advent of the helicopters, it is everyday business.

When sufficient sections of the Fliegende Steg were put in place over a river or other waterway, the troops could cross with dry feet.

The task was to airlift a footbridge, consisting of several parts, and transport it to the point where it was to be used for the crossing of a waterway. The so-called Krämer Department, headed by *Herr* Wrede, was credited with the invention of this equipment. It consisted of a gangplank, with floats attached every 2-3 metres (6.6 to 9.8ft). Its buoyancy was so high that soldiers were able to walk across at a spacing of one metre and, in order to transport it by air, it was fitted with several pairs of wings.

I performed a large part of the trials required for this invention, by flying from Ainring to the river Salzach. Several tests were also flown from Darmstadt to the old Rhine riverbed. The footbridge was launched in tow behind a He 46 or Hs 126, using a line with a length of 60-100m (196.8 to 328ft). At certain speeds which had been determined by experiment, the whole thing was very stable behind the tow aircraft. The intended dropping zone, which was actually on the water upstream of the intended location of the finished bridge, was approached in a normal descent. Then, as soon as the section made contact with the surface of the water, the line would be released. An anchor was attached to the end of it, which immediately dug into the riverbed, securing the section adjacent to the proposed site of the crossing. Upon contact with the water, the wings unlocked, fell off, and floated away. When the current was fairly mild, the footbridge could be put across the river in a relatively short time. For example, we managed to deliver and build a footbridge across the old Rhine near Stockhausen in less than half an hour, by using three tow aircraft.

The *DFS* 228

In 1941, the Department of Aeronautics at the *DFS*, headed by *Dipl.-Ing.* Felix Kracht, was tasked by the *Reichsluftfart-Ministeriums* (Ministry of Aviation) to develop an aircraft capable of operating at unusually high speeds and altitudes. It was to be designed to reach the highest possible speeds at low wing loading, flying at the edge of the stratosphere, and was to be able to achieve the longest of ranges by using the optimum lift / drag ratio. The biggest headaches were the rescue of the pilot in case of emergency, the air-conditioning of the pressure cabin, and selection of the engine. The only type of propulsion which could be practically considered would be a rocket engine which would work independent of oxygen-rich air. Using the *Mistel-Kombination* up to an altitude of 10,000 to 11,000m (32,809 to 36,090ft) was another prerequisite.

When, in 1943, the project was raised to a high priority, construction was expedited and designated *DFS* 228, resulting in a prototype. A Do 217 was specified as the 'mother' aircraft and, following separation from it, the unarmed *DFS*228 was to climb, using the rocket engine, to its calculated ceiling altitude of 22,000m (72,180ft). There, using its aerial camera, the high altitude reconnaissance 'plane was to take pictures until it had descended to 12,000m (39,371ft) in the glide. At that flight level, the rocket engine was to be re-ignited to thrust the aircraft to an even higher ceiling of 23,000 – 24,000m (75,461 to 78,742ft), attainable because of the reduced gross weight, due to fuel used in the initial burn. An operating altitude over 12,000m (39,371ft) was safe, being, at that time, well out of reach of anti-aircraft guns and fighters.

By using the engine several times, a distance of nearly 1,500km (932 miles) could theoretically be covered, well outside enemy defence capabilities. The pressurised cockpit, containing the pilot, could be jettisoned when required, making a long free fall stabilised by the use of a small drogue 'chute. A barometrically-controlled automatic release device actuated the large emergency parachute. For normal landings, the *DFS* 228 was equipped with a wide, hydraulically extendable skid.

The *DFS* 228 V1 was first flown in the autumn of 1943 as a test aircraft without a pressurised cabin, and with a standard fuselage nose and cockpit. It was launched, using the *Mistel-Kombination,* from Hörsching airfield where, three times, I piloted the Do 217 carrying the *DFS* 228 up to its engine-start altitude. The actual flight trials were performed mainly by Gretchen Ziegler and F. Winter. Later, deployment of the trials of the *DFS* 228 from Hörsching to Hildesheim and Rechlin resulted in the total loss of one of the trial aircraft during an air raid at Rechlin. Later, one of the *DFS* 228's which survived the war was seen at an air display in the UK. Also, at the end of the war the Americans secured the plans for the *DFS* 228. After the end of the Korean War, one of the leading designers from Lockheed, C.L. 'Kelly' Johnson, came up with an aircraft looking very much like the *DFS* 228: the U 2 was built under top secret conditions in Johnson's workshops, and will be well known to readers because of reports about its reconnaissance flights over the Soviet Union, and, in particular, the incident involving Gary Powers.

The DFS 228 in Mistelschlepp with a Dornier 217 K-3. From this starting point altitudes of 10,000 metres were reached. Any resemblance to the Lockheed U2 is probably far from coincidental.

Fernsehn-Lenkung gesteuerter Gleitbomben – Television Guided Glide Bombs

The progress of war required the Department of Flight Equipment to deal with the guidance of glide bombs, which were to be released from aircraft and aimed at ships, as well as the guidance of rockets fired against aircraft. Furthermore, it developed equipment for the training of gunners in the use of guidance systems, and this included the so-called target overlay guidance, television guidance, and the guidance beam system.

The special department for the trials of television guidance was installed within the *DFS* in 1942, and was headed by Dr. Trutz Fölsche. A *DFS* 230 cargo glider was fitted with a television transmitter, and a Ju 52 had a receiver installed. After release, the cargo glider was guided to the target via the television pictures received by the Ju 52. The theory was that, in an attack using this kind of weapon, the command aircraft would be able to lay off at a safe distance from the target area, without having to expose itself to enemy defence fire. As a bonus, it would be able to fly in or above the cloud without impeding its ability to guide the bomb.

A large number of the flight trials were flown from either Peenemünde or Kolberg. I took part in these as pilot of a He 111, a Ju 52 and a Do 17. So that our work was not disturbed by military or civil radio transmissions, our flights were mainly over the Baltic Sea. In the second half of 1943, we were well out over the Baltic nearly every day in our He 111 (coded **CQ+VZ**), together with the Do 17 (coded **AO+AI**). The aircraft with the camera flew the course inbound, and the other 'plane, fitted with the receiver, maintained its course outbound. We managed to receive pictures up to a distance of 400km (248.5 miles), and made guided target runs of up to 50km (31 miles). As you can imagine, this was sensational in those days. A glide ratio of 1:10 on the bombs meant that we would be able to release at an altitude of 4,000m (13,126ft) and guide the bombs into the target 40km (24.86 miles) away.

Of the one hundred and nine trial flights which I performed during this project, sixty-eight were over the Baltic. We naturally had sea-survival equipment aboard, such as dinghy, life vest, emergency rations and radio beacon, and nobody was allowed to take part in these trials without wearing a life vest. Our radio operators were Roschlau and Langenbach, the flight mechanics were Kaffenberger and Lohfink, and the trials were directed by Dr. Fölsche and *Herr* Engelbrecht, a member of his staff. Many flights took us all the way out between the islands of Oeland and Gotland, and I can vividly remember one of these flights. We had taken off fairly late at Kolberg, and had arrived at the turning point between the islands at dusk. This meant that the return flight had to be undertaken in the dark. The test had been completed, and the crew were all sitting on the right hand side, looking out of the window. An unusual sight was to be observed, in that the whole Swedish coast was brightly illuminated, and we were able to see every small village. Sweden being neutral, there was no blackout, and the Radio Station at Kalmas was in full operation – just like all the other stations in Sweden – transmitting as normal. Roschlau was able to take fixes which provided an outstanding navigational aid for me. However, it was a strange experience for us to see, to the right, peaceful, brightly lit Sweden, and to the left – total darkness, with a bloody war being waged.

CHAPTER FIFTEEN
Wolfgang Späte
Take-off in the Super-Mystère

I put the following article on paper a few days after I had performed an unusual flight. I was excited, and naturally proud, because I was probably the first German to have flown supersonic. It had been the Germans who, even before the War, had launched aircraft with rocket and jet engines. Before 1945, I had extensive flying experience on both the Me 163 and Me 262, and perhaps one can therefore understand that I have to thank my good fortune, over ten years later, for the opportunity to fly in one of the most modern jet fighters of that time, and to go through the legendary 'sound barrier'.

Earlier, when approaching the speed of sound in an aircraft of conventional construction, a seemingly insurmountable barrier was found as the drag increased. For instance, the Me 163 A would flip over on its side and threaten to break up when it reached a speed of 1,003km/h (623.244mph); it was as if an impenetrable 'wall' of resistance had been reached. However, science has found ways of conquering even this challenge, using special profiles and an even greater sweep for wings; and more powerful engines have made it possible to fly at speeds greater than Mach 1.0.

Note: The speed at which sound travels at sea level is, with standard meteorological conditions, 333 m/sec (1,092ft./sec).

Academic instruction at EPNER, Brétigny.

I had had one year to brush up my knowledge, and to add to it at the *Ecole du PN*, the school for flying personnel at the French Test Flight Centre (CEV) in Brétigny. The time was nearly over; twelve educational and spiritually beneficial months, with not only plenty of work, but also many memorable and educational flights, lay behind me. There was nothing more the school could offer, and the time to say farewell approached. Then I plucked up my courage, and walking up to my instructor, said: 'One trip in the Super-Mystère, a level flight, going through the sound barrier, just once to have an engine with reheat behind me, that would be a very nice farewell present.'

The Super-Mystère was not a training aircraft but, in 1957, it was one of the most modern French prototypes. For approval, my request had to be progressed to the highest authority, but I was encouraged when *Capitaine* Ferrigno, the head of the department of pilot training, calmly remarked, 'Actually, nothing is impossible at Brétigny.' Then, sure enough, *Corv. Capitaine* Mauban, the head of the school, came up to me, nodded and said with a smile: 'Permission for one flight on the Super-Mystére granted. You will have to go to Dassault at Melun for it; have fun!'

Corv. Capitaine Mauban (centre), the Head of the Training Centre, talks with Albert Werner (l) and Wolfgang Späte (r).

I duly reported to the Dassault base, and the first day passed studying the technical and flight manuals. Then, on the next, I stood in front of the sparkling metal bird at Melun, and alongside me was Pignet, the engineer pilot who took care of the Super-Mystère. This aircraft, a IVB2 – No: 03, had been built by the Marcel Dassault company, and was to be mine for one flight.

The French call it 'le Super-Mystère', making the aircraft 'male', and that gender is very appropriate for this aircraft: the highly swept wings, the bullish beauty, the sharp lines of the tail section, and all the other essential parts visible to the eye. I took my time getting to know the Super-Mystère. When you intend to fly, for the first time, an aircraft of a type previously unknown to you, you must familiarise yourself with its constructional conception, as well as its flight characteristics. This means you need to know everything about the operating limitations of the aircraft, such as minimum speed for lift-off and climb, together with the maximum speeds for the approach and landing. You also need to be familiar with the operation and interaction of all its components, beginning with the engine and up to, and including, the last small handle which locks the canopy.

In the single seater there is no second pilot to help or advise if you make a mistake. I inspected the aircraft in every detail from all sides. I sat in the cockpit for nearly two hours and *Monsieur* Pignet patiently reviewed the operation of each lever, switch, button and instrument, until I was sure I had got it. As usual, I had already made a pre-flight checklist for the cockpit, a list of all the things which needed to be done: which switch to operate, which handle to move to which position before starting the engine, taxi-ing out to the runway, lining up on the runway, running up the engine and take-off; and another list for the flight itself. I had prepared similar lists for the predecessors of the Super-Mystère, the Mark II and Mark IV, in which I had made many flights at Brétigny. I had soon been able to play the piano of push-buttons, switches, circuit breakers and lights by heart, and I was completely familiar with the instruments and their indications. Eventually, this meant that I was able to do without the check list. Luckily, there are many pieces of equipment that are commonly used in modern jet aircraft, and which can be found in every newly designed type. This makes it easier to recognise the differences, and to memorise the improvements. But just to ensure I was doing it correctly, I practised performing the required checks a few times with the use of my checklist. When I climbed down the ladder from the cockpit, Glavany, the Chief Pilot for Dassault, walked up to me and said: 'How about it, do you want to take-off?' I looked at the sky, which was covered with clouds at about 2,000m (6,562ft) and replied: 'If it is convenient, I would like to postpone the flight until there is less cloud coverage. Then I

Super-Mystère B2-03 flown by Wolfgang Späte but without the external fuel tanks, thus limiting the flight to half an hour.

would like to climb to 13,000m (42,651ft) and, during my flight, I would like not only to have to fly on instruments, but also to be able to find the airfield fairly easily too.' 'All right,' he replied, 'let's wait for a day when the weather is better.'

The following Wednesday brought a blue sky, a little haze and a few cumulus clouds. That afternoon I sat in the aircraft and prepared myself for take-off. Jean Marie Saget, one of my course colleagues from Brétigny, helped me during the first part of the preparation. The anti-g-suit had to be connected to the proper couplings, the oxygen mask connected to the supply and, not to be forgotten, the emergency oxygen line, which supplied the bottle installed in the parachute pack, had to be connected in case of a high altitude bale-out. I put on my helmet and connected the radio cable to the corresponding plug in the aircraft. The harness was put on and the lock hooked up; it would open automatically after two seconds if I had to bale out. In order to open my parachute automatically, a special lanyard had to be connected to the lock of the harness.

Then the whole cockpit had to be checked, starting from the rear left hand side instrument console, to the main instrument panel, from there to the right console, and all the way to the rear. Each and every instrument, gauge and indicator, warning light and handle, had to be checked for proper indication and position. It took about 8 to10 minutes until I found that the last handle to be checked, the emergency gear lowering handle, was in the proper position. This pedantic precision was life insurance for the pilot. Carelessness or neglect could cost life and limb and, on top of that, an aircraft worth millions.

Then I made my radio check, switched on both sets, and called Ground Control to check the quality of reception and transmission: *'Melun, Melun, ici quatre B deux zero trois – m'entendez vous?'* I asked. *'Je vous entend cinq sur cinq,'* Ground answered. *'Egalement,'* I replied, confirming that I also had the best quality reception. Then everything was set to start the engine: my right hand moved four toggle switches, a green light flashed, then my right index finger pressed the start button. A pointer on one of the instruments started to move, the rpm-indicator of the turbine. Then I began to hear, even through the thick helmet with the tightly fitted earphones, the roar from the discharge of hot exhaust gases. At a predetermined turbine speed, certain switches have to be engaged. The instrument for T-4, the temperature of the exhaust gas in the rear part of the engine, already showed several hundred degrees: growling and howling, the engine was only running at idle rpm. The last safety pins were removed from the undercarriage lever, canopy jettison system and ejector seat firing handle and, lastly, I closed and locked the canopy. I extended the flaps and air brakes for last checks, then retracted them again. 'All clear' was signalled to me, both by the ground crew and via RT, and the tower cleared me to taxi to the hold for runway 29.

Throttle forward, and the engine noise settles to a steady, high frequency hissing. Release the brakes, taxi forward a few metres, then re-apply them, and the Mystère curtseys as the front strut compresses, a routine brake check. Then I continue and turn onto the taxiway, continuing the checks on the move; the gyros for instrument flying are checked for proper operation, the lever for cabin pressure is turned to the Pressure position, hydraulic pressure for the controls, oxygen and other important systems are rechecked and, at the hold point for the runway, I request permission to line up for take-off. A Trident, taxi-ing in front of me, and a Vautour behind, are instructed to wait as numbers two and three after I have departed, and I am cleared to line up on the centreline of the runway.

The control tower gives permission to *'Décollage'*. I push the throttle fully forward, but hold the aircraft on the spot with the brakes. The T 4 indicator rises and, at the required temperature, I move the throttle outboard and select 'P.C.' (Re-heat). The aircraft jolts and I try to hold the brakes with all my strength, but the Mystère is creeping forward, driven by the huge thrust from the engine. It will not be held back any longer, and I release the brakes and am driven forward as though by a giant fist. The runway rushes past under the wheels, accelerating at a fantastic rate. The Mystère is fitted with irreversible servo controls (no feedback from the control surfaces), and so none of the real pressures on the control surfaces are transmitted back to the stick or rudder pedals. I therefore do not notice that I already have effective airflow over the stabiliser, and wait for the speed indicator to reach that which I had noted on my checklist before I lift the nose wheel. However, we are accelerating so rapidly that, as I tentatively raise the nose a fraction, we are already at lift-off speed, and the wheels are off the ground: I am airborne! My left hand is holding the throttle, with the index finger already beneath the undercarriage selector lever. I have just lifted off when I flip the lever up. The automatic undercarriage retraction sequence only takes a few seconds, but I have to raise the nose a little further, in order to avoid exceeding the maximum speed prescribed for the retraction and locking of the undercarriage and external doors.

Giving free rein to the horse, so to speak, I increase speed in a shallow climb to reach the optimum for the climb, then cross-check the most important instruments and indicators: undercarriage, flaps, altimeter, air speed indicator, Mach meter, turbine rpm, T 4, fuel flow, fuel remaining indicator, engine fuel and engine oil pressure, hydraulic pressure for the controls and brakes, oxygen and cabin pressure. (This cross check needed to be performed quicker than I am able to write down the words and you can read them, but there was no cutting corners. Valuable observation time could not be wasted, but still each of these observations had to be precisely carried out. Many things are automated on modern jet fighters and, when all is well, there is little more for the pilot to do, other than to fly. But, if there is a fault somewhere in the complicated mechanism of this thoroughbred, if a temperature is too high, a pressure too low, or one or more warning lights illuminate, this requires action, fast action. The mind has to react instantly in order to find the proper response for the hands, pressing of knobs, actuating or isolating switches and the appropriate positioning of the myriad levers and different handles in the proper order.)

The RT crackles in my ears: 'Undercarriage safely retracted?' They are unable to see me from the ground any longer, as I am rushing through the first small cumulus cloud, looking for a hole in the clouds above through which to climb. The speed which I have already attained in the climb is too high for prolonged instrument flying in cloud, and even higher than the maximum speed we achieved during horizontal flight in the Me 262. What a fantastic climb! A brief look at the VSI (vertical speed indicator) reveals it is against the stop, effectively 'off the clock!' A good minute since I left the runway, and I am already shooting past the clouds, and into the blue skies above. The passage through the clouds is a bit bumpy, the vertical thermal movement of air is felt as turbulence in and around the cumulus clouds, but my sheer speed cuts through the updraughts and downdraughts, feeling like a fast car which suddenly leaves the asphalt for a strip of cobblestones.

'Train bien rentré' (undercarriage up and locked), I confirmed with the tower via RT: the lights in the undercarriage indicators had already confirmed all was well and, in any event, if one of the legs of my tricycle undercarriage had not retracted, or if one of the doors had stayed open or unlocked, it would probably already have been torn off, with consequent secondary damage due to the high aerodynamic pressures. However, everything seemed to be in text book order as I climbed into the sky like greased lightning, maintaining a heading of 290°, the direction of the main runway at Melun.

Besides the check list, I had taken along another piece of paper on which I had noted the flight programme and profile I intended to fly between take-off and landing. As I was converting several thousand litres of kerosene into hot exhaust gases by climbing to an altitude 12-13km (39,371-42,651ft) to fly faster than the speed of sound, I naturally wanted to utilise this flight to maximum advantage: I intended to test a few flight characteristics in order to have a better picture of the aircraft's capabilities. I therefore started with the first point on the programme, for which I had allowed two minutes, trying, 'Actions initiales' (initial control inputs) and 'Stabilité en montée' (stability during climb). I had to be quick whilst performing these exercises if I wished to complete the dozen or so trials listed. There were only a few minutes available for each if I wanted to have at least five minutes left for the penultimate point on my list: breaking the sound barrier in supersonic flight.

A routine check of the instruments indicated that I was just climbing through 10,000m (32,809ft). In the haze below me I could see the countryside, although I was not able to identify its precise location in northern France. Glancing at the compass, I saw that I was still heading 290°, and I began a wide, easy turn to the right. Having rolled out on the reciprocal heading of 110°, I continued the climb. Large city areas could be seen ahead on my track which had to be Paris, and, like a time-lapse film, it passed below. Up ahead, on the left hand side of the Seine, was another concentration of housing and industry; this had to be Melun.

Having reached 13,000m (42,651ft), I trimmed nose down, with the VSI (Vertical Speed Indicator) slowly returning to zero as the aircraft stopped climbing. I continued flying on reheat for a few minutes to accelerate, then deselected the burner, and began my programme. As I looked at the Mach meter to note the speed, I was surprised to see that I had already gone supersonic, the indicator being steady above Mach 1.0. I had not noticed any of the expected signs, symptoms or movements associated with the transonic phenomenon: no pitch-up, no wing drop or any other unusual behaviour. I throttled back, extended the air brakes for a few seconds and bled the speed off to Mach 0.9. With that established, I started my test programme: one minute of this, two minutes of that, turn to the left, turn to the right, three minutes of stability tests, two minutes of phugoide oscillation tests, a little acceleration and deceleration and a bit of up and down. Some of the qualities were obvious, but others were not so clear, and had to be repeated and retested. Then the turn for penetration of the transonic region, and the short supersonic flight.

Again, the obligatory cross check of the instruments: checking of all indicators, a brief look at the oxygen, cabin pressure and engine parameters. Then forward with the throttle and outboard through the gate: the reheat gurgled and the aircraft shot forward but, strangely enough, at Mach 1.0, the pointer of the Mach meter stopped. The average reader of a daily newspaper would have known that the Super-Mystère was easily capable of passing through the sound barrier in level flight, so I wanted to help a little, and pushed the nose down. No improvement, and so I pushed a bit more, but the pointer refused to budge, as though it were glued to Mach 1.0. I tried a few control inputs and was surprised how smooth they were; at lower speeds they had seemed a little too sensitive. 'I am unable to pass Mach 1.0 despite the use of reheat', I told Ground Control in surprise. 'Impossible', came the answer. 'How high are you?'

'Eight thousand three hundred metres,' I replied.

'How much fuel?'

'Three hundred litres in each tank.'

'Climb back up to 11,600 – 13,000m and accelerate again in level flight. It must be a faulty indicator'.

I pulled up, and felt the effect of 'g', proving beyond doubt that my speed must be exceptionally high, more than I had experienced before. A mere fifteen seconds or so later, the altimeter again showed nearly 13,000 metres. I had traded the enormous speed which I had picked up in the dive for altitude and was, once again, established in level flight. The Mach meter had fallen back in the climb, but now started to race forward again, quickly passing Mach 1, 1.05, 1.10, 1.15. Only a few moments earlier it would not move past Mach 1.0. Was it a fault in the indicator, or the curious effect of a shock wave on the nose of the aircraft during transition to supersonic flight which had apparently held us back? I did not have much time to think about it: the Mach meter was reading 1.2, and yet the smoothness of the controls, the stability and the flight characteristics generally reminded me of the behaviour of the good old Kl 35 flying at 220km/h (136.7mph). Only the load factor, the 'g', which either pushed me into the seat or pulled me into the harness when I moved the controls, demonstrated that the speed at which I was travelling was many times higher than that of the venerable Klemm monoplane.

Now I was definitely flying faster than sound, the pointer on the meter gradually moving towards Mach 1.3. At this speed I would not be able to hear the explosion of an atomic bomb, even if it were to detonate behind me; all I could hear were the noises from inside the aircraft. The sound coming from the exhaust of the engine, which can be heard on the ground, cannot keep up with the speed of the aircraft. However, the loss of this noise is not really noticeable because it is replaced, proportionally, by the sound of the air on the nose, canopy and fuselage, dominating the early stages of acceleration, and becoming far louder than the sounds transmitted from the engine via the airframe.

Eventually it just became too much for me or, rather, the fuel state became too little. Every second, the fuel pumps transferred a few litres of kerosene from the fuel tanks to the engine, where they were injected into the combustion chamber and reheat rings, and converted to thrust. The fuel indicators showed a remaining total of 350kg (770lbs), and I reluctantly eased the throttle back, shut down the reheat, and set the engine at idle. One more pull-up to reduce speed, quickly into level flight, and slow down near to stalling speed. Even though time was short, and the approach and landing had to be prepared, I wanted, as the last point of my test programme, to check the aerodynamic behaviour at slow speeds down to the stall. Despite the low fuel state of the aircraft, I was surprised at my own calmness and cool head. Everything up to then had gone as smoothly as clockwork, and I could not imagine that anything could now go wrong. Happy with my slow speed and stall tests, I pushed the stick forward and went into a steep dive, heading towards the airfield at Melun, lying ahead of me – air brakes out. *'Melun tour, ici quatre B deux zero trois – une minute vent arrière'*. One minute later I turned from downwind to base leg at 400m. *'Train – volets – sortis'*, I said (gear and flaps down and checked). I crossed the field boundary at only a few metres, air brakes out, a short flare over the runway, and the wheels gave their first squeak upon touchdown as they smoothly contacted the concrete at high differential speed, leaving small black tyre marks on the runway.

I taxied back to the Dassault hangar, shut down the engine and opened the canopy, my head buzzing with thoughts: thoughts about that highly interesting and, until then, unique flight which had enabled me to experience so many new and remarkable things. Very pensive, I realised how little I had seen of all the difficulties and problems this aircraft had undoubtedly caused during its development. None of the theoretical or conceptual battles in the design offices, none of the inevitable technical problems during the construction of the first prototype in the workshops, none of the months of hard work by the trial and test pilots. I was only able to feel a very tiny part of all this during that very exceptional flight...

CHAPTER SIXTEEN
Wolfgang Späte
X 113 Am

Writing my books and articles for magazines, I have often regretted not having kept a better diary of my flying experiences. When, towards the end of my flying career, I had the opportunity to fly the very first tests and trials of a new and interesting prototype, I decided to take extensive notes of the day's events. With the help of these notes I was able to accurately record events during the trials of the new aircraft, including all its successes and setbacks.

Twenty years after the War had ended, on 2nd July, 1965, during a solemn ceremony, an Me 163 was put on permanent display in the *Deutsche Museum* in Munich. We congratulated and warmly welcomed the designer and spiritual father of this tail-less aircraft, Dr. Alexander Lippisch, who, by then, was over seventy years of age.

Wolfgang Späte (r) with Dr. Alexander Lippisch.

The ceremony would have been incomplete without Dr. Lippisch, which was why we had invited him back to Germany from his residence, far away in the USA. As a successful designer of both gliders and powered aircraft he had, prior to World War II, found numerous supporters. Not only those who were in a position to fly his aircraft as pilots, but also those who wished to see elegance of shape and line, as well as the stunning realisation of new ideas in aircraft design and construction. His ability as a designer to freely interact with pilots, and others from the aircraft industry, was obviously a skill Dr. Lippisch still retained in 1965. The pilots present in Munich were all happy to have him in their midst, and to have a beer with him in the *Hofbräuhaus*.

While we enjoyed the convivial company, as well as the refreshing drink, I looked over the rim of my glass and asked Dr. Lippisch what his ideas were, what he had invented in the intervening years, and what he was going to do until his return flight to the USA. He replied that he had planned to have a chat with Claudius Dornier about a very interesting new idea and, by the tone of his voice, it was clear that it was to be something unique. Maybe something as revolutionary as the Me 163 which we were to see installed in Munich. 'When I come to Troisdorf, on my return journey,' he said, 'I will probably be able to tell you more about it.'

When, a few days later, he came back and was sitting with me, *Der Alte* (The Old Man) was seething with anger. After putting a few probing questions to him, I found that Claudius Dornier had listened to what he had to say, and had then suggested that he should donate1,500 Marks to the men in the flying club of his Friedrichshafen factory, for them to build a small test model, using Dr.Lippisch's blueprints. That, Dornier had apparently commented, would be all he could do for him. He had said that *Bodeneffekt* (ground-effect) – the new concept Lippisch wanted to explore – had been extensively tested forty years earlier using the low-level stump wings on Dornier flying boats...

'Pure envy by the competition!', hissed Lippisch.

Gradually, I learned that Lippisch had begun to develop a vehicle which was half aircraft, half ground-effect flying boat. Inch by inch, I managed to draw him out, and he told me that, even before World War I, it had been found in wind tunnel tests that the lift values of a profile increased considerably when a reflecting surface was moved towards a model from below. A Finn by the name of Kaario had patented a *Stauflügel-Schlitten* (Airfoil Sledge) in 1935. Post-war, an Englishman had the idea of building the Hovercraft which, initially, was fitted with fuel-guzzling compressor engines. As a result, they turned out to be far too noisy and had only a short range. The US Navy built and financed several tests with SES vehicles (Surface-Effect-Vehicles) to improve them. Despite the millions of dollars expended, these projects were abandoned every time, because the prototypes had somersaulted during their first launch and ended up as total losses after crashing into the water, sometimes with fatal consequences. Nobody had seemed to notice that the designers and constructors were not systematically solving the problems; for example, the correct centre of pressure. Lippisch became very agitated and said, shaking his head, 'Everything is really crystal clear when you think about it. These so-called "inventors", huh!' I told him that, if he was able to do any better, I wanted to know and, without another word, he handed me some photographs. They showed a vehicle which more resembled a kite than a well designed aircraft, but it obviously flew, and he called it the X 112.

After the War, Dr. Lippisch had been taken from a US P.O.W. camp, initially only for questioning, but was soon selected by American industry as someone who had something to offer. He was first employed by the Collins company, as were many other German scientists and specialists. Nearly every large company, depending on its budget, had hired one or more German scientists straight from the Prison Camps. Collins himself had picked Dr. Lippisch, despite the fact that his company built radios and Lippisch was an aerodynamic engineer. 'Can you build me a boat, fast enough for me to test my newest electrical equipment for the Navy?', he had asked Lippisch. Throwing himself into his new task, Lippisch researched all available literature on the design of fast boats, and took a critical look at those available at the time. Assimilating all this information, he then designed and constructed a very fast boat. He and Collins nearly broke their necks during the first test run, as their boat almost lifted off the waves, responding to ground-effect at high speed.

This made Lippisch think, and his ever-enquiring mind began to study the phenomenon of ground-effect. Finally, he started his calculations, resulting in a practical design. This was hand-built as a scale model in Collins' workshops and named the X 112, and it flew beautifully, right from the start. 'Tell me,' I said, interrupting Dr. Lippisch's explanation, 'What about the waves? Your *Aerofoilboot*, as you call it, glides on an air cushion, close to the surface of the water. If there is suddenly a gust of wind, what does the pilot do in order not to crash into a wave? Water is as hard as rock at that kind of speed...!' Lippisch explained: 'The thickness of the air cushion on which the ground-effect craft floats is dependent on the wingspan of the airfoil. If you wish to have the waves of the open sea, such as the Atlantic or the Pacific, at a safe distance below you, you must have wing spans of sixty metres or, even better, a hundred metres (196.8 or 328.1ft). But then you have vehicles in which you can transport a thousand people and more, or perishable goods of equivalent weight. The cost per ton per mile would not be much higher than transportation by ship. But you would able to go from Hamburg to New York in about thirty hours...'

I felt as though I had received an electric shock: indeed, here was something which could definitely be called a 'gap in the market', or at least the means of filling it. I remembered that, thirty years earlier, Lippisch had tried hard to sell the tail-less aircraft as the pinnacle of aircraft design until he was finally given the facilities to build the Me 163. When three hundred of the series had nearly been finished they realised that the advantages of such an aircraft were more than outweighed by its disadvantages. No one has built a high-performance all-wing aircraft of that type since. The trials of the Me 163 had cost money, but did not really harm anyone. Was this to be a similar case? It was not for me to pass judgement; I only saw myself called upon to help an inventor who had been denied a breakthrough with an excellent idea.

Two years later, I managed to prise a research contract from the *Verteidigungsministeriums* (Ministry of Defence) for this project. There was not really that much money available and, initially, only 300,000 *Deutsch Marks* were granted, but a few hundred thousand more were added later. One of the largest aircraft manufacturers in Germany considered this peanuts, and was not the least interested, saying: 'Something of this nature would cost three million if we were to do it...' But Rheinflugzeugbau (RFB), a small subsidiary of VFW Focker, happily accepted. This was their first research contract with the Ministry of Defence, so they were not choosy, and Dr. Lippisch was just the man to help achieve good research results with even the smallest of budgets. As in his early days on the Wasserkuppe, he had radio controlled models built and tested, and collected accurate data in the wind tunnels at Darmstadt: the results of these tests were more depressing than encouraging. Even though we had called upon the best and most successful of Germany's model makers, there was a mysterious pitch-up which made the models flip out of control. The model experts shrugged their shoulders and drove home, leaving us with the leftovers and the debris of the models.

Because of all this, we had already used more of the money from our small budget than we had intended. Accordingly we held a pow-wow, and decided that, with the rest of the money, we would build a bigger model, just large enough to carry 100kg

Dr. Lippisch takes a critical look at the model.

(220lbs), equal to the weight of a pilot, including a life vest, and flight instruments. If the pilot went at it carefully, and did not break his neck immediately, he should be able to tell what made the *Aerofoilboot* so unpredictable. For some time we tried to find the man who was to have the honour of being the test pilot, but without success. It then occurred to me that there was no one better suited to this task than myself, and nobody objected!

In early October, 1970, the man-carrying model, designated X 113 Am, was dismantled and transported by road in a removal van, from Mönchengladbach to the Bodensee (Lake Constance). The small 'm' in the designation of the X 113 Am stood for 'mini' but, despite this, its wingspan was just under six metres (19.69ft) and it had a length of approximately eight-and-a-half metres (27.89ft) which made it a trifle bulky when negotiating bridges and passing through tunnels. When I arrived by car at the Bodensee on 14th October, there was already a last minute panic. Someone had (fortunately) found that the elevator trim had been connected the wrong way round, and Hosemann had to work far into the night to correct this fault. In the meantime, Schönfelder and I looked through several water sports shops and marine suppliers, to find a life vest. Wearing a parachute during these flights was not practical due to the lack of space. I was already bumping my head on the roof of the canopy and, at the other extreme, I could reach the nose with my feet. In any event, at the low altitudes at which I was to be flying, a parachute would only have been practical if used in conjunction with an ejector seat. However, the seat would probably have been as heavy as the whole X 113 which, when manned and fully fuelled, weighed 266.86kg (588lbs). We eventually found a life vest which seemed suitable and weighed only 700 grams (about 1 Ω pounds). It contained a small compressed air bottle which was supposed to inflate the vest automatically after being in the water for two to four seconds. After the completion of the trials, and for a wager, Schönfelder wanted to test the automatic function of this vest by jumping into the water. When he had been in the water for five minutes, and the vest had not inflated, he swam back ashore. It required copious amounts of *Glühwein* (literally glow-wine – spiced, mulled wine) to thaw him out. By then it was November, and the water temperature was just over 9°C (48°F).

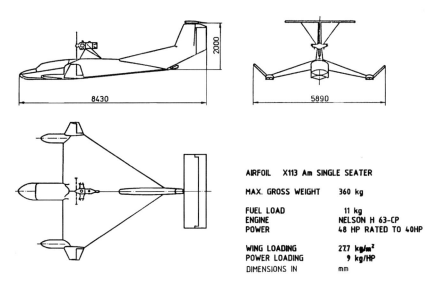

AIRFOIL	X113 Am SINGLE SEATER
MAX. GROSS WEIGHT	360 kg
FUEL LOAD	11 kg
ENGINE	NELSON H 63-CP
POWER	48 HP RATED TO 40HP
WING LOADING	27.7 kg/m²
POWER LOADING	9 kg/HP
DIMENSIONS IN	mm

Three elevations of the X113 Am.

On October 16th, 1970, we were hoping for calm air, but there was a strong wind, the waves were being blown into white caps, far too strong for the first taxi and take-off trials. But even if the winds had been calm, we still would not have been able to fly. The day before, it had been the trim on which the men had worked, as busy as bees, until very late; then it took another half-day to find the total weight and the precise centre of gravity. Without exact determination of the centre of gravity, it would have been irresponsible to fly. The wind tunnel tests had already indicated that we only had longitudinal stability if the centre of gravity (CG) was located at 20% of the mean aerodynamic chord. This chord line is measured from the leading edge of the wing to the trailing edge at the rear. Schönfelder, Krüger, Hurzler and Hosemann were weighing, using two decimal scales and a spring balance. The scales were on loan from Schnezenhausen, one from where the RFB crew were staying, and one from a workshop at the nearby Dornier factory, obtained for the price of a bottle of *Schnapps*. The weights that came with the scales were insufficient, and we therefore made up lead weights, each weighing 10kg (22lbs).

Hosemann was busy moving weights and weighing; weighing and moving weights. Schönfelder was giving orders and taking notes, as well as calculating both with and without his slide rule. During all this he alternately cursed the scales, the weights, Hosemann and the centre of gravity which, just to help the situation, was different every time. When they thought they had established it, they detected an error in the scales. This was naturally Hosemann's fault, because he earned less money than Schönfelder. The whole weighing and calculation procedure began again, and this time CG was not located at 20.6%, but at 23.8%! This was, we hoped, wrong, and a check revealed that the aircraft was not sitting perfectly level on the scales. During the first weighing session the tool box had been under the tail, so back it went. When due allowance was made for the box, the weight distribution showed a CG of 20.1%. Not one ounce of ballast was required in the nose of the airfoil. Perfect!

We were finally ready for launch: however, the wind had increased and the willow trees on the shore of the lake swayed back and forth. What good was a blue sky laughing down at you? The lake had to be smooth when I started my first flight trials.

October 17th, 1970. Dawn's early light crept across the lake from the East at 06.30 hours. The previous day I had set 06.00 hours for the team to meet on the mole and have the aircraft ready. At 04.45 hours the alarm clock went off in my hotel room, and I opened the window to see beautiful stars in the clear sky and not a breath of wind. The weather could not have been better for our first launch. Shortly after, my car stopped on the gravel of the beach promenade near Kressbronn. The lake lay glassy calm and, across the path, the contours of a tall building looked like a gigantic rock in the night. There was only one light showing, on the third floor, centre wing; Dr Lippisch's flat. His wife was up as well, and took good care of us, serving hot coffee, bread, sausage, eggs and all the other ingredients of a good pilot's breakfast. Then, back in our car, we raced through the quiet streets of Friedrichshafen to Immenstaad. It took until 8 o'clock to run up the aerofoil's engine for the first time. When warm, it ran up to 3,200rpm and it was time get the *Kahn* (old tub) into the water. In the meantime, Luxemburger and von Schlachta had arrived with the boats, and I held a briefing. Schönfelder and Ransleben (the cameraman) were to follow the accelerating *Aerofoilboot* with their boat closely on the right side. Von Schlachta, accompanied by Hosemann, Hurzler and Krüger, with their slower dinghy, were to follow on the left side as quickly as possible. If we were successful, they were to stop when they reached 2km (1.24 miles) from the starting point and wait. Fabian was to stay on the mole as rear guard.

The X 113 was lying in the water with its nose pointing out onto the lake. One of the men, wearing waders, was standing in the water, holding onto the wing-tip to steady it. Hosemann put a dinghy into the water and we climbed in and rowed to the other side of the craft. Having arrived, I very carefully climbed aboard: the dinghy was very much less stable than the larger rowing boat, and I needed to be careful not to slip and fall into the cold water. A few moments later, I was sitting on a thin piece of cloth inside the fuselage, preparing myself for the flight.

I strapped the knee board onto my right thigh, and checked that the pencils were in place ready to make any notes. From a small pocket on the knee board, I pulled out a ring with four spikes protruding from it, and stuck it onto the right side of the board, ready for use. This ring, with its spikes, was to help me to break the acrylic glass canopy if the aircraft should come to rest upside down and / or the canopy locks would not open. Connecting all the straps of the harness to the central lock on my abdomen, I pulled them tight and tucked away the radio cord so that it did not interfere with the movements of the stick or the throttle. Finally, I positioned a small ball, hanging on the end of a very fine rubber tube, which was the trigger for a camera. This camera was installed 'looking' over my right shoulder, and when I squeezed the ball, it triggered the camera, taking a picture of the instruments. Considerations of weight forced us to use this method of data registration, which added only a few extra grams. The flying boat itself was already 45kg (99lbs) heavier than planned during construction, and this was why, at least initially, we could not afford to take along an oscillator with all its additional instruments, weighing up to

50kg (110lbs) in total. Nor did we have sufficient electric power to operate this type of additional equipment, because the aircraft did not even have a generator.

Ready: I brought the canopy around, but did not close it immediately as, due to the low outside air temperature, it would quickly have fogged up inside. Constraints of weight and power prohibited installation of a demister to keep the windows clear. Also, as long as the canopy was open, I had a bit more headroom. The seat was installed steeply reclined because of the narrow diameter of the fuselage. As a result, I was lying nearly flat and, when the canopy was closed, I touched the acrylic panel with my forehead as soon as I moved my head forward an inch.

The tow rope was hitched-up at the bow and, in order to keep clear of the fishing nets, buoys and anchored boats, von Schalchta pulled me out onto the lake with a small, but fast, boat. Ten minutes later we were a good distance out and I released the tow. A slight breeze had come up, and the X 113 immediately turned to the right, but there were only harmless little waves, rolling smoothly along the skin of the craft. Closing the canopy, I noted the time of cast-off, and had already tested the radio by speaking briefly to the team on the boat as I was towed out onto the lake. I then switched the radio off, because the battery for the radio and the starter was not powerful enough for extended use.

Fuel shut-off valve open, all controls clear, and the rudder extended into the water. I pressed a small pea-size button, and the electric circuit became live. Two small switches were turned, and the dual ignition circuits were closed. Next to them, on the instrument panel on the left hand console, were two push-buttons for decompression and starter. I pressed them both, and the engine turned a few times and started up perfectly. It ran up to 1,200 and then to 1,500rpm, and the *Aerofoilboot* began to move forward quite smartly. I did not want to taxi too fast, as I wanted to give the engine time to warm up first so, in an effort not to drift too far from the starting point, I tried to force the boat into a turn by deflecting the keel-rudder sharply to one side. It didn't work; the rudder was obviously too small. Due to the weathervaning effect of the tail, the boat was only deflected away from the wind by about 20°, using the keel rudder.

The engine had already warmed up to 100°C (212°F), and I was unable to see any of the motorboats, which had already fallen back on the left and right. After retracting the keel rudder, I slowly increased engine revs to 2,500rpm, and the boat accelerated, the ASI (air-speed-indicator) moving away from zero. The floats on both sides started to lift from the water and, when I applied some left rudder, I felt the *Aerofoilboot* begin to react in the vertical axis, the trailing edge of the wing lifting from the water. At that moment, Schönfelder called on the radio from his escort boat: 'Trailing edge at water level coming clear, but only by a fraction.'

The ASI showed 40km/h (24.85mph), and I could tell from the splashing under the wings that an air cushion had probably formed, but my instincts told me my craft was sitting back, producing a high angle of attack for the wing. I did not want to take off in this configuration for fear of progressing to an immediate loop, but however hard I tried to push the stick forward, the elevator had no effect. After approximately one kilometre (.621 mile) of taxi-ing, I broke off and had them tow me back to the starting point.

On the next run, exactly the same thing happened, and I stopped the run at about the same point and awaited Luxemburger's boat, with Lippisch and Schönfelder, as it approached. They wanted to know what was wrong, and why I was not advancing the throttle more. 'Because,' I told them, 'that was what I wrote into my test-flight plan.' In my own mind I was thinking: 'Why should I have to do so much explaining?' The first Lippisch ground-effect boat, the X 112 which he built at Collins', flew well right from the start. The pilots had not expected anything else, and had just taken off and flown. The X 113 led us to expect worse. Most probably she was going to reveal some very nasty habits from the outset. That was why I had decided to start off very carefully, just as if I were breaking in a young mustang. Moreover, I remembered my friend and Chief Pilot in Mönchengladbach, Helmut Knöpfle, saying to me in his Swabian dialect as I left, *'Weischt du, daß des Wasser jesusmäßig hart sich, wenn ma mit eim Flugzeug nein fällt? Und arg kalt isch halt au scho…'* (Do you know that the water will be as hard as rock when you hit it with your aircraft? And it is already very cold…)

The cardinal problem during the trial of this *Aerofoilboot* was that the pilot was forced to operate it in ground-effect, very close to the water's surface. It was probably very stable in flight, sitting on the air cushion which formed under the wing. In normal circumstances it maintained this attitude by itself, or returned to it after being temporarily displaced by gusts of wind or control inputs. The pilot did not have much time to worry about anything but keeping the aircraft from making hard water contact, or even slicing under the surface. With a conventional aircraft, he took off and climbed to a safe altitude, and, if anything went wrong , he had a safety margin in which to recover, and in case of dire emergency, a parachute as a last resort. A bale-out from the *Aerofoilboot* was just not feasible.

In the meantime, I had been towed back to my starting point for the third time. Again the canopy closed above me and I started the engine. It was still warm, and so I advanced the throttle and watched the revs build, not pausing at 2,500, but letting it run up to 3,000 and, as I gathered speed, the indicator moved a fraction more to 3,100rpm. Then I could feel what full power meant for this small *Stauflügelgefährt* (channel wing) aircraft[1]. Suddenly it had a much better attitude, rising up in the water, but with the angle of attack nowhere near as steep.

It moved forward easily under full power and, as I glanced at the ASI from time to time, it rose to 50km/h (31.07mph). The boat jumped from wave to wave on the trailing edges of the wings, and there was quite a racket as the waves struck fuselage, floats and wings. It sounded as if I were sitting in a kettledrum, even though the waves were not much higher than 10 cm (4 ins). The boat was not pitching any longer, but had adopted a curious rolling motion. Then I suddenly remembered that the empennage was only supported by a thin member. Fortunately, a mirror had been mounted in the cockpit to enable the pilot to look at the tail, without having to turn round. A glance was enough for me to see that the rudder and elevator were fluttering like flags in a storm. I looked forward again, just as a wave bounced the craft into the air; an instinctive pull on the stick, the jolting stopped and I was flying. I saw the airspeed indicator jump to 65, then to 70km/h (40.39 to 43.49mph). I immediately reduced the power and held the boat just above water level, feeling it responding, albeit sluggishly, to elevator inputs. The waves were starting to hit the undersides of the wings with increasing frequency, and I began to notice splashes from right and left as the floats regained contact with the water. After a flight of 300 metres (984ft) I throttled back, and the craft settled back onto the surface of the Bodensee.

I repeated these jumps twice, only to extend the last one to

[1]**Channel Wing** – a wing with a concave under-surface which is designed to encourage airflow under the wing to create ground-effect, rather than airflow over the wing to create lift. Also known as ram-air effect.

a distance of 500m (1,804ft). Whilst doing so, I took great care only to gather sufficient speed to make the transition to ground-effect. When, during a third jump, I reached 90km/h (55.92mph), I immediately pulled back the throttle and, having flown half a kilometre, the Airfoil settled back onto the water, jolting and rattling loudly.

By then, I felt a little more secure in the knowledge that at one time, during the last flight, I had at least reached a height of 50 cm (1ft, 8 ins.), and flight behaviour had remained absolutely normal. We then had to discover if there was a change in the longitudinal moment when we increased the height above the water. This must have been the case with the smaller models, because they climbed away until they were flying 2-3m (6.56 to 9.84ft) above the water, at which point they apparently became uncontrollable. Clearly, I did not want to end up in a situation like that, and therefore resolved to fly carefully and, at the first indication of pitch-up, to return to the safety of the water and ground-effect.

Shortly after 12 o'clock I was sitting, once more, tightly strapped into the pilot's seat of the X 113, and von Schlachta was towing me out to the open waters. I released the tow line and checked that I had radio contact with the escorting boats. Having started the engine and warmed it up, I lifted off the water at 12.35. This time I flew at reduced speeds of 60 (37.28mph) and 90km/h (55.92mph) over a distance of one kilometre (3,281ft). All my concentration was focused on flying slowly and staying close to the water; the maximum height flown must have been about 80 cm (2ft 7.5 ins). The *Aerofoilboot* behaved surprisingly good-naturedly and no abnormal flight characteristics were observed. Recording the test for later analysis, I had several times pressed the little ball which triggered the camera installed in the cockpit.

Again, the escort boat brought me back to the start point and, at 13.00, I taxied out for the next take-off. In the meantime, the wind speed had increased and I could see the odd white-capped wave. The beat of the waves on the boat were quite strong, and I was glad when I could lift clear of the water. I pulled the elevator fully aft because the steadily roughening water was pounding hard on the boat during take-off; this time I did not go straight back down onto the water, but flew toward Friedrichshafen and its harbour mole. I had headed along this extended stretch in order to test how far I was able to climb away from the water before the predicted changes in stability occurred.

Very slowly, I let the boat climb to a height about 2 metres (7ft) and then carefully lowered it back to the surface. Nothing went amiss. Confidently, I lifted the *Aerofoilboot* away from the surface a second time; again, normal behaviour up to 2-3m (6.56 to 9.84ft). The next time at that height, I lowered first the left wing to the water surface and then the right. I observed normal flight behaviour in the longitudinal axis, even during those manoeuvres. As an experiment, I even started rolling into turns.

It was not possible to make a definite statement about lateral control after only two changes in bank, but I was highly relieved that the abnormalities demonstrated by models were, then, absent on the larger model. I also tested the rudder, finding that in level flight over the water there was not much response. To change the heading, one had to roll into a bank, just as with a conventional aircraft. I landed 3km (1.86 miles) away from the starting point.

I was then feeling sufficiently confident to attempt a turn on the next flight and return to the start point, whilst beginning to examine the flight characteristics at 3-4m height (10 to 14ft) Thus, at about lunch time, I was still floating across the Bodensee on my air cushion. The wind had become so strong that I was doubtful about taking responsibility for the launch, especially when I thought about the fact that the Ministry had not granted us the money for *Unterwasserversuche* (underwater trials) or even *Bruchausgeben* (crash tests); however, they wanted to see test results. Still in two minds, I pushed the throttle forward, the engine turning at a little over 3,000rpm. Again I reached 60km/h (40.39mph), but was unable to lift clear of the water in those waves. The tail was contorting tremendously and I chopped the throttle. How long and how far she had jumped, and how wildly the tail had been shaking, I did not know – my poor X 113! However, before we had lost too much speed, there was a mighty wave from which I pulled up and away. I had come free, airborne again, but what was the speed? The ASI showed zero, and I assumed the pitot tube had filled with water. Maintaining level flight for two to three minutes, the ASI cleared and I settled to 80-90km/h.

When the flight was stable, I started a left turn: 'Just stay close to the water,' I thought to myself. The nose of the boat was turning at a snail's pace because I dared not make too steep a turn. The first and most important rule for me was to stay close to the water where the craft would be under control. I wondered if I was already too high? Despite the waves, it was not easy to estimate height in the turn, particularly since I was forced by the designer to lie nearly flat in the cockpit. In that position, gauging altitude is definitely not easy! To my astonishment, I realised that I had to fully deflect the ailerons to achieve a bank angle of 30°. 'Splish,' went the left float, as it made a slight but noticeable contact with the top of a wave. This proved that I was at the correct height, close to the water. I had not intended to make contact with the water, as it could have destabilised the flight, with dire consequences. 'Splash,' the float touched a wave top again, also unintentionally. However, this seemed harmless enough, and had absolutely no effect on the attitude of the craft. The float bounced easily off the water, just as though it were a rubber mat. Nevertheless, as a precaution, I pulled the stick back and increased the height by about a metre, finding that I was able to maintain the bank without using so much aileron.

From then on, I had more time to look into the aerodynamics, and quickly realised that *Bodeneffekt* had a stabilising influence on the channel wing aircraft, inasmuch as it tended to lift a wing that had been lowered. Or, using a different example, when a turn was made during a roll, with one wing dropping lower than the other, the air cushion tended to counteract the drop, not letting the wing touch the surface of the water, and returning it to almost level flight, once the control input was relaxed. Similarly, the closer I was to the surface of the water, the more aileron input I had to make to achieve a roll.

It was only when I could think clearly about it that I realised what was happening but, at the time, I just reacted instinctively to the behaviour of the aircraft. At that moment I was trying to maintain my left turn until the shore came, once more, into view.

It had probably only taken a few minutes, but it seemed as if an eternity had passed until I saw the escort boat in my peripheral vision, appearing from the left. I flew past it at close range and started a right turn. Initially, it seemed as if

The X113 Am making a right turn early in the trials.

249

the X 113 was slightly more reluctant to turn to the right than to the left. However, I soon found that when I was close to the water it was harder to roll into a bank, but when I maintained a height of 2 metres (6.56ft) she turned as easily in either direction (for the reasons outlined earlier).

I was beginning to fly more confidently, and was becoming less apprehensive about the craft doing something unpredictable. At that point I began to wonder if the predicted changes of flight characteristic would appear as soon as I had climbed completely clear of ground-effect? If that was the case, at what height above the water would it happen? Flight trials with the models, together with the wind tunnel tests, had led us expect pitch-up to occur at a height of 4-5 metres (13.12 to 16.40ft). Lippisch thought it would be safer if we did not 'stretch the envelope' that far, that early. I believe he was feeling the heavy weight of responsibility bearing down, and did not want me to attempt anything unnecessarily dangerous. However, the answer to the question was of the utmost importance to him, and therefore of high priority.

After due consideration, I decided I was ready to have a go. I had accrued some fifteen minutes of flying time and my mind was made up; I was going to extend the climb until the first real indications of instability manifested themselves. I flew the *Aerofoilboot* away from the escort boat for two minutes, then back, and very slowly pulled the craft up away from the water in small steps, metre by metre, watching everything like a hawk. Finally, I reached a height over the surface of the lake which was far greater than my total wing span, at least 8 – 10metres (26.25 to 32.81ft). I still experienced the same aerodynamic behaviour as at the surface, in that we were still flying slightly nose down, and this could not be trimmed out using the horizontal stabiliser due to the location of the CG. Aileron and rudder worked as well as in ground-effect, but at that altitude there should be none. I also noted that I had to maintain full power in order to sustain level flight.

I allowed the stick to slip forward, and the nose went down smoothly without any problems as we approached the water again. At 3-4 metres (9.84 to 13.12ft), I rolled into a steep turn with 45° of bank. The *Aerofoilboot* turned almost 'hands off' at this level, and the climb out of ground-effect which, before, had seemed so critical, even dangerous, proved no more problematic than a stroll by the lake. Now that it was behind me, I felt exhilarated: so many things actually prove easy when, initially, they have seemed fraught with potential problems. However, many questions remained unanswered: where indeed was this fantastic ground-effect? Where did it begin? Where did it end? While I was sailing along in the direction of Friedrichshafen, an idea occurred to me, and I decided to test it immediately.

The existence of ground-effect could only be proven by the fact that, in the turn, the inside, lower, wing was apparently raised when flying close to surface level. And, equally, when landing, the long flare when a few pounds of thrust could keep airborne a craft whose total weight was 345kg (760.58lbs) tended also to support its existence. All I needed to do was increase the airspeed until I reached equal aerodynamic pressure, so as to equalise the nose-down moment by generating higher lift through higher speed. Then we would be able to see at what height the boat would stabilise, and that, surely, would be the most effective level of ground-effect. This theory seemed logical enough to me, and I felt I had no other option than to test it. Racing along, close to the deck, I had to maintain more than 90km/h (55.92mph) because, at that speed, the boat began to strike the waves as soon as I tried to let go of the stick (due to the tendency to drop the nose). I pushed the throttle forward, and at 100km/h (62.14mph), was able let go of the stick and the boat flew itself, even though it was very close to the water.

During the debriefing in von Schlachta's caravan, we were all very happy about the fantastic results of the day, but one matter remained unresolved: why were there such obvious differences in flight behaviour between the scale models and the X 113 with its six metre wing span? For a while, Dr. Lippisch stared out through the window, across the lake to the Swiss Alps. 'There is only one explanation,' he said. Then, turning towards us, he continued: 'It is the difference in the *Re-Zahl*.'[2] 'Thank God!' I thought, 'that I did not think about the differences in the *Re-Zahl* before I took off this afternoon!' With that, I left for bed at the *'Gasthof Adler'* where I quickly fell asleep, having consumed three good size Bavarian Beers to celebrate the day's results.

By 23rd October, 1970, we had had a five day break in the flight trials. The weather had become cold and stormy and, during these stand-down days, the question arose as to whether

---

[2]***Re-Zahl*** – German abbreviation of Reynolds or Re-Number. An aero-engineer named Reynolds listed and classified the relationship of hydraulic and hydro-pneumatic pressures on surfaces by number.

we would be able to continue the trials. However, the weather gods were merciful, and on the 23rd they let the lake smile a little. X 113 was back on the mole and ready for launch, just as though the bad weather had not set us back at all.

We had made the best of the down time too, as several jobs on the airframe of the test vehicle could not have been postponed any longer. Among other things, we had found that the vessel had become 4kg (8.8lbs) heavier, and concluded that there must have been a leak somewhere which had to be drained before proceeding. The CG was too far forward, which accounted for the tendency for the nose to pitch down throughout flight. The effectiveness of the rudder for taxi-ing in water was far from satisfactory, and the rear-most section of the fuselage seemed to remain glued to the water's surface until forced aloft. (Lippisch believed that a sharp aerodynamic trailing edge would work wonders.)

Our team had worked devotedly on all these things, sometimes far into the night. Having made the major changes, other minor corrections were then required, but by ten minutes past six on the morning of the 23rd I took off to the west, with a slight northerly wind on my starboard side. I flew a rather long stretch in level flight, taking me along the beach in the direction of the escort boat, which I could just make out on the horizon. The engine was running at 3,100rpm, and I had had a clean, uncomplicated, take-off. Again, the question came to mind, where did ground-effect begin, and where did it end? This was the first priority on my list. I climbed to five metres (16.4ft) and, to satisfy myself that the aircraft was responding appropriately to the controls, I turned it through all axes: rolling the wings left and right with aileron, and using the rudder with varying inputs, I induced a larger or smaller yaw in the horizontal plane. I decided to descend because, at a height of five metres, I felt I was flying a conventional aircraft with no ground-effect to be felt and, at that altitude, I had to maintain more than 100km/h (62.14mph); any slower, and the aircraft did not fly so well. Close to the water, and with a speed range of 70 to 100km/h (43.5 to 62.14mph), flight was most comfortable. My conclusion was that this was probably due to ground-effect manifesting itself.

Returning close to the surface of the water, the aircraft maintained 110km/h (68.35mph) for a while, and I noted that equal aerodynamic pressure must have been achieved. It seemed that one did, indeed, have to get very close to the water – and overcome the natural apprehension regarding the close proximity of one's rear-end to its rock-hard surface. Familiarity gradually eased my anxiety, and I began to accept that my nether regions were passing over the surface of the lake with only 10 to 15 cm (4-6in) to spare. I was already so *abgebrüht* (hard boiled) that a few centimetres of air cushion seemed to me like 100% life insurance. Even when I saw a bow wave appear before me, running ashore from a far-off ferry, approximately 15-20 cm high (6-8in), I retained my confidence in the air cushion beneath the wings, 'It will easily lift me over the wave,' I comforted myself. 'Even if it doesn't, what can a few centimetres of water do?'

Seconds later, there was a terrible impact on the bottom of the boat, the trailing edge of the wing, and the floats. It felt as though I had hit a sea mine as the shock-wave shook the boat. I reached for my glasses, which had been dislodged from my nose, adjusted the knee board and, a few seconds later, seemed to have overcome the shock. The X 113 appeared to be all right, and I thought to myself: 'If there is a hole in the boat, I will most probably only notice it when I land!'

The wave had probably been only a few centimetres higher than the bottom of the boat, but the ground-effect did nothing to help lift us over the top of this steel-hard obstacle. Any more solid a contact than that would probably have inflicted spinal injury, and I speculated what effect such impacts would have on a larger boat and passengers?

The escort boat was still far to the left of me, and so I was able to proceed according to my flight plan, trying to force myself back to the reality of my task. A few moments later, I was back in the middle of my test-programme, searching for the most effective level for ground-effect. Again and again I pulled the boat up to one-and-a-half metres (5ft) and tried to stabilise it; logically, it had to be possible to use the aerodynamic effect in such a way as to maintain a consistent, safe height above the water. However, the *Aerofoilboot* sank back down, close to the surface, and stayed at a height of 15-20cm (6 to 8 ins), no matter whether I flew at 100 or 120km/h (62.14 or 74.57mph).

Just as I had focused all my attention on my flight tests, the engine behind me began to complain, and I gingerly cut the power to allow the *Aerofoilboot* to drop onto the surface of the lake. To my relief, there was no sudden in-rush of freezing water, and I sat there in contemplative mood, 10km (6.21 miles) from my starting point. Eventually, von Schlachta came steaming along to tow me back to the Dornier mole.

In the afternoon, all appeared to be well again, and I ran up the engine prior to the next flight. At six minutes past three, I advanced the throttle to maximum and took off. I had arranged with Ransleben, our photographer and camera operator, that my take-off would be parallel to the large boat on which he had taken up his position, lifting off as I came abeam. No sooner said than done, I set my course to pass only a few metres to the side of the escort boat, and directly in front of the all-seeing eye of the camera. The sky was blue, the shore lines were a riot of autumn colours, and the water was reflecting this colourful mirror image, as well as that of our chamois-coloured aircraft. If this was not a setting for absolutely beautiful pictures, I didn't know what was!

Even at this low altitude there was little remaining ground effect.

It was a successful start, and I pulled up a few metres to perform a steep turn. Pleased with myself, I watched the lower float chase across the water; then the engine cut out again and I was forced to land. Later in the afternoon our little monster was ready again, sitting in the water, waiting. It was just past four when I climbed into the cockpit and cast off. The early sunset of late October was already approaching, but the beautiful atmosphere of autumn, harvest and warmth still lay over the lake. A clear blue sky domed above the near glassy calm *See,* and the sun was already sitting deep down near the edge of the water.

We lifted off into the evening sun, smoothing the waves behind us, the boat obediently descended to water level, and the flight trial began. I soon let go of the stick and left the *Aerofoilboot* to itself and ground-effect. In some parts, the lake was as smooth as a mirror, and it was therefore not too easy to estimate height within a few centimetres. Some Naval glider pilots have encountered unintended, unwanted and most uncomfortable contacts with the water in such conditions, and more than one did not survive the experience. The *Aerofoilboot* seemed able to estimate this apparently critical height above the water, and controlled it apparently by the utilisation of ground-effect, entirely on 'autopilot'. It was the easiest thing in the world to cruise along a smooth surface, not too high and not too low; the only obstacles to be avoided were, obviously, the waves.

My height above the water remained steady at 5-15 cm (2 to 6 ins.), or at least that was what the observers told me by radio. Sometimes, the boat inexplicably climbed to 30 to 40 cm (12 to 16 ins.) as if by magic, then calmly settled down again to the previous minimum altitude. I had not touched the stick for minutes, except when I'd had to make a turn, in order to fly back toward the escort vessels. Each time I flew past the boat upon which Lippisch was observing, I raised my hands to indicate that the *Aerofoilboot* was flying itself. *Der Alte* would, I thought, be happy – maybe even as happy as me – but my joy was clouded by the inescapable fact that this lift enhancing ground-effect phenomenon only paid off effectively at the lowest levels. The air cushion was so thin that the keel of the airfoil cut into the glassy skin of the water, drawing a long line – just like a diamond scoring a pane of glass.

Then I felt the temptation to throw caution to the winds for a few minutes by showing off a little as a finale: I reasoned that the spectators would enjoy such a display as much as I – as long as I made no mistakes. I pushed the throttle fully forward, turned, and headed toward the large escort boat. Rushing toward it, I could already make out individuals on the deck: Ransleben was fumbling with the camera, Lippisch was staring spellbound, Luxemburger was trying desperately to start the engine, and Schönfelder was waving frantically for me to deviate to one side and avoid ramming them like a Kamikaze pilot and killing everyone. Then I pulled back on the stick and, just like a champion show-jumper, X 113 raised its nose and soared over the launch. 'Now you've seen the bottom of the boat too!', I chuckled to myself.

As it had gone so well, I banked around for a second, and then a third run. The sun was almost touching the horizon, and I would soon have to end the day's flying, but there was still time for a nice closing effect. I wanted to see how suited the *Aerofoilboot* was to conventional flight, away from the air cushion and ground-effect. The engine was roaring at full power, and with 120km/h (74.56mph) on the ASI I let the machine climb away. The VSI (vertical speed indicator) showed .5-.75 metres/second (100 to 150ft/pm), and I lifted away from the water in the direction of the Dornier site. When I arrived, I was flying at an altitude of about 120-150m (393 to 492ft), and knew exactly how the old flying pioneers must have felt when they had climbed to such *adlergleichen* (eagle soaring) heights. For quite some time I had not appreciated the delight of an altitude of 150m! Down below, they were just closing up shop and everyone stopped and waved at the little *Lärmerzeuger* (noise machine) above. The escort boat was already moored at the mole below, and I throttled back to idle, letting the engine recover from the strain. Just like a hang-glider, the X 113 descended to meet its shadow below. Making a wide turn around those who remained on the water, I eventually landed nearby.

Representatives of the Press were present on 10th October, bringing their photographers along. My exhibition the previous evening had probably been observed and reported back, and the sensation had attracted the pack. Of course, real achievement counts and should be appropriately recorded and reported, but it is the flourish which really engages their attention. Possibly the Dornier-Systems Press Liaison Department had had a helping hand in it, even though there was nothing exciting to be reported from that side of the factory. So maybe Dornier had beaten the big drum for us, and caught some of the limelight for his company as a spin-off.

Dr. Lippisch patiently answered all the questions: as an experienced inventor, he knew that the best patent was worthless unless properly sold. I assisted as best I could, and he finally agreed that the trial flights planned for the day were to be flown close to the shore for the benefit of the Press, but before this came the questions: 'Was our craft not identical to the hydrofoil boats which could be seen on the Rhine near Bonn and Cologne?' 'No,' replied Dr Lipisch, 'we are the competition for them.' He explained further: 'The hydrofoil boats cannot exceed 60-80 KIAS (kilometres/hour IAS) and run profitably with a conventional submerged propeller propulsion system. This is because water cavitation affects the efficiency of the propeller and limits the top speed of hydrofoils. The *Aerofoilboot* moves along above the water with an unsubmerged aero propeller and, therefore, cavitation has no effect.'

'But don't the air cushion boats invented by the British use the same principle?' 'No,' we asserted, 'we are also competition for them and, in some respects, superior. The hovercraft produce their air cushion with fuel-guzzling jet turbine engines, which limit them in speed and range, whilst the *Aerofoilboot* forms its cushion aerodynamically, by its forward motion across the water. It can, therefore, be much faster than other vessels, theoretically reaching speeds of up to 200 – 300 knots, although requiring considerably less propulsion power than a ship and, therefore, less energy – fuel. As you know, the ship is still the most economical means of transport, being the least expensive per tonne per mile.'

'Aren't the waves a problem in flight?' asked another reporter. 'Not at all,' I lied in a tone of complete conviction, 'you have an elevator to adjust the distance from the water as you please.'

At the same time, I was thinking to myself, 'Dear God, give Dr. Lippisch, or any other designer, a viable solution so that we can produce a practical air cushion, and *really* fly at a great enough distance from the water to avoid those very hard waves.'

My tests had already shown clearly that the X 113 had to stay too close to the surface of the water in order to be completely practical. It was becoming clear that it would be necessary to develop new wing shapes, with completely different profiles, and to start the whole thing again from scratch, using small and then larger models, wind tunnels, measurements, more calculations, and new money from someone's research budget. Would we get it? Most probably not when we put the cards on the table and reported: 'Programme completed. Gained very interesting knowledge, but it just does not work in quite the way we thought.' So we had to appear totally optimistic, and demonstrate that any short-comings could be overcome. I was, therefore, very careful in what I told the Press.

Later that day, I climbed into the cockpit of the X 113 and strapped in once more. I had become well acquainted with our *Aerofoilboot*, and at twelve o'clock sharp I lifted off the water and, for an hour, pulled out all the stops in my flight programme. Time after time I attempted to stabilise the boat at a greater distance from the surface, using the air cushion, but every time it descended right back onto the smooth surface of the Bodensee, patiently lying there in the still air.

As I taxied back to the mole, shortly after one, I felt grateful. After a life full of experiences in gliding, and flying all kinds of powered aircraft; after flights which took me past the speed of sound, and above the troposphere, I had then had the privilege to work on a highly interesting project, sitting as it did on the borderline of aircraft / boat design and construction. We had progressed well during the time on the Bodensee, and had gathered important knowledge, information and data. We were like salmon working their way up-river against the current, jumping the waterfalls as we went, with some successes, some setbacks. We had not managed to get all the way, but we had jumped a lot of waterfalls, and gone a long way up the river. Maybe we could reach the top, at the next attempt?

CHAPTER SEVENTEEN
Dieter Thomas
The Equator Concept

Today, when a large aircraft manufacturer, such as Airbus Industries or Boeing, develops a new aircraft, one can rest assured that dozens of firm orders will be placed well before the prototype has made its maiden flight. That is, well before the flying qualities, performance and general airworthiness of the particular aircraft have been demonstrated in flight. Modern computer-aided design and manufacturing, and an army of engineers, as well as the vast experience of the manufacturer, make it possible to take this enormous economic risk. When it finally comes to the first flight of an aircraft which has been developed in this way, it is not unusual for the crew to fly it for hours without any major problems. This, at least, is what the Chief Test Pilot will tell the public at the Press conference following the event.

When considering the development and production process of smaller companies today, things are much as they were in times gone by. Only in very rare cases does a newly designed aircraft go through flight testing without major modification and only then, after confirmation of airworthiness and performance, can it be offered for sale.

One typical example of the contrast between the initial concept of the designer and the cruel reality of initial flight tests was demonstrated in the 'seventies, when Günther Pöschel of Ulm, West Germany, designed the unique P-300 Equator. Following an extensive market survey by a leading German aviation consulting agency, it appeared that there was a potential gap in the market for a single engined aircraft of modern design, capable of carrying six to eight passengers. Pöschel designed and built this aircraft, using fibre glass and a patented propulsion system. The aircraft was to combine the following advantages:

- *High cruising speed due to laminar airflow wing and fuselage, together with a constant speed propeller set high on the tail-plane.*

- *Composite construction, also allowing for use as an amphibian.*

- *Wing tips designed as retractable floats.*

- *A powerful fuel-injected, super-charged piston engine, installed in the centre section of the fuselage, immediately behind a pressurised cabin, allowing guaranteed cruising at comfortable IFR – levels.*

- *Low noise level in the cabin.*

- *Good visibility for crew and passengers.*

Flight testing of this aircraft did not prove very easy, and the task was therefore delegated to Dieter Thomas who, at that time, was already an experienced test pilot with the DFVLR (Deutsche Forschungs- und Versuchsanstalt für Luftfahrt und Raumfahrt – the German equivalent of NASA, based in Oberpfaffenhofen). He was a graduate of the French Test Pilots' School at Istres, and was eager to complete his first full test programme, as well as supporting the project with all his skill and knowledge. Later, Dieter Thomas became Dornier's Chief Test Pilot and undertook the maiden flights on a further six prototypes.

Here is his report on the Equator:

I n the autumn of 1970, I first set eyes on this new machine, approximately five months prior to its maiden flight. I liked it at first sight, since its concept appeared unique on the well trodden path of modern business aircraft design, and was aimed at exploiting the largely undeveloped market for seaplanes and amphibians.

Dieter Thomas.

Günter Pöschel was determined to fly the prototype himself; as the designer and an enthusiastic pilot, he felt fully qualified for the job. That lasted only until the day when, during a high speed taxi test, the aircraft suddenly became uncontrollable. When that happened, a multitude of problems came to light, which I will discuss later. It speaks well of *Herr* Pöschel that this incident helped him to make a clear-cut decision: he called on the *DFVLR* at Oberpfaffenhofen, near Munich, for help with the flight tests. Ferdinand Schatt and Arno Brünner, who were responsible for the Flight Test Department at that time, proposed me as the test pilot, and also managed to have the executive committee of the *DFVLR* agree to give any further support which might be required. Pöschel Aircraft Manufacturing Limited signed the flight test orders with the *DFVLR* on 13th November, 1970 and, at the same time, applied for a provisional flight permit from the LBA (*Luftfahrt-Bundesamt* – the German equivalent of the CAA or FAA). Things now became a serious reality for me, and I decided that my first priority was to have a good look at both the aircraft and its designer, and to become better acquainted with them.

The P – 300 Concept

Looking at the concept superficially, one tended to classify the aircraft as yet another on the long and exotic list of designs created by the post-war German aircraft industry, which were singularly ingenious, but which remained hard to sell. This impression was more apparent when reading Pöschel's first conceptual study, dated 1967. In his opinion, most of the established designers had always accepted far too many compromises: in contrast, Pöschel, at this stage, was not willing to accept any compromise, and was dedicated to perfecting every detail.

The most striking feature of his design was the location of the propeller, mounted, as it was, in front of the tail assembly. This construction only made sense if operation on water was the main goal, rather than an option. This 'option' also led to the decision to build the aircraft in fibreglass, to resist corrosion when operated in salt water. In order to better understand the results of the flight trials, I should mention that the aircraft was not equipped with ailerons for its first flight. It had only roll spoilers on top of each wing and, in this configuration, Pöschel saw the possibility of using the whole of the trailing edge of the wing as flaps.

SEQUENCE OF FLIGHT TESTING

Preparation for First Flight

From 11th to 20th December, 1970, an extensive range of taxi tests was performed at Laupheim airfield near Ulm. The following problems were identified:

> The fuel, which was carried in two integral wing tanks, sloshed around inside the tank during manoeuvres, despite a lateral stabilisation system. Separation into several smaller tanks would have been too time consuming; therefore Pöschel simply emptied and disconnected the wing tanks and installed an auxiliary tank in the cabin.

The control column could not be fully deflected due to the proximity of the pilot's legs, and there was very little room between the side wall and the centre console. The installation of a control yoke, replacing the stick, alleviated this problem.

Engaging the special clutch, connecting the engine and the propeller drive unit, created considerable problems (adjusting the clutch plates, specifying the flyweights and the power of the recuperator). An additional rpm indicator was installed, showing both the speed of the engine and propeller, and was required to give the pilot a positive indication that the centrifugal clutch had engaged correctly. Later, during the trial phase, the speed at which the clutch engaged was reduced from 1,500 to 1,200rpm. This was to avoid the continuous use of wheel brakes and / or reverse thrust / pitch, produced by the high residual momentum of the engine. To prevent the clutch disengaging during flight, a flight idle stop was added to the throttle quadrant. A similar stop was required to prevent inadvertent selection of reverse pitch which would, if engaged in flight, have had catastrophic consequences.

On 19th December, a further problem was revealed during the first short hop into the air. The aircraft lifted off very nicely but, shortly after closing the throttle to idle, it abruptly attempted to rotate nose-up (tail-heavy tendency). This required the immediate application of full down elevator to keep the aircraft level, and this position had to be maintained all the way to touch-down. Any relaxation of the pressure let the nose rise abruptly. What had happened? As the tail-heavy rotational moment did not occur immediately after throttle reduction, but approximately two seconds later, the lack of thrust momentum could be the only cause. It was concluded that the constant speed propeller had, briefly, slowed too much to maintain the set rpm. This set the pitch of the propeller rather flat, but still in the positive range; however, it felt as if reverse pitch had been applied. The fact that this pitching-up momentum could not be compensated by full elevator deflection revealed a second problem. The elevator control linkage had too much inherent elasticity. Full nose-down control input on the yoke did not produce full deflection of the elevator control surface as the aerodynamic pressure increased. This problem was solved by completely redesigning the elevator kinetics, and by increasing the depth of the control surface from 30% to 40% of the chord. On 20th February, 1971, during the last of the pre-flight hops, an elevator trim setting for both take-off and landing was established. The P-300 was then cleared for its maiden flight.

The date of 27th February was set, and the chase 'plane, rescue helicopter and airport crash and fire crew were standing by. Ground control and written recording of the trial were undertaken by Ulrich von Meier. Ulrich and I had already performed several simulated first flights, both during our time at the French Test Pilots' School, and as the designated Dornier test team on the Franco-German Alpha-Jet Trainer. The weather report offered full VMC (visual meteorological conditions) with only a light crosswind of 4 kts. Just before three o'clock in the afternoon, I was able to lift off without problems. However, immediately after becoming airborne, a wild gyration through the sky ensued. The first input of roll triggered a chain of events which I still find difficult to describe. The aircraft motion could best be described as 'reeling'. Initially, I tried to reduce this by applying deflections up to full roll control. Instead, the reeling intensified and Ground Control advised me to stop using roll control, and to use only the rudder. This worked very well, but it was not until reaching 2,000ft that I gained full control of the aircraft, and managed to initiate the first shallow turn: then I was in a situation where I could carefully examine the spoilers and roll control.

The following extracts from the flight test report, together with a brief description of the problems encountered, may help to provide a simplified explanation of the events described above: During small roll control inputs, the spoiler on the top of the wing extended. This should have reduced lift and, effectively, lowered the wing in the turn. However, it did not 'spoil' the lift as intended, but at low settings aerodynamically increased the thickness of the wing and, therefore, produced lift. When the spoiler was deflected more than 15° it actually did spoil the airflow, causing the wing to drop, as intended. This characteristic made the aircraft virtually uncontrollable and, in any event, no further tests could be performed during this first flight due to the oil temperature of the lower gear box exceeding the limits after only five minutes. Approach and landing were performed without using roll control: fortunately, the rudder was very effective, and also induced sufficient roll for directional control and turn. (Roll is a secondary effect of yaw because one wing tends to fly faster than the other and generates more lift).

The remedial actions initiated by Günter Pöschel immediately after this first flight were decisive and radical. Whilst completely understandable from his point of view, they detracted considerably from the original concept.

- The spoilers were made inoperative.

- The flaps which extended along the whole trailing edge of the wing were cut, and the outer parts redesigned as conventional ailerons. On the remaining section, which now formed the flaps, the maximum extension was reduced from 45° to 39°.

- The lower gear box was fitted with cooling fins.

- A further modification, which was to have a considerable influence on the second flight, was the installation of a concentric double elevator trim actuator, offering a manual back-up trim, in case the electric trim circuit should fail.

The second flight test phase was initiated on 25th May and, again, began with initial taxi tests, this time performed at the *DFVLR* in Oberpfaffenhofen. The second flight took place on 3rd June, and I found I could easily lift off at a speed of 95 kts. I was immediately impressed by the new roll control, and content with the flight performance during the initial climb. However, after accelerating to 100 KIAS (kilometres per hour indicated air speed), and initiating a normal power reduction, the tail-heavy pitching moment rapidly developed, requiring a substantial down-elevator input for correction. The physical effort required to maintain this correction was very high, but when I tried to relieve it by using the trim, there was no response, either from the electrical system or the new mechanical back-up. As my arm muscles were only capable of about fifteen push-ups, they soon started to tremble, and I had to think of something quickly. The old Piper Cub came to mind because, in that aircraft, the elevator trim had cable sometimes started to slip on its wheels when the elevator forces were too high. I therefore progressively released the elevator pressure, again producing a severe pitch-up, but as soon as the control force reached zero, I trimmed forward for all I was worth, saving the day.

This flight also had to be cut short, because the engine oil temperature had risen rapidly to 140°C. After landing, we attempted to solve the problem of the apparent fault in the elevator trim setting. We needed to find out why such a relatively high input of up-elevator trim was required to lift the nose wheel off the ground, especially since it proved too much for the initial climb. Some further taxi tests provided the answers:

> At full power, the nose gear strut was fully compressed, and the aircraft acquired a negative angle of attack during the take-off run, effectively sticking to the runway.

Following rotation and lift-off, the airflow became normal, and the longitudinal control forces, i.e. the pitching moment, changed dramatically. The problem had been isolated, and the solution was very simple: the pressure of the nose gear suspension strut was increased to its maximum, and this resulted in a positive angle of attack for the wing whilst the aircraft was still on the ground. Subsequently, only minor trim changes were required during the next series of short hops into the air, during one of which I was able to fly the aircraft precisely at a height of 1-2m (3-7ft), for some 600 metres (1,969ft) down the runway.

Eventually, we were able to perform six longer test flights in June and July, producing a total of three hours flying time. During these flights, we carried out initial tests and research of the flight characteristics and performance, but only after the engine cooling problem had been solved by changing the air inlet and exhaust for the cooling fan, and installing a larger oil cooler. Within a flight envelope of 72 to 115 KIAS, the aircraft was perfectly stable in the longitudinal axis. The effectiveness of the elevator was satisfactory and, in cruise configuration, as well as with the flaps at 15°, aileron input produced mainly yaw, and very little roll. Rudder input rolled the aircraft into the proper direction without producing any significant yaw. Only when the flaps were lowered to 30° did the aileron and rudder controls operate normally, and the induced effects reduce to a minimum. However, the secondary effects produced during changes of power were a real nuisance. Power reduction resulted in a pitch-up movement and a yaw to the left, whereas adding power caused the nose to drop and the aircraft to yaw to the right. It became obvious that a rudder trim, which was not initially specified, had become necessary. After this trial phase, flight tests were suspended for eighteen months for major modifications to be made.

The P-300 Equator in flight, Dieter Thomas at the controls.

During this period, the aircraft was fitted with a new tail, replacing the conventional horizontal stabiliser/elevator configuration, and its profile was changed. New Fowler flaps were installed, and equipped with electric drive and spindles. The ailerons were enlarged and interconnected to the flaps extension, with a differential overlap. Balance weights were fitted to the ailerons, and the slots between the ailerons and the wings were closed. The rudder was newly covered and fitted with a trim tab, operated by a wheel on the centre console. The main landing gear locks were modified, lowering the fuselage about 100mm (3.9ins.) and, at the same time, the nose wheel steering was permanently modified, giving the P-300 Equator a positive angle of attack on the ground. The elevator and ailerons were fitted with a push rod system, and the cockpit controls were permanently modified from stick to control yoke. The cabin tank was replaced by two separate auxiliary tanks in the wheel wells, each containing 33.5 litres (7.3 imp. gal. 8.8 US gal.). The wheel bays were closed off, and the undercarriage was fitted with a streamlined fairing. The pilots' seats were fitted with a vertical adjustment, in addition to the existing horizontal alignment. The aircraft was equipped with a 12 channel ABC test recorder, together with a Dornier flight logging system installed in the nose. A test probe was connected to a double pitot tube, including devices for the automatic recording of AoA (angle of attack) and side-slip. Finally, the wingtip floats were replaced by lighter wing tips.

One of the leading German specialists, Walter Stender, carried out flutter calculations and vibration tests, and some of the previously mentioned modifications were the result of his findings. On 26th January 1973, the first test flight in the new configuration was performed at the *DFVLR* in Oberpfaffenhofen. After lift-off, a slight pilot-induced elevator oscillation occurred at a speed of 85 KIAS, which could be corrected by pulling back sharply on the elevator control. It subsequently turned out that the new all-flying elevator was a touch too sensitive. The new ailerons were a real improvement, resulting in a correct rolling movement, followed by only a very slight induced adverse yaw. The rudder initially produced a yaw in the proper direction, followed by a strong induced roll in the direction of the rudder input. Unfortunately, when the rudder was released, the aircraft did not return to its initial configuration, but showed a tendency to further increase side-slip (directional instability); this was more pronounced at flap extensions of 15° or more. During this first flight, we initially encountered difficulties in matching propeller and engine rpm during power changes. Throughout several attempts the engine raced alarmingly and, after landing, a large amount of abrasion was detected in the clutch casing. The lack of directional stability was blamed on the new nose extension. During the second flight, with the extension taken off, and a keel installed under the rear fuselage, a slight improvement was noticed. The aircraft had neutral stability, but could not in any way be classed as stable. The elevator became less sensitive, so that it actually became the best control surface, following the increase in the ratio between control wheel and surface deflection.

An additional flight expanded the envelope to 140 KIAS, but the first performance test with full engine thrust showed a somewhat disappointing result. At an altitude of 5,000ft, in standard atmospheric conditions, the maximum speed appeared to be only 131 KIAS. After recalculating the engine data, it turned out that only 235hp was available instead of the claimed 295hp. With a power setting of .75 x nominal, we achieved a stabilised 126 KIAS.

At the end of this new trial phase, the purpose of the initial flight tests with the P-300 had generally been achieved. Sufficient data had been collected to enable construction of the second prototype, incorporating all the necessary modifications. After Günter Pöschel's familiarisation, the first aircraft was released for limited test operations which included additional pilots. These flights were executed mainly to prove the reliability of the drive shaft system of engine and propeller. Two well performed, but involuntary, forced landings in a field outside the airport boundaries, precipitated by the loss of propeller control, put a certain drama back into the programme. The problem in directional stability was more or less solved by a ghastly-looking extension of the vertical fin, coupled with a change in shape of the wingtips. Only constructive suggestions by *Herr* Stender allowed the original shape of the tail section to be retained. These included increasing the leverage induced by the empennage, and raising the dihedral of the wing by 1°.

In conclusion, I would say that, although not immediately successful, the initial flight test phase of the P – 300 not only proved the patented Pöschel concept of mounting the propeller on the aircraft's empennage, but also that composite construction was a viable option for large piston engined aircraft.

CHAPTER EIGHTEEN
Helmut Treiber
Elimination of Aileron and Elevator Flutter

With the end of World War II, the construction of small sporting planes had reached rock bottom in what was to become the Federal Republic of Germany, a position from which it really has still not recovered. However, in a different sector, German aircraft designers have reached a leading position in the world: that is, in the design and construction of gliders. Looking through the registration lists of the world gliding competitions in the last few years, it is apparent that more than 90% of the aircraft competing were built in Germany. The few other types came mainly from countries of the Eastern Bloc.

A high percentage of the gliders produced are intended for export, and all require a quality control check by qualified engineers. These high-grade German products are by no means inexpensive, and therefore require intensive quality control. The following chapter describes the resultant flight trials.

Dipl.-Ing. Helmut Treiber was a member of the German National Gliding Team from 1971 to 1979. He is now an employee of the Schempp-Hirth Aircraft Company and has accrued over 5,000 hours of glider flying, as well as many hours of powered flight. Through his extensive flying experience, and by virtue of several years work in scientific research at the University of Braunschweig's Institute of Aircraft Design and Construction, he has become an outstanding expert in the evaluation of flight characteristics.

Helmut Treiber.

In 1981, a Cirrus VTC glider was brought to us for repair. It had a broken elevator and elevator drive on one side, as well as damage to the rudder. The pilot's report stated that, during a high speed dive, powerful vibration had occurred in the fuselage, immediately followed by loss of control in the elevator and rudder. He was able to make a reasonable landing, despite the fact that he was unable to lower the undercarriage because he had to hold the canopy closed with his free hand. The deformation of the fuselage caused by the vibration had been so powerful that the canopy had been sprung from its framework .

After completion of the repairs, I decided to test the sensitivity to flutter of the rudder and elevator, within the permissible speed range, in order to discover why this phenomenon had occurred. It was not quite clear whether, perhaps, the elevator drive had broken, causing flutter, or whether the flutter had broken the drive. Therefore, after releasing from the tow aircraft at an altitude of 2,500 metres (8,202ft), I began 'exciting' the rudder by rapid alternating movements of the pedals (trampling), and also by abruptly deflecting it to its limits. Up to a speed of 150km/h (93.2mph) the rudder showed erratic oscillation, being controlled by the damper installed in its linkage. However, at higher speeds, oscillation was continuous and increasingly pronounced: it remained undamped at or above 200km/h (124.3mph).

Next I excited the elevator by hitting the stick. At 180km/h (111.85mph) I noticed slight vibrations in the elevator control, and at 220km/h (136.7mph) there was instant elevator flutter, noticeable because of a rattling sound in the aircraft, as well as rapid oscillation of the stick (fore and aft). I immediately grabbed the stick and recovered smoothly. The flutter persisted down to 180km/h (111.85mph) and, although I found no anomaly during recovery, I continued the flight carefully. After landing, I noticed that the shell of the elevator had broken next to the fuselage. The elevator and rudder flutter was eliminated by the following measures:

> Rudder: The mass-balance weights in its nose were increased, and the brake 'chute was removed from its lower section.

> Elevator: We were not able to increase the mass-balance weights, due to lack of space in the elevator nose. Therefore we calculated the dynamic mass-balance (using the W. Stender method) for the elevators, and mounted a mass on the tips of the elevator, protruding forward. A flight trial proved these measures effective. As expected, no signs of flutter were noticed in the elevator up to speeds of 250km/h (155.35mph), 30km/h (18.64mph) more than maximum permissible speed, and the aircraft showed well balanced and damped oscillatory behaviour.

Helmut Teiber taking off in the SB9 to perform flutter tests.

Problems During Spin

In 1969, during the IDAFLIEG-Meeting at Braunschweig, I had the opportunity to perform a flight test and demonstration of the general flight characteristics of an AN 66 (designed and built by A. Neukom). This Open Class glider had essential features such as camber flaps and Schempp-Hirth air brakes, as well as a pendulum elevator. After one hour's flying in good gliding weather, and with a 2,000m (6,562ft) cloudbase, I began an approach to the stall in level flight. As the stall performance was acceptable, I entered a spin in which I wanted to complete two full turns before recovering. Following the first turn, the aircraft quickly levelled out, the pitch reduced from 10° to 0°, and it became very quiet. I had the feeling the aircraft was rotating as if flat on a saucer. My first reaction was to neutralise the rudder, which had been fully deflected opposite the direction of spin. Simultaneously, I centred the elevator, which I had pulled back fully aft. There was no reaction, and so I pushed the stick fully forward and waited for the pitch to increase. Again, no reaction! I quickly considered alternatives to baling out. Obviously the aircraft was far too tail-heavy, and had entered a flat spin from which recovery was impossible using normal countermeasures.

I released my harness and slid as far forward as possible, in order to make the aircraft more nose-heavy; however, despite maintaining opposite control, there was no change in spin attitude. It was time to consider leaving the aeroplane, since I had already lost 1,000m (3,280ft) during the spin, and the ground was coming uncomfortably close. As a last resort, I thought of extending the air brakes. For one thing, the airflow

271

over the wings might be affected in such a way as to increase the pitch, something which had been observed when extending the Schempp-Hirth air brakes. On the other hand, the turning axis during a flat spin normally lies outboard of the fuselage, and so the air brakes would have a different speed of airflow. If the spin axis were located in the area of the inside wing, the outside air brake would have a higher speed airflow, thus producing more drag; in this way the rate of rotation could possibly be slowed down. After extension of the air brakes, and two more turns, the nose slowly started to drop. Then, suddenly, the rudder responded and the turn stopped. At this point I was able to recover the aircraft, approximately 700m (2,297ft) above the ground.

Following the relief I felt after having recovered from this dangerous flat spin, I noticed that the air brakes would not retract, no matter what I tried. The linkage must have locked in the fully extended position, and I immediately turned towards Braunschweig airfield. I soon realised, however, that I would not be able to reach the field from that altitude, because the approach took me over a large wooded area. I decided, therefore, to land in a large field next to the motorway which offered me a clear approach: I flew the circuit and approach by the book, and even remembered to lower the undercarriage!

After rolling to a stop, I took a deep breath before reaching up to open the canopy, but, rather disconcertingly, found that I could not unlock it. Now this really was ironic: I had landed safely, but was unable to get out. I was horrified when I thought of my situation a few minutes earlier when I had been ready to abandon the aircraft during the spin: had I not been able to correct it, I would have been unable to open the canopy! Again and again I tried to open the lock until it finally released, and I managed to get out.

I later learned from Neukom that the AN 66 had been freshly painted before my flight, but had not been reweighed following the paint job. Subsequently it was shown that the centre of gravity had moved aft, well out of the permissible range, and that this displacement of the c of g had been responsible for the problems during my spin.

Spin Characteristics with High Asymmetric Loads

On flights with gliders having a wing span of 15m (49.2ft), flying with the water tanks either completely full or completely empty, normal behaviour was noted during spin entry and recovery. For research into spin characteristics, using asymmetric loads, we took off with both tanks full, and emptied one in flight. This indeed was a very unrealistic operation, because I had to cut through the pipe connecting the wing tanks, in order to enable only one to drain. The highly asymmetric load (the wing carrying water ballast was twice as heavy as the empty one) was indicated by the requirement to maintain half deflection of the ailerons in the direction of the light wing, in order to keep the aircraft level.

After entering the spin over the heavy wing, the aircraft went into a flat spin with erratic turning motions. Recovery was achieved after two turns, using opposite rudder and full up-elevator to achieve a steeper attitude. However, the aircraft still made one and a half more turns until rotation ceased and it could be recovered.

In a later flight, these trials were repeated to research different aileron deflections during spin. The spin was again entered over the heavy wing, and the aircraft went into a flat spin attitude, where the wind noise reduced considerably. After recovery (two turns), the aircraft continued for three more turns. This continuation of the turn after recovery seemed too long for me, so I repeated the trial: spin entry, flat spin and recovery after two turns, but no reaction from the aircraft in the three turns which followed, not even with the stick fully forward. I suddenly remembered an earlier flat spin with a Swiss glider, where deployment of the air brakes had helped recovery. The aircraft which I was now flying had large air brakes, so I could expect a slowing down of the turn and a change of trim to nose-heavy. I extended the air brakes and waited: it took a further five turns before the aircraft lowered its nose far enough for the rudder to become effective, and the turn could be stopped. Since I had started the spin trials at an altitude of 3,000m (9, 843ft), there had been enough time to try the different counter measures and recover.

CHAPTER NINETEEN

Jean Marie Saget
'Vive l'aviation.' From the Diary of a Test Pilot

It gives me great satisfaction to be able to include the following extract, which I translated and edited from the original French, at the end of this book. During this process I tried not to lose any of the vividness of Saget's autobiography, which describes in such a natural style the life of a European Test Pilot, so characteristic of aviation in post World War II Europe. It is, therefore, entirely appropriate that this last contribution comes from my neighbouring France.

Jean Marie Saget shortly before his flying display at Le Bourget 1983.

My parents came from Burgundy, and I was born in Paris, on 17th March, 1929. My youth and schooling were spent partly in Paris, and partly in the Bourgogne. Events which cast shadows over this otherwise happy time were the appearance of the *Front Populair* (Popular Front), the Spanish Civil War, and World War II. I was only eleven years old at the time of the German Invasion but, like many of the children of my generation, these events left their mark.

When, today, I think back to the beginnings of my forty years experience of flying, I imagine they would be similar to those of most other pilots. From the time I was a small boy I was fascinated by flying, an enthusiasm which was not to be appeased. I buried myself in every aviation publication available, and built models – including some of aircraft I hoped I might one day fly. I practised parachuting, and built an ultra-light glider with which, fortunately, I only fell flat on my face, having experienced my first spin.

After spending a year at the Air Force Academy at Salon, I was seconded for further flying training to the USA. This eventually provided me with a piston engine rating, and qualified me for entry to Fighter Command. In May, 1952, I was attached to Number Two Fighter Wing, where an extraordinary atmosphere existed, mainly due to the influence of those we youngsters called *Les Anciens Combattants* (The Oldies) who had fought in the war. For the most part things went well, but one day I was ordered to report to the Commanding Officer after having flown a simulated low-level attack in an aircraft from the Aero Club. His caution was short and to the point: 'If you continue to mess around like this you'll be sent to Air France!' I adopted the suitably humble posture situations like this require.

In September 1952, as is traditional for most Pilot Officers, I wrecked my beautiful new Aronde car on a bend in Vougeot, collecting at the same time a sizeable blow to the head as well as a broken arm and leg, requiring five months in hospital. I took advantage of that situation and got married in December, returning to full duties in January. On 14th July I flew over Versailles for the Parade, preceded by the most spectacular gaggle of forty-eight F 84's and our twenty-four Ouragans criss-crossing between the cloud layers.

Because the wing had grown considerably, the following year was filled with basic training for new crews but, by August, many of the pilots of II/2 were on holiday. Two pilots were required for the Paris – Cannes race at the end of the month, and *Capitaine* Groullier asked me if I was keen to fly. Naturally I jumped at the opportunity, and for two weeks I buried my head in the performance tables of the Ouragan (made available to us for the first time), studying the results of the climb trials, calculating fuel consumption and memorising the course. On the day of the race I met Flight Sergeant Cassagnes, also from II/2, who said: 'There is a rumour that *Monsieur* Dassault has a contract in his pocket for the winner!'

When I arrived in Nice, I was somewhat surprised to hear that I had flown the best time. During the preparations for the flight, Cassagnes and I had both flown the route using the same calculations, and our flight times had differed by only two seconds at the most, over a distance of 730km (543.6 miles). On the day of the race he had, unfortunately, got lost in the mist just prior to entering the leg to Palm Beach.

During the official reception, a man in a white dinner jacket approached me and said: 'So it was you who won the race?'

'*Oui Monsieur*,' I answered.

'Well, then, we shall meet again,' he said, leaving me to ask my neighbour who the mystery man was. Imagine my surprise when he said, 'That was *Monsieur* Marcel Dassault, Member of Parliament!'

I thought no more of this incident until the end of September, when Colonel Tuffal, Head of the Dassault Flight Test Department, had me called to the telephone and offered me a job as Trials Pilot. I briefly took stock: 750 flying hours, deputy formation leader and barely five years in the Air Force. What they said in the 2nd Wing, and pretty much what was said throughout the other fighter wings, was that test pilots were not to be taken too seriously. I felt rather young and inexperienced, but above all, the morale and spirit was excellent in my present posting, making it difficult to consider leaving. However, after being introduced to *Monsieur* Dassault at the company's Head Office in Paris, I accepted the offer, entrusting my future to divine providence. On 1st May, 1955, I became a civilian again, with a total of 950 flying hours.

My first flight was on the Nord 1100 at Villaroche, then on the Mystère II, serial number 02, equipped with a Tay engine and an asymmetric wing section – a wonderful, well balanced aircraft which turned better than the Ouragan. It was to be a long time before I flew an aircraft which impressed me as much.

I was sent to Bordeaux to be trained for acceptance flights and inspections of the MD312, Ouragan, Mystère II and IVA, under the tutorage of two old hands, G. Brian and D. Rastel (both of whom were twenty years older than myself). As a pastime, I acted as a flying instructor at the Dassault Aero Club, and taught my young wife to fly in an NC858. Then, in the autumn, it was back to Villaroche, then on to Istres for the winter 'campaign', test flying the Mystère IV B, fitted with the ATARF engine, and equipped with re-heat. Following a cold spell in February, which brought temperatures of -15°C – together with 60 knot winds from the Mistral, gusting up to 100 kts. – I went to Villacoublay for a blind flying course, then on to Brétigny to take the Test Pilots Course. It was there that I again met *Commandant* Julienne, former Commander of the I/2 Cigognes, and also *Major* Werner of the West German *Luftwaffe*, who would later be involved in two incidents in the Balzac 001.The course was livened up by the jokes of F. Plessier, and the contact with so many foreign pilots, but I really wanted to get back to proper test flights at the factory, for which I had acquired such enthusiasm.

The Federal Republic of Germany was thinking of replacing its F-84s and F-86s with a newer fighter, and *Major* Werner was tasked by the *Führunsstab der Luftwaffe* (Luftwaffe General Staff) with the assessment of the Balzac, which was still in trial status. He arrived at Istres in December, and our first problem was to get his massive figure into the relatively small cockpit of the aircraft. We succeeded reasonably well, and he then proceeded with his test flight. All went well, and Werner had accelerated to 600 kts at low level when he most probably grabbed the stick just a bit too hard, and initiated violent Pilot Induced Oscillations (PIO) in the elevator. Grabbing wildly at the controls, he succeeded only in closing the throttle and cutting off the engine! This actually proved beneficial, because the aircraft slowed down and the PIO finally ceased. *Major* Werner recovered his composure and reported his problem over the radio, part of his message being: '...*die Fahrwerksanzeige ist runtergefallen...*' (...the gear indicator has fallen down...) *Herr* Borsdorff, a German engineer working for SNECMA, translated this, much to our surprise, as: 'He has the gear on his knees...!' Luckily the ATAR-engine was very simple to re-ignite, and with instructions via RT on which button to press, was soon running again, and not a moment too early. Werner made a

fairly good landing, but the wing fairings were somewhat
distorted by the enormous g-forces induced by the oscillations.
He delivered the heap of 'scrap' back to us, and drove his
massive body back to Germany. We later installed a pitch
damper on the elevator, just for him!

The *Major* returned in the Spring, and on this occasion one
of the main undercarriage legs broke off on landing, producing
a spectacular ground loop. We were just two months away from
the maiden flight of the Mirage IIIA 01, the aircraft with which
we were going to be able to offer Mach 2 capability. However,
following Werner's 'inspections' on the Balzac, we felt unable to
include the German *Luftwaffe* in our plans...

A few years later, I heard more about the flying adventures
of *Major* Werner. Flt.Lt. Cockerill reported thus on Werner's
first flight on the English Electric P 1: 'During the briefing we
suggested that he should take off without the use of re-heat,
because the undercarriage needed to be retracted before the
aircraft reached a speed of 250 KIAS.' (Here I would comment
that, when you know the English, you understand that was
exactly what they meant, and it was an important detail of their
take-off instructions.) However, on his very first take-off, the
Major immediately advanced the throttle to re-heat. The
following story circulated for some time in British test pilot
circles: 'The last we saw of him, he was at 20,000ft in a
perpendicular climb, still trying to retract the undercarriage...'

> *Note by Wolfgang Späte: It is said that the Lockheed
> company had to put two F 104s on the casualty list, following
> similar 'inspection' by the Major. For as long as he lived, his 'acts
> of violence' were never made public, and a veil of silence was
> drawn over them. The demand for historical accuracy requires
> us, however, finally to expose this secret.*

Kpt.Lt (Lieutenant-Commander) Picchi joined Dassault
specifically for the trials of the IVM 01, but had to be discharged
from the Company after only three months, due to ill health.
This meant a move for me up to the number one position on that
project, and I made the first take-off in the IVM 01 at Villaroche
on 21st May, 1958. 20th June saw the first appearance at Le
Bourget of the IVM 02; on 7th July the same aircraft suffered a
complete brake failure, and I rolled out into the grass at the end
of the runway at Villaroche, fortunately with no damage.

In the autumn of 1959 we began the exploration of high

altitude in the Mirage III A 02. Roland Glavany had left the Company and René Bigaud soon replaced him as Chief Pilot. He entrusted me with those trials, together with Gerard Muselli and, later, Elie Buge. On my first flight to 58,000ft I took no more than 2,200 litres (484.22 imp gal. or 581.24 US gal.) of fuel and successfully made a level run at Mach 1.8. On 3rd February, 1960, I made a flat-out climb without the aid of booster rockets. Following a run-up at 40,000ft, I climbed until the engine stalled at 73,000ft, indicating Mach 2.0: what an aircraft!

On 8th February I made a check flight using a booster rocket which was to simulate the zoom climb. The plan was to accelerate again at 40,000 feet, and then pull up at an angle of 20° and continue the climb at Mach 2.0 to 60,000ft. (Later, during the real zoom climb, the stick was pulled all the way back, achieving a climb angle of 45° which, in theory, would have taken the aircraft up to 105,000ft travelling at Mach 1.) From Nice, I headed west, accelerating using full thrust and, at 40,000ft, overhead Istres, ignited the booster rocket, reaching Mach 2 with a fuel reserve of 250kg (550 lbs) on each of the two indicators. After pulling up for about thirty seconds, several explosions shook the aircraft. Red lights came on and warning horns sounded all around the cockpit. I shut down the engine and the rocket and pushed the nose down, trimming into normal cruise attitude, whilst turning roughly into the direction of the Company airfield. There was a layer of cirrus cloud below me, and I was not quite sure of my position, but by the time I had taken an easterly heading, I found I had about 50 NM to run, with some 50,000ft to trade for distance, which wouldn't be enough. I remained on course for Istres, but knew that if the engine did not re-light, it would mean either crashing or baling out, using the ejector seat and parachute. If I wanted to play it safe, I could opt for making a glide approach at Montpellier, which only had 1,700 metres (5,578ft) of runway at that time, but I felt that should be sufficient. Hasty calculations revealed that even if I could re-ignite the engine I would probably not have enough fuel to take me safely back to Istres, and so I decided to play safe and landed at Montpellier, following an uneventful re-light of the engine. The local Aero Club pilots were somewhat amazed to see a 'Man from Mars' climb out of the cockpit. Later, we learned that the aircraft had climbed to over 70,000ft.

Several flights followed with vibrations occurring when the

stick was pulled to the fully aft position, but without the explosions. On 20th February, the aircraft reached 81,600ft travelling at Mach 1.55, and I already had my finger to the engine stop lever because the turbine speed had risen to 8,850rpm. At 8,900rpm I was obliged to shut her down, and there was just sufficient time to have a quick look up and see that the sky above me was indeed very dark compared to the bright horizon. Seconds later, the rpm began to decrease, a clear indication that I was losing height. During the evaluation of this flight we discovered that our problems stemmed from the tremendous delay in airspeed indication. The intake cone for the engine was in the position for Mach 1.75 when the aircraft was flying at a speed of approximately Mach 2.15, at an altitude of 60,000ft. That caused problems with the air intakes, and we reasoned that it should be sufficient to manually move the engine intake cone to the position for Mach 2.15 during the pull-up and just leave it there. However, Dassault felt that these pull-ups and zoom climbs were dangerous and, since the Sputniks and Uri Gagarin had been launched into space, there was no point in climbing to 105,000ft with an aircraft: he therefore called a halt to all such trials, which was a major disappointment for us.

On 12th September 1961, I took off to test the possibilities of extending the known flying boundaries of the IV Maircraft. The IVM05 was loaded with an AS30 missile under the right wing and an AS20 under the left. During the supersonic dive the aircraft suddenly veered hard to the right, and I immediately recovered to level flight. My first thought was that something was wrong with the underwing stores and, sure enough, although the AS20 was in its normal position, the AS30 was partly detached and pointing 45° out to the right. I could barely maintain level flight using full throttle to produce 250 KIAS at 15,000ft, and that only by applying full left rudder. I tried the emergency jettison, but only the AS20 dropped off and this did not improve my situation in any way, so I decided to land. However, the right leg of the undercarriage was obstructed by the AS30 hanging sideways, and could only be lowered about halfway. Nonetheless, I decided to proceed, and immediately after touchdown the machine broke away to the right, towards the grass and, miraculously, the nose of the AS30 dug itself into the ground, abruptly thrusting the wing up and giving the gear just enough time to lock down. I was back on three wheels, very close to a point where the runway widened at a taxiway. Without any further problems, the aircraft was taxied onto the tarmac, looking the worse for wear, but a lot better than it would have if the AS30 had exploded! Jaques Lemanon had, with his usual presence of mind, sent out Viron, our photographer, with his camera; he returned with some very interesting footage.

On 27th September, my diary showed the first flight of 'Asterix', the Mirage 5 J 2, which had a fixed 'moustache' to improve low speed handling. The first thirty seconds of this flight were very uncomfortable. Sudden transverse oscillations evoked old memories of the IIIV, topped by oversensitive lateral control of the aircraft. Several modifications were to follow. Later, the Mirage III R344 was equipped with a retractable 'moustache'.

J.Coureau, following his brilliant initial flights on the Mirage G, was appointed Chief Pilot, and suggested that I look after the Mirage F1. I accepted enthusiastically because I was just grinding my teeth following the sad end of the IIIV. So, on 20th March, I lifted off for the first time in the F1 02, which had been modified considerably, based on the experience gained with 01. From the beginning, I felt at home in this great little aeroplane, making Mach 1.5 on the second flight, and Mach 2 on the third, just two days later. The Dassault company stood a good chance of receiving an order for series production from *L' Armèe de l'Air* which until then, had only had the Jaguar. Coureau did the fourth flight, and J.F. Cazaubiel told me that the next would be a demonstration before an official from the Ministry of Finance. April 2nd was the day and, after take-off, I remained out of sight, practising aerobatics for ten minutes. Then I came back to demonstrate the prototype overhead the runway but, unfortunately, with some restrictions still in operation.

With effect from 1st July 1971, I was appointed Dassault's Chief Pilot, succeeding Jean Coureau, who had retired on health grounds. A period of training for our flying personnel followed. The three older Test Pilots' activities were limited to 'flights without risk', even though experience showed that in our line of work difficulties usually arose during the so -called 'normal' or 'low risk' flights. Our old friends, Henri Suisse and Marcel Tixador finally ended their test-flying careers on their 60th birthdays, and were replaced by young pilots, thereby creating a large age difference.

A new year, 1972, and on 23rd March I began performance flight trials, including a climb to 50,000ft at Mach 2.0, achieved in 5 minutes and 7 seconds from brake release. What a machine! Unfortunately, the Air Force was only interested in the transonic air-to-air combat region at that time and, with its high wing loading, the G8 was definitely not the most suitable aircraft. Nevertheless, we continued to investigate the problems of the air intake at an altitude of 50,000ft., flying between Mach 2.1 and Mach 2.2. Due to the nuisance of the sonic booms (supersonic shock waves striking the ground), we were finally asked to take our flights further away from the area. From that day on, high speed flights were only permitted out over the sea.

On July 13th I undertook my first flight with the G8 02. On 29th November, we flew a demonstration for Gretchko, Minister of Defence of the USSR. We wheeled out our complete 'armoury': Jaguar, F1, and G8. The Marshal courteously explained that in the Soviet Union there were at least ten types of aircraft with variable wing geometry. During the visit to the factory at Villaroche, the President of SNECMA offered refreshment to the Russian Marshal, who asked: 'And what do you have to drink?' 'Champagne, Minister,' replied Villarouche. 'What!? A firm as big as SNECMA, and no Cognac? Champagne, diss iss waaater!'

Following the demonstration, the Marshal had a watch presented to me. However, due to an unfortunate design fault involving the hands, it stopped every six hours – I suppose it was the thought that counted!

In September 1978 I was again at Farnborough, this time in a sparkling new Alpha Jet E 2, straight from the factory in Toulouse. After returning from England I departed for Cairo for a demonstration of precision firing and aerobatics. We were warmly welcomed by our friends Fakhry, Samir Fahrid and Abeel, and began the practice flights immediately, taking off from Almaza with Samir Fahrid in the rear seat to familiarise me with the gunnery range at Bilbeis. After having fired the rockets and guns, we returned peacefully to Almaza, topping-off our day with a slow roll and break from inverted flight (as practice for the aerobatic demonstration the next day). I asked Samir to fly the traffic circuit a trifle wider, to avoid making long finals, as the aircraft was still rather heavy and it was a hot afternoon. During the turn onto finals, Samir added some power, resulting in explosions and a rise in T 4 (exhaust gas) temperature. My initial thought was that we had stalled one engine, so I reduced the throttle on the suspect, and then slowly advanced it again: there was no pick-up, just a further series of explosions, and then I noticed that the second engine would not exceed 70% rpm, and was starting to issue explosions as well. Things were getting very serious, because we were a fair distance from the runway, and losing height at an alarming rate. I considered retracting the gear to reduce drag, but realised it wouldn't work because we were too low, at 600ft. and dropping like a stone! I shouted at Samir: 'Eject, eject, eject!', and his seat left from behind me immediately; I took one last look at the altimeter and to my horror saw that the needle was dropping past 300ft. Glancing over the side, I confirmed what the instrument indicated, that I was already too low to eject. I was heading for the main gate of a military camp, guarded by a soldier with his rifle dutifully at the slope, standing smartly to attention. A second soldier, wearing a red scarf, realised the danger and dashed away to the right, and I managed to turn away so as not to run him down. The ground was coming rapidly closer, and ahead there was little to encourage me. Several deep ditches and large piles of gravel loomed; large, approximately 10ft high – anti-tank defences. I was only too aware that the metal of the aircraft's nose was very fragile and thin: my last conscious thought was the disappointment of having to end it all that way.

Everything went blank, but I regained consciousness after the initial impact, and found my machine sliding along very close to the ground, having lost its undercarriage. It was hot,

The emergency landing short of the runway at Almaza, Egypt.

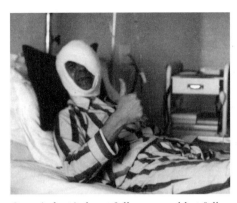

Saget in hospital, not fully recovered but full of optimism.

and I would have liked to have stopped the aircraft, but was unable to. I sat tight and finally executed a ground loop to the right. The 'plane came to a halt, just 100ft from a tented camp, where young soldiers were having a nap. The time was 3.20 p.m. I looked up and saw five curious faces, all alike, wearing berets and moustaches. My admirers had broken open the canopy with a stone. At that moment I was unaware that they had also triggered the ejector seat by moving the seat firing handle out of the way. Luckily, the gas charge had escaped through the bottom of the firing mechanism, which had been extensively damaged in the landing, thus preventing the seat from hurling myself and my friendly helpers through the air. Yes, miracles do still happen! Unfortunately, Samir sustained a severely injured leg, his parachute having only just opened as he touched the ground.

I escaped with a fractured cheek bone, a few broken ribs and bruises all over my body. Two months later I was flying again in the Aero Club. By December 15th, I was back on my first trial flight: I thought to myself, 'Life is beautiful – now, doubly so!'

The first flight with the Super Mirage 4000 was made on 9th March 1979; a wonderful aircraft! What joy, what pride, to be trusted with an aircraft of such quality! To be the bearer of the hopes and aspirations of the Dassault Company! The maiden flight and initial test flights were easily performed; clearly a successful design. During the sixth flight, I reached Mach 2 within 2 minutes. The 4000 was demonstrated at Le Bourget – though still with a few restrictions imposed on it. Full clearance for the 'Fly By Wire' control system was still to be granted but, what an aeroplane: we were well equipped to stand up to the competition. When releasing the brakes at reduced take-off weight it felt like being kicked in the backside. I had not experienced anything like it since my Mustang flights. It took me a few flights to master the aerobatics, since letting the aircraft have its head also meant problems in slowing it down again. Eventually I managed the vertical 8 straight after take-off. At Farnborough, I reduced the 8 to a loop, the cloud base being at only 2,000ft. The top of the loop took me to 2,500ft, straight into the clouds. A split second of doubt, and then I continued my loop, pulling a 27°/28° angle of attack (the automatic AoA limiter had not been installed at the time), and the aircraft recovered smoothly at 500ft without penetrating the prescribed minimum safe height.

Flying supersonic, the 4000 was a lion. From the moment of brake-release up to 50,000ft at Mach 1.8, she took a little more than three and a half minutes. At 40,000ft it was easily possible to maintain a climb rate of 40,000ft/min! During the observation of my flight in the telemetry office, with a foreign committee watching, something interesting happened. Distracted by a small problem with my HUD (Head Up Display), I noticed, a little late, that the aircraft was climbing faster than usual. I levelled off at Mach 2 with more than 60,000ft of altitude, dressed only in a summer flight suit! From that day on, I rolled inverted at 48,000ft and pulled the stick fully aft when I saw the pointer of the altimeter passing 50,000ft. That way the overshoot was limited to a minimum. This performance was achieved using two of the first M 53 Dash 2 engines, whose thrust was significantly less than that predicted for the production line engines.

In the transonic speed range at 40,000ft, it was still possible to pull just over 4 g. That had not been seen since the Mystère II, and the visibility from the pear-drop canopy, starting as it did at elbow level, was so fantastic that one always had the feeling of being on top of the situation.

During a ferry flight to Farnborough on 27th August, 1980, I was impressed by the precision of the flight controls: I flew with great ease in close formation at 40,000ft, and at an easy cruise of Mach 0.92. I could raise or lower the position of the aircraft by 10 centimetres (4 inches), and the aircraft adhered precisely to control inputs, and stayed in position. Later, flying at 45,000ft, the steering was nearly as precise. A 'well done' to our engineers and technicians.

On 30th October, 1981, we ferried five Super Etendards from Cazaux to St. Nazaire, under the strictest secrecy because the aircraft were destined for delivery to the Argentine Navy. Upon arrival we were welcomed by the local Press, who seemed very well informed about the whole affair. To top it all, on the

The Saget family, centre Madam Saget who gave up flying to become a house wife.

return flight we flew under the bridges of St. Nazaire in our small commuter aircraft.

On 25th February, 1982, I logged my 10,000th flying hour. By a remarkable coincidence I was flying the Mirage 4000 and my son, Claude, received permission to accompany me in a Mirage 3 E. He was a pilot in the III/2nd Squadron, Alsace, based at Istres at the time. It was one of the most wonderful moments in my flying career. On that day I flew as lead of an eight ship formation, each aircraft with a member of my family, including my sister, at the controls. We later celebrated this unique event with our friends.

At the Salon, Charles Hernu, the Minister of Defence, had observed my aerobatics in the Mirage 4000, and spontaneously recommended me for the Cross of The Legion of Honour, which was later presented to me by *Monsieur* Dassault.

The 4000 did not take up all my time; I also took care of the main programme for the Company, the Mirage 2000. On completion of an uneventful flight in the second prototype, 02, the engine failed as I was turning finals for my approach. It was time for rapid decisions: no chance of making the field, I was already low on speed and, at the time of engine failure, had only 800ft. altitude. 'Just like Cairo!', I thought. I quickly tried the re-light procedure and switched to additional fuel, but it was all too late; another glance outside confirmed that I had to abandon the aircraft immediately! A last cryptic message on the RT: *'Je saute!'* (I'm jumping), caused tremendous excitement in Ground Control, as everything had been going so well until then. With one hand I tried to pull the upper firing handle (starting the ejection sequence with some seats), before remembering I was in a Mark 10! My hand went down to where the firing handle was located, the other holding the stick fully aft. Bang!, and I felt myself accelerate up the guide rails, smoothly clearing the cockpit. I observed myself rising above and clear of the aircraft, the drogue-'chute opening to stabilise me horizontally, before the main 'chute was released and I separated from the seat. My harness straps jerked firmly and I glanced up to see the comforting sight of my fully deployed canopy. To my right, the aircraft impacted the ground and bounced only once, bursting into flames on final contact. Several seconds of peaceful descent elapsed, and I landed on the only small area of level ground amidst the rocks and bushes. Upon landing, I broke two dorsal vertebrae, probably because I had not released the seat pack containing the dinghy and the survival pack; I had had very little time and had also been distracted by the crash of my aircraft.

The last formation flight in a military jet.

December 24th, 1985 marked my last flight on a military combat aircraft. Valliéres was at some pains to ensure I understood that I had more than passed the age limit. As my swan song, I was permitted to mount the best horse in the stable, the Mirage 4000, on which a new trial series was being initiated. One last time at Mach 2, one last fly-past in four ship formation; the three young pilots at my side had rather touchingly arranged it all without my knowledge. Back on the ground, I was briefly overcome by sadness, but after about thirty seconds I was once more on an even keel: I had realised that it was no use regretting what could not be changed. 'What cannot be cured, must be endured.'

I handed over my seat as Chief Pilot to Guy Mitaux Maurouard, who would soon start the trials on the Rafale, the bold new hope for Dassault for the Nineties, and stepped back into the ranks, as is the custom in the holy orders of monks. A new horizon opened up before me, luckily stocked with the most beautiful aircraft: Mystère 10, 20, 50, Falcon 900 and the Atlantique.

I was confident that I would be granted a few years of test-flying yet, and therefore decided to make the best of what was available in the field.

Thus the beginning of the year 1986 found me with the Falcon 900 in skies throughout the world.

Here's to life!

Two old friends, Wolfgang Späte and Jean Marie Saget.